W9-BTD-121

FIRE BASE
ILLINGWORTH

Also by Philip Keith

Blackhorse Riders

FIRE BASE ILLINGWORTH

An Epic True Story of Remarkable Courage Against Staggering Odds

Philip Keith

St. Martin's Press
New York

www.stmartins.com

Library of Congress Cataloging-in-Publication Data

Keith, Philip A.

Fire Base Illingworth : an epic true story of remarkable courage against staggering odds / Philip Keith.—First edition.

p. cm

Includes bibliographical references and index.

ISBN 978-1-250-02495-4 (hardcover)

ISBN 978-1-250-02496-1 (e-book)

1. Fire Base Illingworth, Battle of, Vietnam, 1970. 2. United States. Army. Armored Cavalry Regiment, 11th. 3. United States. Army. Cavalry, 8th. Battalion, 2nd. Company C. I. Title.

DS557.8.F57K45 2013

959.704'342—dc23

2013023488

St. Martin's Press books may be purchased for educational, business, or promotional use. For information on bulk purchases, please contact Macmillan Corporate and Premium Sales Department at 1-800-221-7945, extension 5442, or write specialmarkets@macmillan.com.

First Edition: October 2013

10 9 8 7 6 5 4 3 2 1

This book is dedicated to all the valiant warriors who fought at FSB Illingworth on April 1, 1970. Their courageous examples of what American warriors can do under the direst of circumstances should be celebrated for all time.

I also want to dedicate this book to my son, Pierce. It is my fervent hope that he will never have to be in a position to face what the men at Illingworth confronted; but, if fate should decree otherwise, I hope that he will remember the stories of these men and, in his turn, serve his country with honor and courage.

CONTENTS

FOREWORD

The Vietnam War continues to provide interesting and relevant material to authors, like Phil Keith, who have that rare ability to discover and describe exceedingly poignant, little-known circumstances that blend together to highlight the fortitude, heroism, and sacrifices of the American soldier. Another factor that helps make Vietnam such a fertile ground for masterful narrators like Phil can be traced to the fact that this conflict differed significantly in scope and purpose from one year to the next, and from one region of the country to another. No two situations were alike.

The involvement of the United States military in Vietnam grew steadily, beginning with a modest advisory effort starting in the late 1950s. That small start grew until by 1965 our total force expanded to more than a half a million service members on the ground in country. While some detachments continued to train the South Vietnamese Army, the primary mission morphed into one of carrying the heaviest burden of the fighting against the Viet Cong and the North Vietnamese Army. It is in this environment, in April

1970, which Phil Keith the author of this book zeroes in on actions that involved three company-sized units, totaling less than three hundred soldiers.

Mr. Keith had already written two successful fictional novels when friend and well-known author Tom Clavin urged him to try his hand at nonfiction. When Phil asked Tom what he should write about he received this advice, "Write what you know. You're a Vietnam Veteran, write about Vietnam. There are many stories about Vietnam that still need to be told. You'll figure it out and you'll know it when you see it." As luck would have it, two days later, Phil read a story in the *New York Times* about Alpha Troop, 1st Squadron, 11th Armored Cavalry Regiment. According to the article, President Obama was about to award the Presidential Unit Citation to this intrepid band of troopers for a rescue operation they had conducted almost forty years prior in Vietnam. What had they done to deserve this honor—and why were they being recognized so belatedly? Phil knew immediately that this was a story he should tell.

The result was the publishing of his highly successful and widely acclaimed 2012 book, *Blackhorse Riders*. The narrative details the heroic efforts of Alpha Troop, accompanied by "A Company" of the 2/8, as these men forced their way through the jungle to come to the aid of another company that had become entrapped by an entire North Vietnamese regiment. This action occurred on March 26, 1970, yet it took another four decades for the whole story to emerge and for these brave warriors to finally receive the accolades they deserved.

While researching *Blackhorse Riders*, it came to Phil's attention that just a few days later, in the early hours of April 1, 1970, at an isolated jungle outpost called "Fire Base Illingworth," many of the very same soldiers became involved in an even more intense action. Equally significant was that the opposition turned out to be the very same enemy regiment they had tangled with five days prior.

Phil Keith has been thorough and persistent: By locating dozens of surviving individuals who were there, and directly involved in the fighting, this chronological tale superbly describes the challenges faced on an almost daily basis by American units serving in Vietnam at that time. Of special note is that Phil was able to locate and obtain the views of the former NVA regimental commander whose unit attacked Fire Base Illingworth. These observations by a former enemy commander are rare indeed and add significantly to the tale.

The strength and appeal of Phil Keith's work lies in the number of firsthand accounts that he has acquired through his painstaking research. These individuals cover the complete chain of command. The interviews attest to the immense sacrifices made by our citizen soldiers at a time when the nation was deeply divided over our involvement in Vietnam. The hardships endured by these men far away from home became their routine. No one went to Vietnam to become a hero, but Phil Keith has masterfully captured the essence of what it takes to be one in this superb recitation of men doing their duty. This is a must-read for anyone interested in the true nature of what the U.S. Army faced during some of the toughest days of American involvement in Vietnam.

Major General Michael J. Conrad, U.S. Army (Ret.)

General Conrad, as a Lieutenant Colonel in April 1970, was Commanding Officer of the 2nd Battalion, 8th Cavalry, 1st Cavalry Division, and in command of Fire Base Illingworth at the time of the events described in this book.

AUTHOR'S NOTE

This book picks up where my previous book on Vietnam, *Blackhorse Riders,* ends, but it is not a sequel in the traditional sense. *Fire Base Illingworth* is about a completely different set of circumstances in an entirely new setting. What makes it seem similar is that some of the same soldiers who were directly involved in *Blackhorse Riders* are once again at the heart of this story.

In *Blackhorse Riders* we learned about the men of Charlie Company, 2nd Battalion, 8th Cavalry, and their escapades during late 1969 and early 1970. At the beginning of this time frame, these soldiers were known as "Lucky Charlie" by their battalion mates. Through nothing more than the luck of the draw, Charlie Company seemed to get the easiest marches, the least combative patrols, and all the breaks. Then, on Valentine's Day 1970, all that changed. The odds caught up with Charlie Company with a vengeance. By the end of the following six weeks, Charlie was vastly understrength and had gone through considerable tribulation. The January rosters had turned over nearly 100 percent, and most of the turmoil had been due to combat casualties. Back at the Replacement Center, where new men were still pouring off the transports from America, Charlie Company was given the unwelcome sobriquet of "the Company of the Living Dead" and had become an outfit you wanted to avoid getting orders to if at all possible.

On March 20, the company was assigned to conduct another grueling patrol in War Zone C, near the Cambodian border. The men were tasked with sniffing out enemy infiltration routes and uncovering supply bases. Eighty-seven soldiers started out on that patrol. Because there were insufficient officers available, some sergeants were pressed into service as platoon leaders. Many of the men were "newbies," raw replacements, soldiers shoving off on their first combat assignments.

On March 26, after two days of picking up incontrovertible evidence of nearby enemy activity, Charlie Company made contact with the NVA (North Vietnamese Army). They had, as it turned out, walked straight into a cleverly laid trap. It really wasn't their fault: They had been told to press on despite the ominous signs, and the NVA, masters at this kind of warfare, knew Charlie was in the area. The NVA determined that if the Americans kept moving in their current direction they would eventually come across the well-hidden NVA compound—it was simply too big to miss. Given the high probability of discovery, the NVA decided to stack the deck in their favor: They began laying down clever but irresistible markers that would pull the Americans along in the direction the enemy wanted them to go. The path that the NVA laid out was straight into the maw of a storage complex guarded by dozens of stoutly built bunkers. Every bunker was positioned to give the NVA interlocking fields of fire using an array of machine guns, AK-47 rifles, and RPGs. Their aim was to swallow up this entire company—kill them all if they could, but if not, take the survivors prisoner. That way, their secret jungle location would remain just that.

Within moments of coming across this massive defensive position, Charlie Company was surrounded, outgunned, and outmanned by seven or more to one. They were in deep, serious trouble. They hunkered down and called for backup. The only nearby force with any conceivable chance of reaching them and rendering assistance was Team Alpha, which consisted of Alpha Troop, 1st Squadron, 11th Armored Cavalry Regiment and Company A, 2nd Battalion, 8th Cavalry Regiment, 1st Cavalry Division. Team Alpha had been formed a few days prior to March 26 by the 2/8 Battalion Commander, Lt. Col. Mike Conrad, as an experiment in joint infantry-cavalry maneuvering. Capt. John Poindexter, commanding officer of Alpha Troop, was the senior officer and in command of the team.

Alpha Team was about three miles away, temporarily encamped in a dry lake bed. The hybrid outfit was configured with half a dozen Sheridan tanks, sixteen M-113 ACAVs (armored cavalry assault vehicles), and a line company of straight-leg infantry. Capt. Poindexter, and Capt. Ray Armer, CO of Company A, were monitoring the radios and aware of Charlie Company's desperate situation. Poindexter and Armer agreed that something had to be done. Poindexter, acting on his own initiative, told his men to "saddle up." Subsequently, Poindexter and Colonel Conrad discussed the situation by radio and Conrad directed Poindexter to get Team Alpha moving toward Charlie's position.

The immediate challenge was the terrain that lay ahead. Four to five kilometers of choking vines, giant hardwood trees, thick bamboo, and tall grasses separated Alpha Troop from Charlie Company. There were no roads or precut pathways. The only way to reach Charlie was to do what they called "busting," or plowing straight through the jungle.

Exhibiting superior determination and exercising incredible force of will, Alpha Team plunged ahead. They were bedeviled all the way by overheating engines, nearly impassable jungle, and the threat of ambush, but they managed to locate the stranded men of Charlie after five hours of extremely tough busting. Then, in order to extract the grunts, the cavalrymen found it expedient and necessary to engage the entrenched enemy in a pitched battle. Captain Poindexter felt he either had to force the NVA to flee or, at minimum, push them back far enough to keep them from being a threat to the rescue operation and any subsequent withdrawal.

Captain Poindexter lined up his nineteen battle-ready tracks in a wide arc across the front of the NVA complex. At exactly 1700 hours on March 26 he ordered a full combat assault. This was very much in keeping with the unofficial motto of the Blackhorse Regiment: "Find the bastards, and then pile on." For the next two hours the cavalry, with the support of their attached infantry and the survivors of Charlie Company, went at it hammer and tong with the NVA. Neither side gave much ground, and both sides suffered. Finally, after doing all he and his men could do, and realizing that they were only creating more casualties, Poindexter decided they had done enough. They had, after all, completed their primary mission: They had rescued Charlie Company.

With ammunition stocks approaching critical levels, many soldiers needing urgent medical attention, and darkness approaching, the only rational course of action was to disengage and return to the Team's temporary base at their former night defensive position. Poindexter conferred with Conrad, who agreed with the assessment, and by 1930, the Team began the extraction process.

When it was all over and the rosters checked, Charlie had been reduced from eighty-seven men to thirty-nine effectives. The fight had cost them two KIAs and forty-six men wounded badly enough to require extraction from the field. The day after the battle, Charlie was helicoptered to regroup and recuperate at an FSB (fire support base) christened Illingworth. Their own battalion had carved this temporary fortress out of an open plain nine days prior. The base was roughly five miles away from the tussle in the jungle they had just endured.

The survivors of Charlie were relieved to be within the confines of a more fortified position—one bristling with artillery, populated by a few tanks and ACAVs, and constantly resupplied by helicopters bringing the mail, hot chow, and cold drinks. In reality, however, they had just leapt out of the frying pan and into the fire, but they wouldn't know that and feel the flames until five days later. This is the scenario that makes *Fire Base Illingworth,* on the surface, seem like a continuation of the action in *Blackhorse Riders:* The same hard-luck company of infantrymen is once again caught in the death grip of a maelstrom that threatens to sweep them away. The grand irony, of course, is that these men were supposed to have been rebuilding their strength in a relatively safe haven. Instead, as they will soon discover, they have been placed in an even graver situation and are about to do battle with the very same enemy troops they had barely escaped five days prior.

A small portion of Alpha Troop ends up at Illingworth, too, but not by choice. The contingent consists of three of the unit's Sheridan tanks, Alpha Troop's (unarmed) M-577 command track, one deuce-and-a-half mechanic's truck, and one M-113 ACAV. All three of the Sheridans had sustained damage during the March 26 mission to rescue Charlie Company. One tank, A-19, was virtually useless, its power pack completely fried, rendering it immobile. Another Sheridan, A-18, had towed A-19 out of the jungle to Illingworth but it, too, had an engine that was problematic and prone to serious overheating. A-37 had taken a direct hit from an RPG, killing the tank commander and shattering its .50 caliber mount and gun. These near-derelicts were parked out on the berm at the northeast corner of Illingworth, awaiting repairs. They might not be mobile, but two of their main guns could be made to function, if they could be powered up—which was somewhat problematic. Fortunately, the cavalry contingent did have one .50 caliber machine gun, plus fifteen troops to add to the roster of defenders if they were needed. They would be.

On the other side of this combat equation the enemy had to be factored in: They were the 272nd Regiment of the 9th Division of the North Vietnamese Army. These men had been the opposition at the battle in the jungle with Alpha Team on March 26, and they were bloodied badly (eighty-eight graves were discovered in the after-action policing by Alpha Troop on March 28). Was retribution on their minds? Possibly, as we shall see. They were certainly not too happy at having their supply cache discovered, and they undoubtedly perceived that FSB Illingworth was a threat to their continued operations in the region. In short, there were certainly very plausible reasons for the NVA to initiate some action, and they did. In the early morning hours of April 1 they poured out of the tree line determined to overrun and capture this nettlesome and seemingly vulnerable American outpost.

Blackhorse Riders told the story of March 26, 1970, from the personal perspectives of the men who fought that battle. The narrative is woven completely from what those men saw and heard, boots on the ground, as they battled the jungle, the enemy, and their own apprehensions. That approach worked well, so I am going to do the same again here. This book will once again be my narrative, but it will consist mostly of the firsthand stories of the men who fought, endured, or died at FSB Illingworth.

I will admit, though, that the text of this book turned out to be more difficult to pull together than I first anticipated. Let me explain: *Blackhorse Riders* is extremely rich in the actual recollections of the men involved, and I had the benefit of many wonderful interviews and one-on-one conversations with the soldiers participating in those events. In addition, there was a very robust collection of official documents, sworn statements, written records, and carefully researched material to go along with the story arcs. This happy situation—for an author—was due principally to the enormous efforts at rebuilding the official record of Alpha Troop's exploits in March 1970, shepherded by Mr. John Poindexter and his assistants during the period from roughly 1999 to 2007. This group carefully constructed a dossier to support their case for an award of the Presidential Unit Citation to Alpha Troop based on their actions to rescue Charlie Company on March 26. Mr. Poindexter and his team generously shared their efforts with me as I constructed the book *Blackhorse Riders*. Happily, their quest for the PUC was ultimately successful, and, in the process, they made life infinitely easier for a documentarian like me.

In the case of *Fire Base Illingworth,* the story is very different. First, there is great inconsistency in the official army documents relative to the events surrounding the Illingworth saga. Between the Operational Reports, Daily Staff Journals, reports of lessons learned, routine requests for supplies, status of forces documents, recommendations for medals and awards, and many other bits of the paper trail, there is plenty to read and review, but there is much more disagreement on times, dates, actions, and even names and spellings than a careful researcher would like to see. Even the name

Illingworth is very frequently misspelled (or mispronounced) as in "Illingsworth"—with an unnecessary *s*—or even "Ellingsworth" or "Ellingworth." Several official army reports state, without hesitation, that "no"—as in zero—enemy troops penetrated the perimeters of the fire base on the night of the battle of April 1. There are photos taken immediately after the battle that clearly show otherwise, and the men who fought there are in near-unanimous agreement that the official reports are incorrect. The commencement of the bombardment of Illingworth by the NVA was stated as 0200 in one report, 0217 in another, and 0250 in a third. A critical event—the detonation of a huge stockpile of howitzer ammunition during the battle—was reported at 0317 and 0250. One journal even records the time of this explosion as midnight. In several reports, D Company of the 11th Armored Cavalry was misidentified as A Company (there is no A Company in the 11th) or A Troop. On the night of the battle A Troop was many klicks away chasing other NVA components.

Some of the errors can be attributed to innocent mistakes: Recordkeeping in the field, at the time, was haphazard at best, and dotting i's and crossing t's was and should have been considered secondary to the necessity of staying alive under very difficult wartime conditions. I could not find any effort to purposefully obfuscate or deceive, with the possible exception of the comments made relative to whether the enemy had penetrated the compound. I did find some considerable effort to downplay the casualties and gloss over some of the obvious errors in judgment, but nothing that would rise to the level of terrible military blundering.

As with all engagements in all wars, the details we think we know, even from firsthand experience, are always subject to memory modification as time goes by. Some of that has happened here. I even interviewed a survivor whom three other battle participants swore they had seen killed. These judgmental mistakes should be viewed, of course, in light of the horrible conditions these men endured.

There is another key difference between the two narratives that I feel is important to touch upon, and it concerns pride of accomplishment. The men who participated in the events depicted in *Blackhorse Riders* felt a great deal of immediate satisfaction for the rescue operation they effected. In addition to the many thumbs-up and backslaps they received from the men they saved, every trooper knew he had participated in something special, something more important than the monotonous but dangerous routines they had become used to slogging through. This action was something unique, one that produced an immediate tangible result. Those who were rescued would have undoubtedly perished or become POWs if the cavalrymen had done nothing. By and large, the troopers from the 11th ACR who were involved in the actions of March 26 have always been eager to share their stories. They have also been warmed in the late-life glow of belated but sweet recognition. Going to the White House to receive the Presidential Unit Citation in October 2009, and standing with the president of the United States, was for many of these men the experience of a lifetime.

The men who fought at Illingworth see things differently: Theirs was a battle for their own survival, and the reasons they had to endure these deprivations are still not clear to most of them. They do not see their victory as an accomplishment, except in terms of making it out alive. As a result, I found there was still a great deal of reluctance to talk about Illingworth and to reopen the psychic wounds that some of these men have been dealing with for more than forty years. These men are not going to Washington to receive any additional honors from a grateful nation.

This is unfortunate. What the soldiers in this story did at

Illingworth, as I shall try to show, was nothing short of miraculous. More than just beating back a determined assault, they performed numerous acts of incredible bravery. An outfit cobbled together, composed of disparate units that had never worked in unison, defeated the best efforts of a crack regiment of frontline North Vietnamese troops—and did it while being outnumbered by at least two to one. That, to me, is pretty impressive. I would like to help these veterans better understand their place in the Vietnam narrative and to show the rest of the world how these courageous Americans reacted to incredibly bad combat odds and still managed to succeed.

—Phil Keith

Southampton, New York

September 2013

DRAMATIS PERSONAE

Names are listed with their ranks and assignments at the time of the story. Men whose names are in italics were killed in action at FSB Illingworth on April 1, 1970, and are listed with their ranks at the time of their burial (several were posthumously promoted). Names appended with an asterisk have died postbattle.

1st Cavalry Division, Airmobile

Major General Elvy Roberts, Division Commander*
Brigadier General George Casey Sr., Asst. Division Commander*
Colonel Morris J. Brady, Division Artillery Commander
Captain (Father) Patrick Boyle, Division (Catholic) Chaplain

1st Brigade, 1st Cavalry Division

Colonel William V. Ochs Jr., Commanding Officer*
Captain Joe Hogg, Cobra Pilot, Airborne Rocket Artillery, A Battery, 2nd Battalion, 20th Artillery: "Blue Max"

2nd Battalion, 7th Cavalry

Lieutenant Colonel Robert Hannas, Commanding Officer

Major Gordon Frank, S-3, Operations Officer, Second in Command

2nd Battalion, 8th Cavalry

Lieutenant Colonel Michael J. Conrad, Commanding Officer

Major Michael Moore, S-3, Operations Officer, Second in Command

Captain John Ahearn, Artillery Liaison Officer

Headquarters and Headquarters Company, 2nd Battalion, 8th Cavalry

Sergeant David G. Dragosavac

Sergeant Sidney E. Plattenburger

Sergeant Lee Weltha, Supply Sergeant

Specialist Fourth Class Tim Hall, Battalion Radio Telephone Operator

Alpha Company, 2nd Battalion, 8th Cavalry

Captain Ray Armer, Commanding Officer

Sergeant Maynard "Bo" Boedecker, Squad Leader, Plato Platoon

Corporal Billy P. Carlisle

Corporal John James "Jack" Illingworth (listed here, but KIA March 14, 1970)

Charlie Company, 2nd Battalion, 8th Cavalry

Captain George Hobson, Commanding Officer

First Sergeant (Acting) Charles Beauchamp

Sergeant Robert A. Hill

Sergeant Gerald W. Purdon

Corporal Leroy J. Fasching

Corporal Michael R. Patterson

Corporal Klaus D. Schlieben

Specialist Fourth Class Richard "Rick" Hokenson

Specialist Fourth Class Cliff Rhodes

Private First Class Roger J. McInerny

Private First Class Ken "Mississippi" Woodward

E (Recon) Company, 2nd Battalion, 8th Cavalry

First Lieutenant Gregory J. Peters, Recon Platoon Commander*
First Lieutenant Mike Russell, Mortar Platoon Commander
Staff Sergeant James L. Taylor*
Sergeant Randall Richards, Squad Leader, Mortar Platoon
Sergeant Brent A. Street
Sergeant Lou Vaca, M-60 Machine Gunner
Sergeant Casey O. Waller
Corporal Bobby L. Barker
Corporal Nathan J. Mann
Specialist Fourth Class Peter Lemon
Private First Class Ken Vall de Juli

First Squadron, 11th Armored Cavalry

Lieutenant Colonel James Reed, Commanding Officer

Alpha Troop, First Squadron, 11th Armored Cavalry

Captain John Poindexter, Commanding Officer
First Lieutenant Paul Baerman, Commanding Officer (Acting)
Staff Sergeant Joseph Colan "J. C." Hughes
Sergeant Kenneth Ray Hodge
Sergeant Francis "Bud" Smolich, Mortar Section Chief*
Corporal John Lee Smith
Specialist Fourth Class George Burks

D Company, First Squadron, 11th Armored Cavalry

Captain Jerry Hensley, Commanding Officer
First Lieutenant Timothy Brooks, Platoon Leader, 2nd Platoon

Headquarters and Headquarters Battalion, 2nd Battalion, 32nd Field Artillery

Staff Sergeant Lawrence E. Sutton

A Battery, 2nd Battalion, 32nd Field Artillery

Major Thomas H. Magness, Operations Officer*
Specialist Fourth Class Ralph Jones, Assistant Gunner
Specialist Fourth Class David H. Lassen
Specialist Fourth Class Terry L. Schell

Headquarters and Headquarters Battalion, 1st Battalion, 77th Field Artillery

Staff Sergeant Steven J. Williams

Specialist Fourth Class Thomas J. Murphy

B Battery, 1st Battalion, 77th Field Artillery

Captain Arnold W. Laidig, Commanding Officer*

First Lieutenant Cleaveland F. Bridgman

Staff Sergeant Benjamin V. Childress

Sergeant Syriac Hebert

Sergeant Robert H. Lane

Private First Class Thomas R. Bowen

2nd Battalion, 272nd North Vietnamese Regiment

Colonel Nguyen Tuong Lai, Commanding Officer, 272nd NVA Regiment

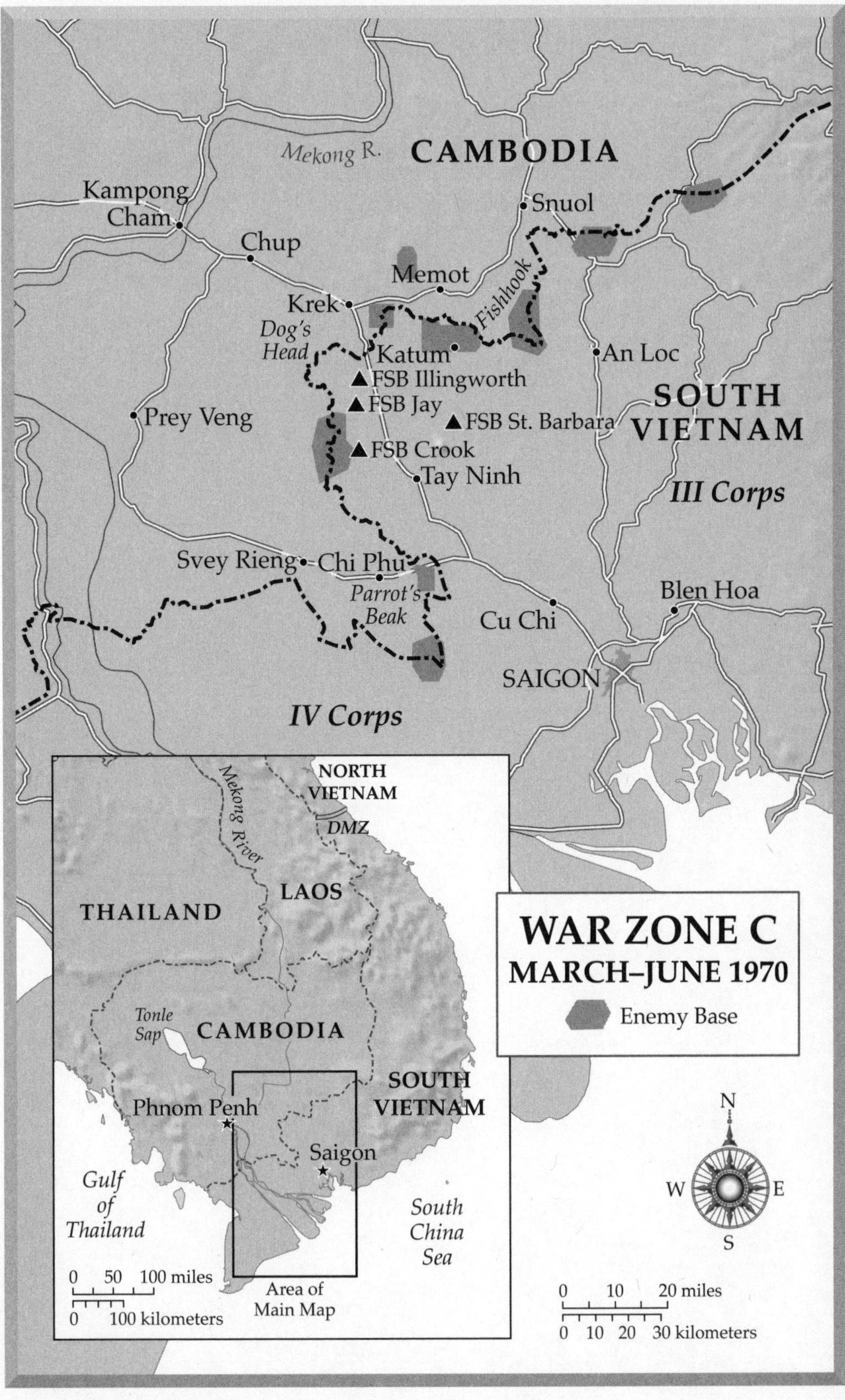
CAMBODIA
Mekong R.
Kampong Cham
Chup
Snuol
Memot
Krek
Fishhook
Dog's Head
Katum
FSB Illingworth
FSB Jay
FSB St. Barbara
FSB Crook
An Loc
SOUTH VIETNAM
Prey Veng
Tay Ninh
III Corps
Svey Rieng
Chi Phu
Parrot's Beak
Cu Chi
Blen Hoa
SAIGON
IV Corps
NORTH VIETNAM
Mekong River
DMZ
LAOS
THAILAND
Tonle Sap
CAMBODIA
SOUTH VIETNAM
Phnom Penh
Saigon
Gulf of Thailand
South China Sea
0 50 100 miles
0 100 kilometers
Area of Main Map
WAR ZONE C
MARCH–JUNE 1970
Enemy Base
N
W
E
S
0 10 20 miles
0 10 20 30 kilometers

1

THE TRAP IS BAITED

IT WAS QUIET, BUT IT WOULDN'T BE FOR LONG. Lt. Col. Mike Conrad, commanding officer of the 2/8, and the senior officer commanding at FSB Illingworth, knew the NVA were out there. His ground surveillance radar had found them stacked up and swarming in the tree line, and they would come boiling out of the jungle and attempt to overrun his undermanned and vulnerable position as soon as they felt ready. That would be just about any moment. He knew he'd get a warning, though—maybe a few minutes—before the assault began. The NVA were experienced, tough, capable, and far from stupid. They'd begin by pounding the bejesus out of Conrad's base with mortars, rockets, recoilless rifles, and whatever artillery they might have been able to drag through the woods and place behind their front lines. They would soften up the Americans before blowing their bugles and charging Conrad's works.

It was 0217, April 1, 1970. Every man on the fire base, about 220 of them, had been woken up in anticipation of an attack. Conrad had demanded that every officer and every sergeant make sure that every man was awake and alert. The "Pipsy-5"* antipersonnel radar that Conrad and his men had deployed to scour their perimeter had initially picked up strong movement right before midnight, especially in the jungle area facing the southwest corner of their pitifully small berm. Conrad did not hesitate. He ordered the Cobra gunships he had standing by to zoom in and rake the tree lines. They unloaded salvo after salvo of rockets and ripped the foliage with their miniguns. Artillery from nearby firebases like FSB Hannas, FSB St. Barbara, and Camp Hazard opened up on the preprogrammed coordinates they had carefully calculated, aiming points designed to support FSB Illingworth. Conrad also unleashed his own .50 cal machine guns and whatever M-60s were available, and all guns poured fire directly into the trees ahead.

No response came back toward Conrad's lines, however, and after a few minutes, the firing of the defenders slowed to a stop. Rotor blades flicked away in the night sky, their sounds becoming faint as they sped away to refuel and resupply. The throaty cannons and mortars fell silent, too. Machine-gun barrels glowed, and the smell of warm gun oil wafted on the night air. The grunts put their personal weapons back on "safe." It became eerily quiet. After a few minutes the night sounds returned. Crickets recommenced their chirping; a

* The AN/PPS-5 (colloquially the "Pipsy-5") antipersonnel radar is a portable detection system about as large as one of today's living-room plasma televisions. It is operated by a crew of two. Like any radar set, it could scan and detect moving or fixed targets and it was used in Vietnam to "hunt" for small groups of men and vehicles, especially those hidden in the jungle. It operated silently and had a range of about 5,000 meters for groups of men and out to 10,000 meters for vehicles. There was a radar set in place at FSB Illingworth, and, according to former Captain John Ahern, the artillery liaison officer at Illingworth on the night of the battle, the radar picked up the first NVA movements in the tree line just prior to midnight. That detection led to the initial bombardment of the NVA positions, which had some effect on their strength and manpower. The troops who manned the Pipsy-5 that night were instrumental in weakening the enemy and saving some of their comrades, without doubt.

monkey screeched in the trees. Within the lines, the men nervously began the never-ending process of wiping down and reloading their weapons. They relaxed—as much as they could given the tension swirling around them. A number of them decided to catch a few z's. Those who could sleep did so in place, boots on, heads resting on helmets or other equally uncomfortable, makeshift pillows.

Colonel Conrad cautiously stepped out from his TOC (tactical operations center) and peered into the blackness. With his RTO (radio telephone operator) at his side he decided to walk the perimeter—again. It would be one more sweep of the interior lines, just to be sure that he and his men had done everything humanly possible to be ready.

A thousand things were racing through Conrad's brain. Uppermost in his thoughts was the fact that as bad as their situation had become, it was exactly what his bosses had wanted it to be. His men were being used as lures, very expensive and vulnerable lures, to draw out the NVA and get them to expose themselves. It had worked, that was for sure, and since it had, Conrad's job had morphed into keeping the lures from being swallowed whole. It wasn't going to be easy.

After his last stroll Conrad returned to the TOC. He decided to lie down and try to catch a few precious moments of sleep. He would not get very much rest. About an hour later, after tossing around miserably on his cot, he was wide awake. At 0217, somewhere out in the inky blackness, he heard them: faint whistles followed by the barking of artillery. Conrad leapt from his rack and tried to race outside. Bad move—he was forced to dive back into the TOC as sheets of steel rained down on his post. The explosions ripped the night sky apart and enveloped the entire compound in deadly shards of red-hot metal.

2

THE FIREBASE STRATEGY IN VIETNAM

By early 1970, "Vietnamization" of the war was in full swing. The "we can beat them" approach of General William Westmoreland, who had commanded all the troops in Vietnam from 1964 to 1968, had proved to be unattainable. Also over was the tenure of his former boss, President Lyndon Johnson. The elevation of Richard Nixon to the presidency, partly based on a promise to end the war, blew sweeping winds of strategic change into the Saigon headquarters of MACV (Military Assistance Command, Vietnam) soon after the 1968 elections. General Creighton W. Abrams was placed in command, and his orders were clear: Hand off the war to the South Vietnamese and get us out with as much dignity and as few additional casualties as possible.

By the first months of 1970, many American units had been issued orders to stand down and get ready to redeploy back to the States. Our staunch allies, like Australia, New Zealand, and South Korea, were peeling away as well. Even at that, over 350,000 army, navy, and air force personnel were still stationed in Vietnam along with about 50,000 U.S. Marines. The main job assigned to all that manpower was to "clear the playing field" of as many obstacles as possible and then turn over responsibility for the war to the South Vietnamese government and the Army of the Republic of Vietnam (ARVN). It would not be an easy task, and many in the American forces were dubious about the potential for a positive outcome.

The skepticism did not come about due to the perceptions concerning the combat capabilities of the average soldier within the ARVN. Just like their opponents, the Vietcong and the NVA, the South Vietnamese were fighting for what they believed in. Generally, the frontline ARVN troops and their junior officers had a decent reputation, and many had fought bravely. The challenge within the ARVN was with the field-grade officers (majors) and above (colonels and generals). The officer corps at the higher levels was riddled with the corrupt and the incompetent. Part of the reason was cultural; this was a society that had been, for centuries, based on the Chinese model, where connections and bribery had played a major role in determining who acceded to the higher levels of power. Another big part of the problem stemmed from the fact that many of the most courageous and competent officers, invariably the younger, lower-ranking ones, were not surviving long enough to get promoted and rise to the top.

This situation might have been able to be corrected if the quasi-civilian governments of the era had had any backbone or moral fiber themselves. As it was, one corrupt regime followed another, and no effective and determined leadership emerged to stabilize the situation. The so-called domino theory, which the war hawks touted and the "peaceniks" derided, ultimately proved to be correct, but in fairness to those who were skeptical, some of the dominoes were just plain rotten.

Via Vietnamization, were we knowingly setting up a "paper tiger"? In hindsight, it would seem that most of the senior leaders of the time would probably have guessed just that, but it wasn't a foregone conclusion. There was a chance for success, albeit a very tentative one. This glimmer of a prospect, combined with the persistent pressure to cut our losses and withdraw, made Vietnamization the plan of the day.

Setting up a clean slate upon which the ARVN could write their destiny was not going to be easy. It centered on using the superior firepower of American arms, principally those on the ground and in the air. The army, marines, and air force, in particular, would police things up one more time, hoping the NVA would not be capable of racking up another set of insurmountable obstacles for the ARVN. This strategy meant locating and clearing as many NVA strongholds, supply depots, and infiltration trails as possible before handing off the baton. It would, in May 1970, be the primary reason for the Cambodian Incursion; but in March, that event was still some weeks away and in a highly classified planning phase.

In War Zone C, where the story of FSB Illingworth takes place, the task of cleanup fell primarily to the 1st Cavalry Division. The "First Team" was a 15,000-man division, primarily infantry, but with a substantial airlift capability. The division's hefty reliance on its helicopters gave it, in fact, an "airmobile" designation. The unit was also augmented by the temporary assignment to it of the 11th Armored Cavalry Regiment (ACR) and a number of batteries from the 2nd Field Force, Vietnam (Artillery). The combined force was a very powerful one with the ability to move fast and strike hard. The division was commanded, at the time of this story, by Maj. Gen. Elvy Roberts.

Roberts was old-school. He had graduated from West Point with the Class of '43 and was immediately thrown into the crucible of World War II. As a paratrooper, he made jumps into Normandy and other parts of France with the famed 501st and 502nd Parachute Infantry Regiments. He fought in the Battle of the Bulge, and by the time the war concluded he had a Silver Star, a Bronze Star, and a Purple Heart to testify to his personal bravery.

Roberts rose steadily through the officer ranks, leading a battalion, then a brigade, and was, for two years in the 1950s, principal U.S. military adviser to the shah of Iran. As the Vietnam War commenced, then widened, he served a tour as an adviser to the ARVN. Most of the army's best officers pulled an adviser's tour at one time or another in the early years of the conflict. On his second tour, he was tapped as an assistant division commander and ultimately the division commander of the 1st Cavalry.

In his turn as head of the division, he was assisted by two ADCs (assistant division commanders), one of whom was Brig. Gen. George Casey Sr. Casey was a rising star in the army—brilliant (he matriculated first at Harvard, then transferred to West Point, Class of '45), popular, fearless, and an exceptional strategist. Although "fire bases" or "fire support bases" were not new in concept, it was primarily Casey's method for deploying them at this point in the war that made them critical to the Vietnamization objectives of the division. The strategy was much more about mobility in Casey's vision than it had been when the U.S. Army's Korean allies had first developed the fire base concept.

Casey was no stranger to Vietnam either. He had served in country previously, not once but twice. For ambitious senior officers, two tours were becoming more or less de rigueur. Casey was being offered a third tour, but three tours would be strictly voluntary—and unusual. This tour, if he accepted it, would give him command of the division, after a few months as an ADC. He said yes. He would, of course, get a second star, making him one of the army's youngest-ever major generals, but he did not accept the assignment for that reason. His notes, letters, and records, as well as the recollections of his many devoted aides and subordinates, indicate that he had a deep, abiding concern for his men. He knew, unquestionably, that the dynamics of the war were changing, and he wanted to see his men get through this difficult transition period with as little hardship and bloodshed as possible. He felt it was his duty to stay with these men, to protect them to the extent that he could, and to get them out of this quagmire as soon as possible.

With the brainy, gifted, and hard-charging Casey as his number two, Roberts didn't have a lot to worry about when it came to making sure that his orders were carried out and that the troops were doing what they were supposed to be doing, albeit under difficult circumstances. Roberts was well aware of the informal chatter about Casey's rising star in the army and his possibly becoming chief of staff at some point in his career. Roberts gave Casey a lot of room to either prove his theories—or hang himself.

So it was that Casey, in early 1970, convened his battalion commanders and basically told them that they were going to do things differently. They would no longer be seeking out the enemy and attempting to engage them in full-on, stand-up fights: They were going to get the enemy to come to them, by luring them out, tempting them with easy targets, then laying on the full, crushing force of the big guns and tactical air.

War Zone C, the 1st Cavalry's primary area of operations (AO), extended from Saigon, north and west, all the way up and through a large bulge in the Vietnamese contour that ended in a jagged and twisted border with Cambodia (see map, page xxiii). The area had once been modestly populated, and the French had built a hard-surfaced road through the region. This highway was designed to carry traffic and commerce from Saigon to the major cities along the Cambodian border and then on to Phnom Penh, the country's hub and capital. One of these border cities, Snoul, would become a prime focal point of the upcoming Cambodian invasion.

The commercial center of War Zone C was Tay Ninh City, but by 1970 it was nearly deserted; the whole region had been a free-fire zone for nearly two decades. The French, the Viet Minh fighting the French, the Vietcong, the PAVN (the People's Army of Vietnam), and, eventually, the Americans had all used the wide-ranging area as a constant battleground. Many cleared areas that had supported productive farms were being reclaimed by the jungle.

War Zone C, which had colorful nicknames for certain facets of its contours—monikers like "the Parrot's Beak," the "Fishhook," and "the Dog's Head"—had become a prime conduit for the northern forces to sneak both men and supplies into the south. The infamous Ho Chi Minh Trail, which snaked down from the north through the neutral nations of Laos and Cambodia to the west, had sprouted tributary pathways throughout the zone. The terrain was riddled with cleverly disguised trails, and the triple-canopy jungle hid numerous caches of supplies and materiel.

The presence of the 1st Cav and, concurrently, the 25th Infantry, had made life much more difficult for the PAVN. Their choices were to relocate the supply routes to Cambodia or to try to continue to push supplies and reinforcements through the zone. Cambodia was the worst of their options: The delays inherent in the longer routes were onerous, and the government of Cambodia was becoming increasingly obstreperous concerning the "invasion" of its territory by the North Vietnamese.

There was another pressing imperative for the NVA to use the routes available to them in War Zone C: Their allies, the Vietcong, had suffered a staggering number of casualties during the 1968 Tet Offensive. The coordinated attacks, flung at nearly one hundred different targets during the Tet holiday, were universally beaten back (including an attack on the American Embassy in Saigon), but there were many desperate battles, and the campaign nearly finished the Vietcong as an effective fighting force. This collapse put the whole NVA strategy in jeopardy, especially in the southern part of the country, and it made the NVA even more anxious to rush men and supplies to the areas in and around Saigon. The trails through War Zone C were still the most expedient pathways.

The NVA, like sharks, were also smelling blood in the water. They believed that the Americans were losing their resolve to fight hard (that proved to be untrue) and that taking just a few more risks, pushing just a little harder, would finish off any determined resistance on the part of the United States and its allies. As a consequence, they elected to continue to use the supply routes, supply depots, and fortified bunker complexes they had peppered throughout War Zone C. In so doing they were, in effect, daring the Americans to deny them the use of these resources.

General Casey certainly understood what the NVA were up to, and he wanted to thwart the enemy's plans for using his AO as a conduit to press the war more effectively. This would mean, of course, that he and his men would have to root out the enemy, one base at a time. Plus, the rules had changed. Casey, Roberts, and the other senior commanders no longer had carte blanche to throw American resources at the enemy in an effort to get them to commit to a fight. The brute-force tactics of hard-charging warfare were no longer authorized. Casey would have to make the NVA come to him, then try to destroy them in a more efficient manner.

Casey came up with a plan. It was bold, innovative, and dangerous, but Roberts signed off on it, and in late 1969 and early 1970 it was put in play. The strategy was based on speed, mobility, stealth, and keeping the enemy guessing—and nervous. Small, company-sized units, both infantry and armor, would be sent out on long patrols to try to sniff out hidden enemy caches and supply routes. Once they were located, air and artillery would be called in to eliminate them. To assist in this process, the artillery units in the division would no longer remain in fixed base positions. They would be broken down into battery-sized commands and moved around like the infantry and the cavalry.

It was a giant game of chess played across a landscape encompassing thousands of square miles. The infantry, just like the queen on the chessboard (which is why the infantry has been dubbed "the Queen of Battle"), would roam wherever it chose. The armored units, acting as knights and bishops, would jump or crisscross the landscape, tearing up the jungle and trying to root out the enemy and expose them to the artillery. The artillery, just like their castled counterparts in chess, would have only a limited range of mobility, but they would be kept moving, every few days, just to keep the enemy confused and on their toes.

The key to the strategy was the fire base, or fire support base, or FSB. The FSB, as stated previously, was not a new concept: Fire bases, many also doubling as LZs, or landing zones (for helicopters, primarily), had been in play for years. Heretofore, however, most of them had been employed as semipermanent or long-term (more than a month) outposts carved out of the jungle or placed atop fortified hills or mesas. They had been intended to bring the war to the enemy and, in some cases, positioned with the express purpose of provoking the NVA and getting them to come out of their jungle hideouts and do battle. Some of these FSBs became large fortresses with complicated installations, heavy artillery, huge landing pads, and hot showers. Several were as large as the entire valley they were staged in. These outposts would be placed close enough, in a perfect world, to provide overlapping artillery coverage from FSB to FSB. They also became spots where companies of infantry could find respite from their jungle patrols and, if they were lucky, a cold beer and a hot steak.

To some, it seemed like the army was repeating a strategy it had become comfortable with many decades ago. The FSBs were reminiscent, in many ways, of the cavalry forts of the old American West, plunked down in the Indian territories that were scattered across the plains.

In January of 1970, General Casey informed his brigade and battalion commanders that they were going to start "busting some serious brush." Casey knew, however, that with the vastness of War Zone C, his men couldn't be everywhere, so he also told them they were going to move fast, hopscotch across the region, set up FSBs, and "kick some ass." He wanted the NVA to be off guard and constantly wondering where the 1st Cav was going to show up next.

The key to Casey's new plan was ratcheting up the FSB concept. With rare exceptions, the 1st Cav FSBs would be installations of very short duration. They would be moved constantly. The hope was to keep the NVA nervous, off balance, and always guessing what the Americans' next moves would be. In theory, this constant maneuvering would not allow the NVA to develop any semipermanent installations either. They would have to continually worry about having their caches of precious materials and ammunition discovered and destroyed. Their previous advantages of being able to remain in fortified and well-hidden jungle hideouts would be negated. Their jungle trails and resupply routes would be under constant observation and continually imperiled.

Under the Casey FSB doctrine, open areas would be selected near where the maneuver battalions of infantry and their supporting helicopters and armor were operating. Bulldozers would then arrive on the scene and begin shoving dirt, carving out large circular areas, approximately 100 meters across. The dirt was pushed up into berms around a perimeter roughly 3 feet high. One or two access openings were made; then headquarters elements, medical facilities, and artillery were moved inside. A tactical operations center (TOC) was established within the new base, usually somewhere near the center. The TOC was dug in and often covered with sandbags and corrugated metal roofing. Some TOCs were made out of CONEX boxes (large, metal shipping containers, such as those used for transocean freight). Machine-gun bunkers were spaced around the perimeter, and gun pits for the artillery batteries were marked and day in.

The 1st Cav, between February 1 and April 30, 1970, constructed and abandoned an astonishing eighty-three FSBs within their AO. One FSB lasted fifty-one days, but that was the exception. A scattering lasted two to three weeks. Most were built and then abandoned in ten days or less, and almost a third of these FSBs were opened and closed in one or two days.

FSBs were, by their very design, out in the open, and the "walls" were only flimsy piles of sand augmented by layers of sandbags piled on top, usually only three bags deep. They would not be able to stand much of a pounding from enemy artillery or RPGs. Given that they were going to be opened and closed with regularity and rapidity, they would not be robustly constructed or surrounded by walls of barbed wire, elaborate fortifications, or overly strong gun emplacements.

FSBs had a secondary purpose, and one that wasn't always popular with those who manned them: They were tempting targets for the enemy. The army absolutely appreciated that a fixed position like an FSB, sitting out in the open and populated by large pieces of artillery and ammunition dumps, would become irresistible to the enemy. As soon as the first mobile FSBs were established, the NVA exhibited a strong inclination to attack them. Although this did, of course, expose the inhabitants of an FSB to imminent danger, it served the very useful purpose of allowing the army to discover where the enemy was as soon as they took the bait. This, in turn, decreased the territory that the infantry had to search and allowed the Americans to concentrate their resources to greater effect.

The army, when establishing an FSB, almost always installed all manner of ground surveillance radars, sensory equipment, and infrared night-sighting devices. The engineers and their bulldozers deliberately left patches of concealment around or near the FSBs, hoping that the enemy would use them as spots for their forward observers and recon troops. When the NVA took advantage of these patches of trees or jungle—which they often did—they soon discovered, much to their detriment, that each one of them had been pretargeted by the big guns inside the perimeter of the FSB or the guns at another nearby FSB. The engineers also carved large racetracklike concentric circles around the FSBs, usually at 100, 150, and 300 meters beyond the firing positions. These circles would be used by airborne observers as range scales and points of reference when calling in TACAIR (tactical air support) or artillery strikes on the enemy.

An FSB was, no doubt, a dangerous place, but one that was also bristling with weapons and equipped with the means to effectively counter the enemy's desire to destroy it. At least, that was the theory.

By late March 1970, the tactics were bearing fruit. Many NVA supply bases had been uncovered, including one that had disgorged an astonishing 250,000 pounds of rice. The NVA were growing increasingly nervous and edgy, and they had started to shove back, thereby exposing themselves to counterattack. This was just what General Casey wanted.

3

"THE PERFECT SOLDIER"

PRIVATE FIRST CLASS JOHN J. "JACK" ILLINGWORTH, FROM NEW Haven, Connecticut, landed in country on January 8, 1970, five days before his twentieth birthday. A scant sixty-five days later he would be dead: killed in a vicious little firefight near the Cambodian border. It was a sad coda to what might have been a life of bright promise. Here is his all-too-brief story:

A small stream ran through a tiny copse near the otherwise dull and dreary Brookside Housing Project in downtown New Haven. Though diminutive, the wooded refuge was still large enough for a young boy to lose himself within, and dream of better days ahead. It was, for him, a magical spot within which turtles and snakes, even an owl with a broken wing, would be found. All of these creatures, and more, came home to the impossibly small three-bedroom apartment crammed with Jack's parents and eight brothers and sisters. Jack was the oldest boy, his sister Judy the oldest of all; then had come the twins, Laura and Mary; followed by Joyce, Frank, Harriett, Cynthia, and Susan.

Jack's parents were Frances ("Frank"), an ironworker, and Muriel, a homemaker (as might be expected with a brood of nine). Unfortunately for Frank, a fall from a second-story work project broke his back in 1959, and he was paralyzed from the waist down forevermore. This ended a proud and boisterous union man's career, and commenced the dark days of drinking and despair that lay ahead for Frank and the entire family.

Jack's sister Laura recalls many drunken nights and weekends, when the New Haven police would come by the apartment and referee. On several occasions, they had to haul Frank off to sober him up and calm him down before he hurt someone. The cops came so many times, in fact, that one officer, smitten by both the family's plight and Muriel herself, offered to marry Muriel to get her out of her nearly intolerable situation. With an admirable degree of loyalty and stoicism, Muriel declined, in favor of her children.

Jack, as the oldest boy, became the family's principal provider. Frank's disability payments would only stretch so far, especially after the tab for alcohol was figured in. As a teenager, Jack would be up at four in the morning, rolling newspapers and making early deliveries. He also worked at the nearby Catholic rectory as a janitor. All the kids worked as soon as they were old enough to hold down even the smallest of jobs.

Whatever precious spare time Jack had, he would volunteer at the local nature center. After Catholic grammar school he enrolled at New Haven's Eli Whitney Technical High School, where he fell in love with both a young Italian girl and carpentry. He demonstrated great skill with wood, finding a trade and something he could do for the rest of his life. Carpenters, especially union ones, made excellent money. This was, however, the late 1960s, and as it would with millions of young men of that decade, the Selective

Service would seek Jack out before he had time to join the carpenters union or marry the girl of his dreams.

As the family's primary source of income, Jack could have claimed exemption from the draft, but he did not. For all his father's challenges and belligerence, he was a veteran who had gone ashore at Anzio in World War II and knew all about combat and the imperative to serve one's country. He had passed this sense of obligation along to his oldest son, and when Jack's turn came, all he said was "I have to do this."

Laura remembers taking Jack to the bus station. He went off to basic training at Fort Dix, New Jersey, in August of 1969. He came home for a few days at Christmas. After the holiday Laura, by then a senior in high school, took him back to the bus station. It would be the last time she would see her big brother alive.

"He was such a handsome boy," Laura remembers fondly, and his youthful pictures attest to that. "He could have done anything, been anyone he wanted to be, but all he wanted then was to be a soldier, a good one, and to do his duty."

Immediately after finishing basic training at Fort Dix, Private Illingworth was given orders to Vietnam. He had expected it—most men in his training battalion were detailed likewise, and even though the direction of the war was changing, its giant maw was still consuming men at an alarming rate. Nonetheless, Jack left confident that he would return, as his letters home continued to attest: letters that included most of the pay he was making in the army.

As soon as he landed in Vietnam, he was sent to a replacement company for further detailing. In late January 1970, right after Jack's twentieth birthday, he was assigned to Captain Ray Armer's Alpha Company of the 2/8.

On March 13, Alpha Company was way out in the boonies on a long patrol that had originated at a fire support base about six miles from the Cambodian border. As the company was crossing a wide stream, they came under fire. Everyone dove for cover or fell back except for one soldier who had already forded the stream and went down in the initial fusillade. Moments later the grunt on the far bank was desperately calling for help. The company's two medics were already busy with other casualties. Captain Armer told the rest of the men to stay put.

Jack Illingworth didn't like lying there and doing nothing while a man was crying for help. His squad leader, Sgt. Maynard "Bo" Boedecker, told him to "chill out" and wait for orders—or the medics. At first, Illingworth did, but no medics came up and no orders came forward. Finally, yelling, "Screw it!" Illingworth leapt up. He zigged and zagged the 20 yards or so across the stream to find the soldier, a grunt by the name of Lockhart, who was badly wounded. With bullets dicing the foliage all around him, Illingworth grabbed Lockhart and slung him over his shoulder in the typical "wounded warrior" carry. Miraculously, he and Lockhart made it back unscathed. Captain Armer was not pleased with Illingworth's disobedience of orders, but, given the circumstances and the positive result, he quickly overlooked his displeasure to concentrate on the actions of a brave soldier. Armer made a note in his day book recommending Illingworth for a Silver Star. The battalion commander, Lt. Col. Mike Conrad, received Armer's recommendation, by radio, that day.

Armer decided to stop the company for the night on the near side of the stream. It was approaching dark, and he felt it best to stay in place and resume the patrol at first light. The company hunkered down and set up their perimeters, expecting the NVA might try to take a run at them during the night. The NVA didn't storm across the stream that evening, but they did take some shots at the Americans. This was probably more an attempt to keep the grunts awake and on edge than a serious effort to do much damage.

Sergeant Boedecker recalls that several men got clipped during the tense evening in the woods, Jack Illingworth among them. It was nothing serious, however, and the wounds were quickly bandaged. The men's psyches were taking more hits than their bodies were. Everyone knew that there would be a major confrontation at dawn, and no one got much sleep.

Early on March 14, Alpha Company was on the move, crossing the stream in force, poking and prodding, looking for the contact they were certain they were going to get. They didn't get very far before firing erupted. PFC Illingworth was helping to man an M-60 machine gun that morning. As he aimed and fired, a B-40 rocket came sizzling out of the jungle.

The rocket hit Illingworth's M-60 a glancing blow and then blew shrapnel in all directions. Jack Illingworth's body absorbed a great deal of the damaging blast. Although the explosion did not kill him instantly, Illingworth received wounds that were clearly mortal. He could not have survived even if the best medical attention had been rendered instantly.

As he lay dying, he called for water. Sergeant Boedecker knelt by his side. He tried to make Illingworth comfortable and laid him on his backpack. Boedecker prayed for Illingworth, not that he would live, but that he would die. As Boedecker later told it, Illingworth was torn up so badly by the B-40 that had he lived, he probably would have regretted it.

Jack Illingworth likely knew, in his last moments, that his life was over, yet he didn't cry out; he didn't bemoan his fate. He died stoically, like the good soldier he had become.

Soon thereafter, Colonel Conrad read Alpha Company's DSR (Daily Status Report) for March 14. On it, he saw the name of PFC Illingworth listed as KIA. He then remembered: *Isn't there something else on Illingworth? Ah, yes, here it is. The same soldier was recommended for the Silver Star.*

Conrad sighed. "One day a live hero, the next day a dead one."

The tragedy was still on Conrad's mind on March 17, three days later, when the 2/8 was establishing yet another fire support base. This one would be astride a trail the NVA had been using to move massive quantities of supplies to their men in the south. Heretofore, the FSBs had been named somewhat quixotically, one time after someone's wife or girlfriend, the next time mockingly, as in "FSB Danger."

Conrad decided that perhaps these installations should be taken a little more seriously. Thus it was that on the 17th, when it came time to designate the newest FSB, Conrad named it Illingworth, in honor of the young soldier who had been so much in his thoughts during the last seventy-two hours.

Who knows what Jack Illingworth would have become had he survived the war? Who knows what any of the 58,272 men and women who are listed on the Vietnam Memorial Wall would have become? Some, certainly, would have become carpenters, like Jack wanted to be. Some would have married their hometown sweethearts, like Jack wished to do. Jack Illingworth made it through 65 days of his 365-day tour, less than 18 percent of his obligated time. On the other hand, 997 men died on their very first day of combat in Vietnam. A sad 1,448 died on the day they were supposed to rotate out and go home. Jack was twenty when he died, but there were many who were younger, including the youngest: Marine PFC Dan Bullock. He was reportedly only fifteen.

Jack's body was returned to his family, and when he was buried in New Haven's All Saints Cemetery he received full military honors. Over one hundred cars drove in the mournful procession to his final resting place.

Later that year, in September, family and friends gathered one more time in Jack Illingworth's honor. This time it was at the New Haven Induction Center, where Jack Illingworth had started his military journey a little more than a year before. The commanding officer of the Yale University Army ROTC Program, Col. Richard R. Irving, presented the Illingworth family with nine medals and decorations Jack Illingworth had won: the Silver Star, the Bronze Star, the Purple Heart, the Combat Infantryman's Badge, the Air Medal, the Army Commendation Medal, the National Defense Service Medal, the Vietnam Service Medal, and the Vietnam Campaign Medal. By this time the family had also received personal letters of condolence from President Richard M. Nixon; Secretary of the Army Stanley Resor; Gen. Creighton Abrams, the commander of all troops in Vietnam; Maj. Gen. Elvy Roberts, the commander of the 1st Cavalry Division at the time of Jack Illingworth's death; Connecticut's U.S. Senator Thomas J. Dodd; and Capt. Ray Armer, Jack Illingworth's company commander.

In addition, because of Jack Illingworth's act of bravery just before he died, he was posthumously promoted to corporal. All of it seemed small compensation to Jack Illingworth's grieving family and friends. Sadly, these sorts of activities would be repeated across the nation over 58,000 times.

30 May 2005

It was a lucky day for me when we met and became close friends. It's been 35 years since my last letter to my old friend Jack was returned to me, letting me know he had been killed. I was not surprised when

I recently read in a book that a fire base was named after Jack. Jack, like the rest of his family, were kind, strong, had a great sense of humor, gave me their love and were always truthful to me. I know, they know, I never forgot them or their son and brother who was taken at such an early age, my dear old friend Jack.

Peace

Russ Horner

The Vietnam Veterans

Memorial Wall,

The Wall-USA.com

11 Jan 2007

Dear John,

With all of this war going on and having a nephew and friends fighting for us I can't help but think of you. It's also two days before your birthday, a day that was very lucky for the rest of us. I love you, cousin, and am very proud of you and THANK YOU for what you have done. I never have forgotten your memorial service. As a young child it left a big impression in my mind and in the minds of the rest of our family. GOD BLESS JACK, see you when I get there. I LOVE YOU.

Your cousin Joann

The Virtual Wall online,

used with permission

4

FROM THE FRYING PAN INTO THE FIRE

ON MARCH 26, 1970, CHARLIE COMPANY 2/8 WALKED INTO A PREVIOUSLY unknown and skillfully hidden NVA supply base. For several days, Charlie had been cautiously patrolling in the immediate area. On the 24th, they had discovered a "trotter," a trail through the jungle wide enough for two men to walk down side by side. This was proof positive that the enemy was in the area, and in strength. Only major supply routes connecting crucial way stations had trails such as this. The scope and size of the installation Charlie stumbled upon, however, was still a shock. The complex was ringed by solidly built and well-concealed bunkers dug into the earth and protected by stout, hand-cut logs. The NVA had set up interlocking fields of fire with their heavy machine guns and RPGs. Defending the base were over six hundred NVA Regulars from the 272nd Regiment. Charlie, on the other hand, was an understrength company of eighty-seven. More than half of the men were newbies. None of the new men had, until then, fired a shot in anger.

Capt. George Hobson was the CO (commanding officer) of

Charlie Company, and he, too, was new—but only to the company. He had taken command from Charlie's former CO, Capt. Joe Gesker, fourteen days prior, after Gesker had been wounded. Hobson was a veteran soldier with enlisted experience before his commissioning and had already served one tour in Vietnam, as an adviser to the ARVN. He had lots of combat savvy, but the situation he and his men found themselves in on March 26 was, to use one of their terms, a real "shit sandwich" of gigantic proportions. In addition to lacking experienced soldiers, Hobson was also shy several officers and senior noncoms. Charlie Company probably shouldn't have been placed in this position, but, as the men were fond of saying at the time, "And there it is."

Hobson was the type of officer (he eventually made a career of the army, retiring as a lieutenant colonel) who believed orders were orders. He might not have wished to be where he was, but he was not about to question his superiors, either. Hobson was gruff, prickly, and a no-nonsense leader. His men did not necessarily love their new commander, but they surely did respect him, and that was just fine with Captain Hobson.

Hobson's commanding officer at the time was the very same Lt. Col. Mike Conrad, CO of the 2/8, who was trying to adjust his battalion to the harsh and extended conditions at FSB Illingworth. Conrad had sent Charlie out from Illingworth to conduct this long, intensive patrol of the jungle near the Cambodian border on March 20. The order he had given Hobson was to "find the NVA and report back." If they did find the enemy they were not to bring on an engagement. They were to step aside and let TACAIR and the artillery pulverize whatever Charlie found.

Unfortunately, it didn't quite work out as planned. Charlie found unmistakable evidence of the NVA when they discovered the trotter. In addition, they uncovered a distinctive NVA radio communications wire hidden along the trail and signs that the NVA were cutting down trees (probably for bunkers) and setting snares in the jungle to catch small animals to cook up with their rice. On March 24, before bedding down for the night, Charlie laid a booby trap along the trotter. It went off about 0200 the next morning, killing an NVA warrant officer. When Hobson's men searched the body of the man at daylight, they found sketches with detailed drawings of FSB Illingworth. This discovery sent Colonel Conrad and the intel officers back at Division into paroxysms of concern. What were the NVA planning? Something, obviously, was about to happen. Although this was good information for the Americans to have, it made Charlie's situation a lot more dangerous. Conrad was even more desperate for Hobson to locate the NVA. He pushed the patrol farther and farther north, toward the border, which seemed, from all indications, the direction most likely to lead to the enemy.

It was. Shortly before noon, on March 26, with Hobson's company creeping silently and slowly along in two parallel lines about 20 yards apart, the entire company walked into a carefully laid trap. They followed the signs—carefully staged by the NVA, it was later discovered—of broken branches, snares, small trails, and pieces of discarded equipment. The NVA, skillfully hidden in the brush along both sides of Charlie's direction of travel, let the whole company pass before pouncing. Once all of Hobson's men were completely inside the enemy's lines of defense, the trap was sprung. NVA at the back end of the complex closed ranks, sealing off Charlie's only avenue of retreat, then all hell broke loose.

One of Hobson's soldiers was drilled through the brain and died instantly. Another had his right femoral artery ripped apart. This poor grunt expired later in the battle. Another dozen men went down with various wounds right at the outset. Hobson had been wise to patrol in parallel lines; this allowed his men to fan out quickly, form a defensive circle, and establish a perimeter. Still, many of Hobson's grunts were paralyzed—not with fear, although that would not have been unusual, but by inexperience. The few veteran noncoms and experienced officers on hand spent precious moments simply pushing and shoving men into better firing positions and then reminding them to shoot. There'd be no "cherries" remaining after this firefight.

Hobson quickly determined that his situation was dire. The NVA had them surrounded and cut off. The enemy was fighting from sheltered positions, most of them firing from within their dirt and log bunkers. Hobson's men were essentially out in the open; if concealed at all, it was only by insubstantial vegetation. He got on the radio and started calling for support.

Colonel Conrad heard the calls immediately. He sprinted to his command helicopter and told his pilot to get him to Charlie's position ASAP. They were soon overhead. Hobson marked his position with smoke grenades. Conrad could readily see that his men were in a world of hurt. There were no landing zones anywhere nearby, and Charlie would not be able to hack an LZ out of the brush anytime soon. Without an LZ, it would be impossible to have helicopters pull his men out and equally impossible to get more troops in.

Conrad did have TACAIR and artillery at his disposal, and he got them moving quickly, but neither the aircraft nor the big guns could do much good. The troops were intermingled, and dropping shells or bombs on the NVA could kill or wound Charlie's men with equal probability. The F-4 Phantoms, the Apache gunships, and the artillery at the nearby fire support bases (including Illingworth) could only pound away at the margins of the fight, where Conrad was fairly sure no Americans would be impacted. Even Conrad's helicopter couldn't get close; the NVA took shots at it every time it came within range. The best Conrad could do was to try to keep Charlie Company supplied with ammo and encouragement and hope that somehow Hobson could find a way to break through the encirclement.

That wasn't going to happen. Down on the ground, Hobson was totally occupied with keeping his men alive—and he wasn't going to try to effect a breakout, either. That would mean leaving behind his wounded, and he was not about to do that. No, they would stay put until Colonel Conrad got it figured out, even if that meant, as Hobson well knew, every man becoming a casualty or a POW.

Meanwhile, about 3 miles away, unbeknown to or forgotten by Conrad or Hobson, was Alpha Troop, 1st Squadron, 11th Armored Cavalry. The headquarters elements were ensconced in a dry lake bed. The maneuver platoons were out on patrol, duties they had been performing for more than thirty straight days. All the men were dead tired. The night before, possibly even because of the fatigue, the troop had suffered a horrific accident wherein a mortar round—undoubtedly defective—had exploded in one of their own vehicles, killing three men and shaking the troop to its emotional core.

Alpha Troop's CO, Capt. John Poindexter, twenty-five, was sitting outside his command track, sweltering in the midday heat, hearing the very same radio calls from Hobson that Conrad was then getting. He grabbed a chart of the local area, and it didn't take him long to approximate where Charlie Company was at that moment. Poindexter could also see clearly that he and his men were the only ones anywhere near Charlie's position. As a precaution, he recalled two of his patrolling platoons and had his third platoon, the one closest to Charlie's assumed location, halt in place and await further orders. Poindexter figured Conrad, who was his temporary boss, would be on the radios shortly ordering him and his men to ride to the rescue.

So they waited, but no one called. Working with Alpha Troop that day was Alpha 2/8, a company of infantrymen that Conrad had assigned to ride along with them, as an experiment in joint armor/infantry patrolling. The CO of Alpha Company was the very same Capt. Ray Armer who had been Corporal Illingworth's most recent commander. He, too, was sitting with Poindexter listening to the radios. Someone had to ask the question, so Armer did.

"What do you think we should do, John?"

The two captains discussed the options, none of them good. They could hold tight and wait for orders, in which case Charlie's situation would only grow more desperate and more men were likely to die. In the army, you typically waited for orders, but this didn't seem right under the circumstances at that moment. They could send a patrol out in the direction of Charlie and probe the situation, to see what the options might be. That might also waste valuable time, and it would certainly reduce the available daylight remaining. Or they could mount up, hell-bent for leather, and make a mad dash toward Charlie, hoping to arrive in time to do something productive and get out of there before dark. The NVA owned the night, and no one wanted to be out in the jungle at night fighting the NVA. Doing nothing felt like the least palatable option, so—orders be damned—Poindexter instructed everyone to "saddle up."

Shortly after giving his men the go-ahead, Poindexter was finally able to reach Colonel Conrad on the battalion net. Conrad was impressed that Poindexter was tracking the serious situation developing and had his Team Alpha on the move. Conrad directed them to continue.

For the next several hours Alpha Team (the combination of the cavalry's Alpha Troop and the infantry's Alpha 2/8) forged ahead, busting jungle. Due to the thickness of the vegetation, the sweltering temperatures of the day, and the overheating engines, progress was not rapid, but at least it was steady. Poindexter radioed Conrad that he was on the way, and Conrad, desperate for any help, heartily approved of Poindexter's initiative—even though it was not clear to Conrad just how this was going to work, if at all.

The forest was eventually conquered at roughly 1630. Then, as Alpha Team neared Charlie's position, they ran into one more tough obstacle. A B-52 bombing mission, sometime in the recent past, had cut a wide swath in the jungle to the rear of Charlie's position. That path of destruction was directly in front of Alpha Team, blocking the route to Charlie Company. The bombers had done a fine job of blowing up the jungle, but in so doing they had left behind a tangle of broken tree trunks and craters big enough to swallow an ACAV whole. The slippery, silted sides of the holes could twist the treads off a track if a driver was not careful. The partial openness of the devastation would also expose the entire column to the NVA. There was no way around the mess, however, so Poindexter told his men to charge across—and they did. Miraculously, no tracks disappeared into any of the giant holes, and no vehicles were disabled by the detritus, the uneven ground, or the NVA.

As the diesel-powered beasts chugged through and into Charlie's lines, they halted and began unloading medical supplies, water, and ammunition. Charlie Company was nearly spent. It was clear that the rescuers had not arrived a moment too soon. Some men were too exhausted to even cheer. The ground was littered with the wounded, and in spots the grass seemed to have been painted red. Incredibly, Charlie had sustained no additional KIAs beyond the two men shot down at the outset of the fight, but it was clear that among the many wounded were a number of men in shock or going into extremis. If help could not be administered soon, there were going to be a lot more grunts in body bags.

At that moment, Captains Poindexter and Armer, joined by a grateful Captain Hobson, had another crucial decision to make: Should they load up the rescued men and make a mad dash back, or should they engage the enemy? Poindexter was leery of leaving an undefeated enemy at his back, one who could sprint through the jungle and lay traps ahead of his tracks or bedevil his men all the way back to their NDP (night defensive position). He was also tempted by the target. They had been chasing this regiment for weeks, and, there they were, right in front of him. Crushing this regiment was one of the main objectives for the 1st Cav at that time.

Poindexter decided to gamble on one quick, hard thrust into the heart of the complex—to go in all guns blazing and do as much damage as he could. If they couldn't beat them, they could at least inflict some serious destruction and give the NVA a reason not to pursue his column. He got on the radios and ordered his nineteen fighting tracks to line up in a wide arc across the front of the NVA bunker complex. When all his tracks were ready, he ordered a full combat assault.

Alpha Troop's Sheridans fired one round after another; the terrifying beehive warheads, with their 10,000 flechettes each, carved giant holes in the jungle. Any enemy troops caught in the path of one of those blasts were instantly riddled with them. (One unfortunate NVA soldier was found, three days later, literally pinned to a tree like an oversized butterfly in a display case. He had been pierced with dozens of the deadly darts.) All the tracks had .50 caliber machine guns, and the ACAVs mounted two more M-60 light machine guns each. Ray Armer's infantrymen went in behind the tracks, adding their M-16 firepower and hand grenades to the mix.

The NVA bent, but they did not break. Although they were outgunned, they had the Americans outmanned. The two sides went at it full bore for two solid hours. RPGs tore into the American lines, wounding many, damaging several of Poindexter's tracks, and killing one brave tank commander. Poindexter was wounded by the same rocket. Men were down all over, and to make matters more complicated, the NVA renewed their attacks on Charlie Company, which was tasked with guarding the rear and the only avenue of egress.

After having a painful arm wound bandaged, Poindexter had to face the realities of the situation. Night was rapidly approaching, he was beginning to run low on ammo, and the men—especially those in Charlie Company—were near the point of collapse. He did not want to be tangled up with the enemy in the dark. That was a losing proposition. It was clear they had done considerable damage to the enemy, and once Alpha Team pulled back, Division would send in TACAIR to blast this base into splinters and chlorophyll, thus eliminating it as a threat. Many of the wounded needed help that could not be given in the field; plus, they had accomplished their major objective: the rescue of Charlie Company. It was a hell of a day's worth of work no matter how one looked at it, and in consideration of everything, Poindexter gave the order to round everyone up and move out.

Darkness fell on the column almost as soon as it started back, effectively stalling it in place, still far from home plate. Poindexter feared the NVA would pounce if they couldn't get some light on the situation. Fortuitously, the mortar section chief, Sgt. "Bud" Smolich, had laid in the coordinates of his remaining mortar track back at the NDP before the column left on its trek. Knowing those coordinates and the returning column's rough position on the trail back out, he could direct the mortar crew at the NDP to light up the sky with illumination rounds in the vicinity of Alpha Team. It worked, and the mortar crew was able to provide enough light for the exhausted rescuers and those they rescued to pick their way through the jungle and back to the NDP.

Charlie Company had gone into the jungle with eighty-seven men: they came out with thirty-nine effectives, i.e., those still standing and not wounded badly enough to require evacuation. Including the two men killed, that was a casualty rate of 56 percent. The injured included Captain Hobson, who somehow went untouched during the course of the main attack but was hit as the column left the scene. He suffered painful shrapnel wounds to the face when an RPG slammed into the turret of a tank next to where he was standing. He probably should have left the company for treatment after the return to the NDP, but he did not. He didn't want to leave his men—what remained of them, anyway. It was an honorable decision but one that would cause him to later lose an eye.

Charlie Company was flown out of Alpha Troop's NDP on the morning of March 27 and taken to FSB Illingworth, only 5 klicks away. Colonel Conrad wanted them off the line after such a tremendous pounding. They were instructed to "rest up." At least they could get a few cold sodas and rudimentary showers. The remaining men were told to guard the southeast sector of the FSB and await further orders. Hobson's first priority was obtaining replacements, and on the morning of March 30 he received the first batch of about thirty.

This restocking of the personnel cupboard allowed several veteran members of Charlie Company, like PFC Ken "Mississippi" Woodward, to rotate to the rear for a day or two to attend to other necessities. Woodward was an RTO in Scotch Platoon. He had reported to Charlie Company in January, which meant he had been through all of the toughest fighting that had been visited upon "Hard Luck Charlie" in the three months since. He had been a firsthand witness to the terrible dismantling of what had been a damn good combat outfit. The company was one-third the size it had been when Woodward joined up, and he had begun to lose track of the faces and names of the men he had seen come and go since.

In the past ninety days there had been engagements where more men had been killed in action than on March 26, but there had not been a fight that had been tougher or scarier. There were times during that very long day when Woodward sincerely believed that his last moments on earth were at hand. Somehow, though, he had survived, albeit not without a few cuts and bruises. At one point in the battle, while helping a fellow grunt to the casualty collection point, he had been slammed to the ground by an explosive concussion and nicked by shrapnel in the left knee and right ankle. The blood flowed freely, but he deemed the wound not sufficient to remove him from the fight.

Now that the company—or what was left of it—was in a place of relative safety Woodward went to his platoon leader seeking permission to go to the rear for a bit. He had a couple of teeth that were bothering him, and he wanted to get them fixed up before humping off into the jungle again. He received permission for what would become the most fortuitous dental appointment in Ken Woodward's life.

5

"BUILD IT AND THEY WILL COME"

THE REVISED FIRE-BASE STRATEGY WAS PAYING OFF—IF, INDEED, making the NVA nervous, angry, and aggressive was considered a good payoff. General Casey was keeping his brigades on the move, and 1st Brigade's 2/8 battalion, under Colonel Conrad's leadership, was hitting the NVA particularly hard; the enemy's casualties were ratcheting upward.

On March 17, the 2/8 abandoned FSB Drum and moved even closer to the Cambodian border in order to establish another fire base right on top of where the intel guys believed the NVA had a robust trail system leading south. As noted above, Conrad dubbed the new FSB Illingworth in honor of PFC (posthumously promoted to corporal) Jack Illingworth.

Another 1st Brigade battalion, the 2/7, commanded by Lt. Col. Robert Hannas, was also moving up. The next day, March 18, they set up shop on a spot about 6 miles away from Illingworth, occupying a former fire support base named Jay. This post had been opened and then closed by the ARVN some weeks prior (chapter 7 has a more complete discussion of FSB Jay). Over the next two weeks, FSBs Jay and Illingworth would operate in concert against the NVA forces infiltrating the area. They would also become entwined in some of the most savage fighting of 1970.

The construction of a fire support base was usually quite a circus, and Illingworth was no exception. First, Division intel picked the geographic coordinates that were most likely to catch the NVA's immediate attention. The FSB would be placed as close as possible to where the NVA were believed to be running men and supplies through the local brush. With the basic coordinates in hand, Colonel Conrad would plant a center stake, the physical spot where the construction process would commence. The outpost would be out in the open so that it could be free of cumbersome obstructions. This would also make the base an inviting target, and as odd as it might seem to some, that was part of the plan.

With the physical spot designated and marked, the engineers would be flown in, followed immediately by a Chinook helicopter dangling a small bulldozer from a sling beneath its belly. The dozer would start from wherever the senior engineer in charge directed, and immediately begin shoving piles of earth outward, forming a huge circle roughly 300 yards across. (Theoretically: By the time the engineers were done at Illingworth, the outer boundary resembled an egg more than a perfect circle.) The dirt berm was to be about 3 feet high.

The next activity was to build out the tactical operations center. The same bulldozer dug a big hole near the center of the base. Large timbers were flown in to span the hole. Sheets of PSP (pierced steel planking), the same kind used to construct makeshift runways and tarmacs, were brought in to lie across the top of the timbers. Finally, several layers of sandbags were filled and thrown on top of the steel planking. A Chinook also flew in a large CONEX box (an empty shipping container), which was plopped down next to the TOC and smothered in sandbags. This would be the battalion aid station.

The icing on the cake was a single, virtually useless, strand of concertina wire that was strung all around the top of the berm. Barbed wire was not very effective at slowing down the enemy unless it was staked down (it wasn't at Illingworth) and complemented with what was called "tanglefoot." A tanglefoot installation placed multiple lines of barbed wire or razor wire somewhere between knee and ankle height across a wide space, typically 8 to 10 feet across. These patches were usually placed near strategic spots, such as the .50 cal bunkers or the TOC. The patchwork quilt of wire was difficult to cross or crawl under without getting all entangled (thus the countrified nomenclature of "tanglefoot"). Installing these types of elaborate wire snares required a lot of time and personnel, neither of which Colonel Conrad had. It also took a great deal of aerial support to fly in tons of bales of barbed wire. Division flight time was then at a premium and therefore unavailable to use for this purpose.

The single strand of wire that was deployed would not be an obstacle of any consequence to troops determined to storm the base, but the wire barrier was visible to a charging enemy. They could not know how extensive (or insubstantial) the wire was, especially in the dark, until they were on top of it. The fear of a substantial wire barrier could cause a moment's hesitation, and that half second might make the difference to a defender. At least that was the theory.

Once these rudimentary preparations had been made, the infantry could dig in. At Illingworth, Conrad carefully placed his infantry assets (fewer than ninety men, by the best available contemporary records) at posts on the perimeter closest to what he figured would be the likeliest points of attack. The infantry officers would then detail their platoons and squads to construct firing positions. Some of the squads were lucky enough to procure corrugated metal culverts—sort of mini-Quonset huts—but most were relegated to piling up whatever sandbags, boxes, used ammo cans, spare timbers, and wire they could scrounge.

By the time all the infantry emplacements were done, there were twenty of them. Each could contain, if fully manned (they were not), between six and nine grunts. Where there were culverts, the men stacked sandbags on top of them three to four bags deep. Men who were left to fend for themselves on the line dug foxholes into the berm. For some reason, there was a scarcity of claymore mines, and until more could be flown in, only a few were placed in front of each section of the perimeter. The total number of claymores, in the collected memories of those who survived the onslaught, was pegged at "a couple dozen." This was hardly enough to deflect or defeat a determined formation of enemy combatants, but certainly enough to catch a few enemies in the first wave.

The fire base had machine guns, but not a large number; the veterans of the battle indicated that there may have been ten to twelve of all calibers. A few M-60s were brought up and placed along the berm, probably no more than six. Recollections count "several" .50 calibers on the line, which included one that had been "appropriated" from one of the inoperable Sheridan tanks languishing over on the northwest corner of the base. There was a quad .50 mount, consisting of four synchronized .50 cals (more on that below), stationed near the 8-inch howitzers.

After the engineers left, the artillery arrived. The same faithful "Shit-hooks" would sling in and disgorge several of the big guns that had been assigned to Illingworth, and others would rumble up in convoy. Eventually, FSB Illingworth would have the following artillery units and field pieces on hand: six 105 mm howitzers from Battery B, 1st Battalion, 77th Field Artillery; three 155 mm howitzers from A Battery, 1st Battalion, 30th Field Artillery; and two 8-inch SP howitzers from A Battery, 2nd Battalion, 32nd Field Artillery. The "redlegs"* also flew in a portable FDC (fire direction center) housed within another CONEX container. B Battery, 5th Battalion, 2nd Field Artillery, sent up a quad .50 gun truck, and I Battery of the 29th Field Artillery provided a xenon searchlight jeep. (These two resources were primarily to support and protect the 8-inch howitzers.) There were also three 81 mm mortars in Echo 2/8's mortar platoon.

The 105 mm howitzer had been around since the early days of World War II in what was called the M-101 version. In 1966 the newer, lighter M-102 model began to be deployed to Vietnam, and it became the ubiquitous and primary workhorse artillery piece for the duration of the war. The M-102 could be towed by just about any truck with a three-quarter-ton capacity or higher. It could also be parachuted into LZs or slung below any medium- to heavy-lift helicopter.

Direct fire (pointing and shooting directly at the enemy) was not the 105s primary purpose, although it could be—and was—used in that capacity when things got dicey. Its main advantage was the ability to fire a lot of shells quickly. The M-102 could fire as many as ten rounds per minute for three frantic minutes, then a sustained rate of three rounds per minute. The 105 fired a 33-pound

* Artillerists had been called "redlegs" since the 1860s for the red stripe Civil War gunners wore down the seams of their uniform trousers. This stripe was used to distinguish the artillerists from the infantrymen.

projectile out to 7 miles but was more normally used in Vietnam for closer-in work. A standard crew was eight men per gun, but there were seldom that many gunners available during 105 evolutions with the 1st Cav. A crew of four to six was more the norm.

The 155 mm howitzers were another step up in firepower. There were three 155s at Illingworth, and they were the M-114 versions. These 6-ton guns could fire a variety of shells including high explosive, illumination, smoke, or chemical rounds. Their range was out to 16,000 yards (9.1 miles), and they could fire up to forty rounds an hour in combat conditions. The M-114 was a towed howitzer but could also be airlifted into place. The gun called for a crew of ten or eleven men, but was hardly ever served, in Vietnam, by that many redlegs. Five or six men, pulling double duties, were more in keeping with actual practice.

The 8-inch SP howitzers were the "big boys." So big, in fact, that they had a crew of up to thirteen and were followed around by separate self-propelled ammunition carriers. They could fire powerful 200-pound projectiles over 25,000 meters, (15.5 miles) allowing them to provide long-range cover for infantry units that were over 15 miles away. They were virtually useless for indirect fire; in fact, the two 8-inch guns that were sent to Illingworth did not fire a shot during the battle of April 1, 1970, but there's more to that story, and it will be told in later chapters.

Once the artillery was in place (the 8-inch guns didn't arrive until March 21), FSB Illingworth was a fairly formidable installation, from an artillery standpoint. The 105s and 155s could provide very effective fire support; for example, when Charlie 2/8 was surrounded and nearly wiped out on March 26, the guns at Illingworth did all they could to hold off the NVA until the cavalry could arrive.

Once the guns were placed within the perimeter (except for the later-arriving 8-inchers), the artillerymen began setting up firing solutions for predetermined sites all around the outside of the base. Colonel Conrad had some pretty good ideas concerning where the NVA might establish rocket-firing positions or mortar emplacements, and he gave those coordinates to the artillery. The guns at FSB Jay, FSB St. Barbara, and the other nearby bases were also given the coordinates so they, too, could put the enemy in their crosshairs.

The irony, of course, was that the NVA was doing the same thing. Illingworth was too tempting a target to ignore, and it was certainly no secret where the big guns were being placed and where the infantry had set up their firing positions. The enemy could see every "hardened" position with a good set of binoculars. They had the entire base mapped out, as Charlie 2/8 discovered on March 25. (Recall that papers recovered on the body of a dead NVA warrant officer Charlie had killed in an ambush clearly showed every gun position, every rifle pit, the TOC, everything.)

One more important factor needs to be detailed about the artillery at Illingworth and its ability to participate in the base's defense. This concerns the manning of the guns. The 155s and the 8-inch guns were designed as stand-off weapons. As such, the crews that served the guns worked from upright positions or from perches on the guns themselves. There was virtually no way that the 155 and 8-inch gun crews could aim and fire their guns without being fully exposed. They could have been slaughtered quickly.

In regard to the 105s, however, the situation was completely different. These guns could be loaded and fired even if the crewmen were literally lying on the ground behind the guns. The trails of the guns themselves also provided a modicum of fire protection for their crews. The postures required of the various gun crews would become an important factor in the coming battle.

The cavalry had a presence at FSB Illingworth, although not really by choice. Alpha Troop, 1st Squadron of the 11th ACR, had gotten roughed up on March 26, going up against the 272nd Regiment. They had pulled off an amazing rescue but ended up fighting a two-hour, all-guns-blazing, muzzle-to-muzzle pitched battle before hauling Charlie 2/8 out of the jungle. They were forced to leave one ACAV behind when it got inextricably impaled on a tree stump. Sheridan A-19 had blown its power pack and was no longer capable of movement. Sheridan A-18 had overheated badly going into the fight and then several more times during the main engagement; at one point, its electrical system had caught on fire. Amazingly, even after the tank crew doused the wires with gallons of water and put out the flames, the electronics kept working. By the end of the day, however, it was readily evident that the "old gal" needed some major work. Still, A-18 was able to tow A-19 out of the forest. By the time she got herself and her tow to FSB Illingworth, it was time for the mechanics to work some miracles. The crews of both tanks were told to stand down and await repairs. Several of them were granted R&R and flew off to exotic locations like Sydney, Australia.

Also languishing at Illingworth was Sheridan A-37. It was operable, but no one wanted to drive it. The tank commander of A-37, SFC Robert Foreman, had been the only KIA that Alpha Troop had sustained during the battle of March 26. As Foreman stood in the cupola atop the tank, firing his .50 cal and directing his gunner and driver, an RPG blew through the thin aluminum shield surrounding his machine gun and struck Foreman squarely in the chest, all but cutting him in half. He was a total professional and well liked. His death had hit the troop hard. Several of his companions had removed his body—or most of it—as soon as the Sheridan returned to the troop's NDP that evening. The main gun worked, but the .50 cal and tank commander's perch were smashed badly, so this track was sent to Illingworth for repairs along with the other two Sheridans. On top of the damage, the tank just plain reeked after five days baking in the tropical heat. There were still small pieces of the unlucky sergeant, unrecovered, in the cracks and crevices of the tank's hull. Adding it all up, the crew was "spooked" about getting back in the tank. It possessed "bad juju."

Alpha Troop's M-557 was at Illingworth, too. This track was a modified M-113 ACAV that served as the unit's command and control vehicle. A canvas extension at the rear allowed a couple of men to stand inside, typically the CO and the troop's senior radio operator. The CO (Captain Poindexter) was in the rear getting his wounded arm patched up. The acting CO (1st Lieutenant Baerman) was out in the field with the remainder of the troop. Baerman had no desire to drag this unarmed track around with him, so the M-557 had little to do—except process radio traffic, which it did quite well. The unit's steady and capable senior radio operator, Sgt. Greg Steege, twenty-two, from Denver, Iowa, was in charge of the track in the CO's absence.

An M-113 ACAV from Alpha Troop's 2nd Platoon was at Illingworth as well. Its rear door had gotten stuck in the open position, and in that configuration it was useless for combat, so it, too, was waiting for the mechanics. In the meantime, its guns had been stripped from it and reassigned to the line.

Last but not least, the cavalry had a deuce-and-a-half on hand (a 2½-ton standard truck). It was used for hauling mechanics and spare parts, as well as running errands for anyone on the base who needed a truck.

There were no commissioned officers from Alpha Troop present, so the cavalry contingent's command fell into the lap of S. Sgt. J. C. Hughes, twenty, from Delray Beach, Florida. J. C. was a "shake 'n bake," or "instant E-5," having been sent through accelerated NCO school at Fort Knox. He had missed the "festivities" in the jungle on March 26, having been on an R&R in Sydney. He arrived back just in time to be shuttled out to Illingworth on March 31.

"My timing was impeccable," he would later say with a laugh.

Alpha 2/8 was already back out on patrol, somewhere in the nearby jungle. After their adventures with Alpha Troop on March 26, they were detailed to go back and police up the battle site, which they did on March 28. Immediately after that, Capt. Ray Armer and his men were detached from duty with Alpha Troop and put back into the regular rotation with their battalion. Given the devastation that had occurred to Charlie Company, Alpha Company was the only infantry unit on hand capable of normal operations. So off they went, even though they were short several men.

Charlie 2/8, reduced from company strength to the size of a platoon, received about thirty newbies on March 30, but these numbers would still be insufficient to man the perimeter of Illingworth. To augment his paltry infantry ranks, Lt. Col. Mike Conrad pulled his battalion's reconnaissance platoon, E-Recon, commanded by 1st Lt. Gregory J. Peters, into FSB Illingworth. They had been out on an extended jungle patrol and were due back in soon anyway. The moment they arrived, Conrad assigned them to man the berm and bolster the decimated ranks of Charlie Company. He put them under the temporary command of Capt. George Hobson, CO of Charlie Company and now the base's security chief.

Although E-Recon consisted of only twenty-two men, they were twenty-two of the very best soldiers in the battalion, if not the whole brigade. They would not only be a tipping point in the crucial hours of the coming battle, they would be the bulk of the shield that blunted the NVA attack. The heroics of these twenty-two men would generate one Medal of Honor (SP4 Peter Lemon), two Distinguished Service Crosses (SP4 Casey Waller and SP4 Brent Street), two Silver Stars (Lieutenant Peters and S. Sgt. James Taylor), a Bronze Star with "V" (PFC Ken Vall de Juli), and sixteen Purple Hearts. What would have been the outcome had not these men been at the very section of the berm that sustained the major thrust of the NVA attack?

The actual head count of infantry at FSB Illingworth in the days before April 1, 1970, hovers in the range of eighty-five to ninety. No one is sure of the exact number.

The artillerymen numbered around eighty; the cavalrymen mustered sixteen. With additional men manning the FDC, the TOC, the radios, the mortar platoon, the quad .50, the ground radar, and the searchlight jeep, the total numbers, including the infantry, were close to 215 effectives. This number also accounted for Colonel Conrad and his S-3, Maj. Michael Moore; Capt. John Ahearn, the battalion artillery liaison; 1st Lt. Mike Russell, the Echo 2/8 mortar platoon commander; Maj. Thomas H. Magness, S-3, 2nd Battalion, 32nd Field Artillery, commander of the 8-inch guns; Captain Arnold Laidig, CO of the 1/77 Artillery battery; 1st Lt. Cleaveland Bridgman, the officer in charge of the 1/77 FDC; and a scattering of other artillery officers and noncoms.

So that was it: a decimated line company about half its normal size, augmented by a platoon of recon guys, all thrown together with a few cavalrymen with busted tanks and mixed up with the batteries of several artillery battalions. None of these units had effectively worked with each other before, and certainly not in any sort of cohesive or coordinated manner. Most of the men did not know more than a handful of the others, and there were at least a couple dozen men, including some officers, who had yet to be in a serious firefight.

Outside the berm, staring back at the Americans from the surrounding jungle, was the 272nd NVA regiment. These were tough, experienced front-line troops. Each squad was formed from three-man cells who had trained together since their induction into the North Vietnamese Army. Each three-cell squad was led by a veteran sergeant. These soldiers were in it for life; they would only go home if they sustained crippling wounds or ended up in a bag full of cremated ashes, or when the war ended, whichever happened first. They were skilled, hard as nails, and silent, deadly killers. They were also angry. Their regiment had taken a pounding from the 11th Cav five days before and had tangled with both the 2/8 and the 11th ACR all through February and March. They wanted retribution. They were determined to take FSB Illingworth and kill or capture everyone within it.

6

"IT'S ALL RELATIVE"

WHEN IT CAME TO THE QUALITY OF LIFE ABOARD A FIRE SUPPORT base, all things were relative. Compared to what it was like for the average infantryman out on a long, arduous jungle patrol, a couple of days at an FSB were usually considered a small bit of luxury. At the very least, it was a respite from the constant tension of shoving vines aside and waiting for a B-40 rocket to sizzle out of the teeming foliage and blow you away.

Compared to duty in many of the built-up rear areas, like the big installation at Long Binh, which included air-conditioned barracks, plush clubs, and swimming pools, life at an FSB was only slightly better than living in the rudest native village. It still beat the jungle. Here is a contemporary description from former infantryman John Banicki, who served with Bravo 2/8:

> Fire Support Base (FSB) or Landing Zone (LZ) as they were called earlier in the Vietnam War were where we would rest between patrols. Most patrols lasted from 12 to 15 days out in the jungle

looking for the enemy or his activities. We would then spend 3 or 4 days on a FSB. The larger FSB's would have 105 or 155 mm howitzers, a mortar platoon, command & control bunker, mess hall, medical aid station and other supporting resources. The FSB's were set up to support the maneuvering companies out in the jungle, other FSB's and fire on suspected enemy location's. It was truly amazing how fast and accurate those guys were with their howitzers and mortars.

Our rest period would include pulling guard duty 24 hrs a day. Each infantryman would pull a 1 or 2 hour stint in one of the guard bunkers rotating among all of our enlisted men in the company. The 1st Cavalry FSB's were built in the form of a triangle with a combination sleeping and guard bunker on each corner. There was an M-60 machine gun, claymore mines, starlight night vision spotting scope and a radio in each of the guard bunkers. There also was a shooting range where we would shoot up our old ammunition and make sure our weapons were in good working order.

Then there was latrine duty. When the cut-off 55 gallon barrel became full of human waste we would add fuel oil and a little gas to burn the waste up. THIS DID NOT SMELL GOOD. There also was garbage detail. We would pick up the trash barrels on a mule (small motorized cart) and transport it outside the fire base perimeter and dump it into a large pit where it was later burned.

While on the FSB we would receive mail and any packages from back home. A good cold pop or beer was had by spinning it on a block of ice when we could get our hands on one. We could also take a well deserved shower. This consisted of a tripod with a canvas bucket that had a shower head attached to it. You would stand on a wooden pallet to keep out of the mud. No privacy but it sure felt good. A trip to the barber and medical aid station were usually a necessity. The jungle was not kind to our bodies as in BIG BUGS, man eating ants, leeches and plants that had an attitude. Our feet also took a real beating during the rainy season.

Jim Vinyard was a marine in Vietnam and aboard a fire support base near Da Nang:

> Life on a major fire support base was quite a change from life on a small hill or being in the bush. We had a gasoline generator so we could have electricity. We had a mess tent where you could get a warm meal of something. The cooks did an absolutely outstanding job of disguising food. Many times, I had no clue what I was eating, but it was warm and I did not have to use a heat tab to get it that way. We had an old airplane fuel tank that someone had made into a shower. I was able to put my air mattress on a cot! Ahhh, all the luxuries of home.

Almost everyone who served at an FSB remembers the dirt. Depending on the location of the fire support base in War Zone C, the soil could be brown, red, sandy, or black. No matter where the base was placed, dirt was everywhere and ever present. The soil at Illingworth was mostly light brown, powdery, and composed of lots of fine grit. It was of a consistency perfectly amenable to being blown around in the lightest of winds. Since it was also the dry season, the slightest movement of vehicles or marching men would send clouds of the stuff swirling skyward. When a helicopter landed near the base it stirred up its own dust storm.

Particles of the native earth were constantly in the men's mouths and nostrils, in their clothes, and, most annoyingly, in their weapons. It was a supreme challenge to keep the guns serviceable. Oily towels, rags, and even old uniform parts were draped over the .50 cals and M-60s in an attempt to keep the barrels, breeches, and magazines crud-free—or at least in firing order. As for the grunt's individual weapon, the ubiquitous M-16—well, that was another set of challenges completely.

When the M-16 was first introduced in Vietnam in 1963, it was intended to replace the older, heavier M-14. The M-16 offered a much more rapid rate of fire, but the environmental conditions in country and the ability to fire more bullets faster created problems that no one had foreseen. The powder for the cartridges, at first, tended to burn less cleanly, causing it to build up in the chambers and the barrels. The barrels themselves were more subject to corrosion and fouling due to the hot, damp, humid environment of Southeast Asia. Infantrymen were contending with either mud in the rainy season or dirt and grit in the dry season, but no season was good for the initial models of the M-16.

Here is one tale of a Marine Corps platoon in Vietnam, during the early days of the M-16s deployment, as reported in *Time* magazine in 1967: "We left with 72 men in our platoon and came back with 19. Believe it or not, you know what killed most of us? Our own rifle. Practically every one of our dead was found with his [M 16] torn down next to him where he had been trying to fix it."

By the time the grunts at FSB Illingworth were settling in for the night on March 31, 1970, the M-16's problems had been fixed. The cartridges had newer and more reliable powder, and the chambers and bores were being lined with chrome to help eliminate corrosion and sticking. Nonetheless, as any infantryman will tell you, if you don't keep your weapon clean at all times, you are asking for trouble.

The grit and grime got into all of the other equipment as well: the medical kits, the ground-sensing radars, the radios, the trucks, the ACAVs, and the tanks. It got into the food, too. Anytime a grunt was opening up or heating a C-ration there was always filth in the air. On the occasions when hot chow was available, either flown in from a kitchen in the rear or prepared on-site, it was almost always accompanied by a nondelectable "coating."

Everyone bitched about the dirt and dust, but it was a reality of everyday life on a fire support base. It even became a defining element in the battle that enveloped FSB Illingworth on the morning of April 1, 1970, as we shall see.

Living quarters on an FSB were abominable, at best, but they weren't designed to do much more than allow a grunt to grab a few hours of sleep in a spot where he was not directly exposed to enemy fire. The infantry set up sleeping areas inside the culverts that were placed at intervals around the berm. The artillerymen did likewise, in culverts near their guns. The cavalrymen had the "luxury" of being able to sleep inside their ACAVs or tanks. If fearful of having their metal boxes get hit during the night by an RPG or artillery, they would sometimes stretch out underneath the bellies of their mechanical beasts.

A typical Illingworth configuration consisted of four men inside a culvert with two cots placed side by side and end to end. The culverts were covered with sandbags piled two or three layers deep. The metal half-rounds were often raised by putting either more sandbags or dirt-filled ammo boxes underneath the sides of the shells. This allowed sleeping grunts to have at least a few inches above their heads—space in which to toss while dreaming of how many days they had remaining to DEROS (date of expected return from overseas).

Most men at a fire base went around during the day—and slept during the sweltering nights—bare chested, some junior officers included. This made life a bit more comfortable, if confusing, and it also reduced sweat buildup in the men's uniforms. Since soap and showers were a once-in-a-while luxury, it was essential to try to reduce the amount of body odor. Tight quarters in a culvert at midnight with four filthy, sweat-encrusted bodies packed in was not conducive to a pleasant sleep. Not that the men got much sleep anyway. Between watches, duty rosters, drills, and enemy incursions, it was a rare event when any individual soldier got more than four or five hours of consecutive sleep in a twenty-four-hour cycle.

The officers didn't fare much better. The battalion CO might have the luxury of a cot set up in the corner of the TOC. There might be room for one or two other cots, but they were typically "hot-bunked," that is, shared between officers in a rotating duty roster. FDCs might have a cot or two, if the space had been dug deep and wide enough. Out on the line, a platoon leader might get a small culvert to himself. All in all, it was a rugged, rudimentary, and not very restful existence. On a fire support base, though, sleep was not a high priority.

The ingenuity and resourcefulness of the American soldier has been in evidence since the Revolutionary War, in challenging spots such as Valley Forge, then later on at Vicksburg, Guadalcanal, and the Chosin Reservoir. In conditions like the jungles of Vietnam, far out from the rear areas, on bases like Illingworth, huge tubs of ice manage to show up, along with the occasional crate of fresh vegetables, box of prime steaks, even ice cream and cold beer. Whether that happens or not is primarily up to the local supply sergeant or dedicated mess specialist and their informal networks of swaps, trades, exchanges of favors, or cleverly disguised "appropriations." A soldier cannot, after all, exist on C-rats alone. These tiny slices of life were very important morale boosters.

Not surprisingly, very few soldiers found life at a fire support base desirable or remotely pleasant. It was terrible duty and constantly beset by life-threatening situations. It did bind men together, though, in a *Band of Brothers* scenario where every grunt was forced to focus hard and stay alert.

7

FIRE SUPPORT BASE JAY: PORTENT OF TERROR

As Mike Conrad was busy cobbling together his resources to carve out FSB Illingworth, his counterpart in the 2/7, Lt. Col. Robert Hannas, was settling into FSB Jay, about six miles away—and even closer to the Cambodian border. Unlike Illingworth, FSB Jay was not a new installation. It had been constructed earlier by an ARVN battalion and then abandoned. Hannas and his men were ordered to reoccupy the former fire base after the discovery, nearby, of new infiltration trails and an NVA ammunition depot. The enemy cache had been quite extensive, containing several tons of artillery and mortar rounds, plus a stash of RPGs, grenades, and machine-gun ammunition. Amazingly, a number of the captured ammo boxes were clearly stenciled USA. What the NVA were going to do with American-manufactured ammunition (which would not fit their standard-issue guns) was unclear unless they were planning on capturing a significant number of American machine guns and field pieces, which, apparently, they were.

Bob Hannas was born and raised in Brooklyn and attended

Brooklyn Technical High School and then City College of New York, where he earned both a bachelor's degree and a master's in education. Tall, broad-shouldered, and radiating confidence, he ran a tight ship. He was respected by those below and above him. He understood the realities of shepherding a 650-man battalion of grunts that had come from all walks of life and political persuasions—many of them draftees, a number of them harboring antiwar sentiments.

When veteran CBS news correspondent John Laurence and a crew were detailed to the 1st Cav in March 1970, General Casey sent them to Lieutenant Colonel Hannas. The CBS team wanted to film something that was part news and part documentary, a piece concerning what it was like for the "average grunt" in Vietnam during that phase of the war. Casey and the commander of the 1st Brigade, Col. William Ochs, felt that Bob Hannas and his men were the right guys for this delicate assignment. Laurence and his team spent several weeks in and around the men of the 2/7. Their adventures were recorded and shipped back to Saigon and then on to New York and the *CBS Evening News* back in the States. Laurence wrote a book about his Vietnam experiences, this one and others, entitled *The Cat from Hué.**

Hannas, to this day, is not happy with some items that ended up in Laurence's book. There is a story about Hannas himself, and his wounding at FSB Jay, that was entirely untrue, Hannas says. Another item that irked Hannas, as it did many American commanders, was photojournalists photographing American dead or wounded. The army was sensitive about allowing pictures of casualties to be published at a time when American forces were supposed to be disengaging from combat; and peace talks were well

* The latest (paperback) edition is from Public Affairs, New York (2002).

under way (in Paris). There was a practical purpose to the ban as well: It was entirely possible that some family member would be exposed to seeing a dead or seriously wounded relative on the front page of the local paper or on television before the Defense Department could get proper notices to next of kin.

Someone in Laurence's crew had apparently done some filming that had been banned. One of Hannas's men, who had witnessed the prohibited photography, told the colonel about it. Since there were no film-developing facilities in the middle of the jungle, the photos needed to be turned in and developed at the CBS Saigon bureau. Colonel Hannas offered the CBS crew a ride on his command Huey to Tay Ninh, where they could hop on another flight to Saigon. During the trip the photographer coyly bragged about having gotten some "great shots."

"Oh, really?" Colonel Hannas asked. "How many?"

"Enough for these canisters," the photographer bragged, holding up several film containers.

"Wow, can I see those?" the colonel asked innocently.

"Sure!" the cameraman responded, suspecting nothing.

The photographer passed the metal film cases to Hannas, who promptly pitched them out of the open door of the Huey.

"I got my ass chewed pretty good for that one," Hannas later chuckled, "but I didn't give a shit. They broke the rules."

Hannas didn't have much better luck with the next film crew, although the final outcome was more amusing.

"They sent [Walter] Cronkite out to me, too," Hannas related. "He was looking for a juicy story on drugs or race relations. I told him I didn't have any of those problems, at least not out in the field. He couldn't quite 'get it,' that when you're in the boonies and depending on the guy standing next to you to protect your ass, you don't do drugs if you want to survive and you don't give a crap what color the guy is as long as he's sober and alert. Cronkite started to argue with me. We were standing near a hot chow line—a dinner that the cooks in the rear had made up and flown in, to give the men a hot meal. Right then, here come these four soldiers, filthy and covered in the black dirt we battled constantly. They were stripped to the waist and walking along with their arms thrown around each other, laughing and having a great ol' time.

"Suddenly, they see me, 'the old man.' They stop, smile, and greet me with, 'Hey, colonel, how's it shakin'?' and other informal greetings. You had to stare at them very hard to realize, under all the grime, that two of these men were white boys and two were blacks.

"I stared at them, with a smile, and said something like, 'You men are a mess!' Well, they all looked at each other and started laughing. One of the men then said, 'Well, colonel, black is beautiful!'

"Cronkite was not amused. He accused me of staging the whole scene."

Hannas and his battalion took up their positions at FSB Jay on March 18. Just like Illingworth, Jay was in an open plain and had been set astride what the army believed was a major infiltration route for NVA personnel and supplies. However, Jay was going to be closer to the tree line and an even easier target for any NVA gunners who might be in the area. Hannas was not concerned; he believed he was only going to be in this position for three or four days before picking up and relocating his resources again. In fact, both he and Mike Conrad had already picked out the coordinates for their next two jumps across the region. The Americans had also learned from hard experience and good intelligence that the NVA would invariably take at least five days, sometimes more, to study a new fire base and work up a plan of attack. As long as the battalions kept jumping, it would be tough for the NVA to catch up and pounce.

[Author's note: Part of the reason for this operational caution in NVA regiments was that the units were mostly based on the Russian model of command and control. Only the unit commander himself had any flexibility or initiative, and even that was very limited. Operational orders were typically generated very far up the food chain and then passed down to the field units for execution. This took a great deal of time; plans had to be formulated, information had to be verified, and dispatches needed to be worked up. It was cumbersome and ponderous and allowed for very little leeway. On the other hand, it made it fairly certain that orders would be carried out as issued.]

FSB Jay was smaller than FSB Illingworth, and there were other subtle differences, mostly based on the personal preferences of the commander. For example, where Conrad had dug his TOC into the ground and then covered it with planking, PSP, and sandbags, Hannas preferred having his TOC in a CONEX box, aboveground. He did, however, surround the box with piled-up dirt and sandbags.

As Hannas began reactivating Jay, Conrad flew in to coordinate with him. It was imperative that they confer on their patrol schedules, intended night ambushes, and the placement of their H&I (harassment and interdiction) firing lines. They also wanted to be sure that the other fire bases in the area had them dialed up accurately in regard to covering fire, overlapping fire zones, and mutual support signals. Conrad remembers bantering with Hannas about the "here we go again" nature of their respective positions and the fact that they were being put out there as targets. The two bases, they agreed, would surely draw both the ire and the immediate attention of their foes.

Over the course of the next several days, Hannas, like Conrad, continued to send his companies out on patrols in the immediate area. There were minor skirmishes, but nothing like what the 2/8's Charlie Company experienced on March 26, which ended up requiring the mad dash and rescue pulled off by the 11th ACR's Alpha Troop. After the first full week in place, both Hannas and Conrad began to get a little nervous. They had fully expected to have been told to move to the next position, but no orders came down the line to do so.

Colonel Conrad began pleading with his brigade commander, Colonel Ochs, to let him abandon Illingworth and move on. His sense of urgency increased after he learned from Charlie Company that the NVA had detailed diagrams of FSB Illingworth. The sketches included specifics on the position of Conrad's TOC, the locations of all his artillery pieces, the position of every firing pit, and where all of his ammunition had been stored. Ochs, a veteran infantryman and West Pointer, agreed with Conrad, and they both approached General Casey. Casey took it up with the division commander, Major General Roberts, who, shockingly, demurred. Roberts was satisfied by the action he was getting at and near the locations of these particular fire bases, and he was pleased that the NVA were getting so agitated about them. Roberts felt this was the right approach and the division was getting good results. He ordered his subordinates to keep Jay and Illingworth in place just a while longer.

Conrad had received this startlingly bad news from Roberts directly, at a hastily convened conference in Tay Ninh. Conrad had flown from Illingworth to division headquarters on his command

Huey, full of confidence that he would be moving his men out of the trap he perceived Illingworth had become. Along for the ride (but not participating in the high-level meeting) was Capt. John Ahearn, Conrad's artillery liaison officer. Ahearn had been interested in checking out some new intel on enemy artillery positions, and Conrad said they could do that on the way back.

Ahearn clearly recalls Conrad coming back to the helicopter, after the meeting. Uncharacteristically, Conrad was in a foul mood. He climbed aboard the Huey, slumped down in the jump seat opposite Ahearn, strapped in, and said nothing but a curt "Go!" to the helicopter pilot. His face was dark, and he was obviously distressed. He slammed his fist, hard, into the side of the helicopter's bulkhead. Ahearn had been at Conrad's side for nearly three months by this time, and he had never seen Conrad like this. Ahearn decided to keep his own counsel as the helicopter leapt into the sky. It was going to be a bumpy ride, Ahearn concluded, and not because of any potentially bad weather.

In the early morning hours of March 29, eleven days after FSB Jay was reoccupied, the 3rd Battalion of the 95th NVA Regiment opened a bombardment on FSB Jay that nearly crippled the base. The first rounds slammed into and around the TOC. This was, of course, exactly what the NVA had planned. The antennas came down immediately, and all communications between FSB Jay and other American units ceased. Simultaneously, the NVA battalion poured out of the nearby jungle. Before the Americans had much time to react, they were nearly on top of the berm.

Responding to the incoming that was hammering his base, Lieutenant Colonel Hannas was out of the TOC in a flash, trying to assess the damage done and what he needed to do next. Explosives were going off all over the compound.

"I looked up," Hannas recalled, "and there on the berm, only a few yards away, was an NVA grenadier. He was raising his RPG to fire at the TOC. At the same split second, I raised my rifle. He saw me. For the briefest of seconds, our eyes met. I fired. I hit him squarely in the chest. He must have pressed his trigger simultaneously, but my bullet got to him before the rocket left his tube. The impact of my round must have caused his body to jerk a fraction, but, anyway, his shot was low. Instead of hitting the TOC squarely, the RPG went right into the ground next to me."

Colonel Hannas remembers seeing his right leg go pinwheeling through the air 6 or 8 feet beyond him. He toppled over.

"I didn't really feel any pain, I was just pissed," Hannas said grimly. "A couple of my buddies rushed over and picked me up. One of them yelled something about getting me a medic. I said, 'To hell with that, put me on that machine gun over there, then go get a medic,' or something like that. They started to hoist me over to the gun, which was unoccupied, when another mortar round came in and—blam!—just like that, I was down again, minus my other leg."

Hannas was in deep, serious trouble, and bleeding out quickly.

"Somebody, probably Major Frank, got a medic over to me. Frank and the kid tied off both stumps with tourniquets, somehow. I was going in and out of consciousness. They tell me my heart stopped a couple of times, so they beat on my chest. I remember somebody, once, giving me mouth-to-mouth. I think it was Major Frank. Then someone leaning over me said, 'Oh, God! The old man's dead!' But I wasn't. I could hear everything they were saying, I could see everything they were trying to do to save me. I wanted to scream 'I'm not dead!' but my mouth wouldn't form the words."

Leadership of the battalion fell to Maj. Gordon Frank, Hannas's S-3, who was already slightly wounded himself. The medics picked up Hannas's body and moved him over to the casualty collection area—on the side where the dead were being placed.

The artillery liaison officer at FSB Illingworth, Capt. John Ahearn, who was awake and alert at the ungodly hour of 0420, began to see flashes of artillery and the glow of flares in the sky in the direction of FSB Jay. He called the FDC at Tay Ninh, who, in turn, activated the prearranged firing plan for Jay, which included the guns at Illingworth as well as the artillery at FSB Camp Hazard. TACAIR was also alerted, and within moments a C-130 flare ship was in the air lighting up the sky. Some minimal communications were restored thanks to a tactical radio that had survived the initial onslaught and to the relatively short sight distance between Jay and Illingworth.

NVA rockets, mortars, and well-placed artillery continued to rain down. These rounds would cause the majority of the damage inflicted on FSB Jay that night. The barrage was accurate and effective because the NVA had had so much time to map out their firing plan and be sure they had every target zeroed in. One mortar round struck the ammo dump for the 105 mm howitzers, which blew up in a horrendous roar. Another round hit a supply of 3,000 pounds of C-3 explosive. It, too, went up in spectacular fashion. Since both stashes of ammo had been dug into well-constructed pits, neither explosion killed anyone, although several were injured.

As the barrage was having its desired effect on Jay, a platoon-sized group of the enemy was able to penetrate the berm in the southwest corner. They blew a hole in the wire and charged in. They knew exactly where they wanted to go: straight at the howitzers. Only a determined effort by the artillerymen, who resorted to firing their M-16s and lowering the guns to fire canister rounds, was able to blunt the attack. As it was, sappers managed to destroy two of the howitzers and disable another.

As dawn began to break, so did the NVA attack. The determined defense put up by Hannas's men and the arty guys was nearly superhuman. As it got lighter, the attack helicopters, gunships, and TACAIR fighters could find their targets easily. The communications grunts at the battered TOC were finally able to rig some makeshift antennas and got their radios working again. The artillery, with just three guns remaining, kept blasting away at the retreating NVA, their muzzles at zero elevation.

As a full sun bathed FSB Jay in daylight and upward-spiraling temperatures, a thick cloud of dust hovered over everything. The whole scene was macabre and monochrome, except for one small splash of color: Rising above the detritus of this terrible struggle was an American flag, tied to a sapling, flapping leisurely in the rising heat waves.

As the medevacs flew in and out of FSB Jay with their shattered human cargos, one took off in such a fashion that its powerful rotor wash rolled Colonel Hannas's torso from the pile of dead across the ground and into the pile of wounded. Had that not happened, Bob Hannas might have remained with the dead—permanently.

When the partly comatose colonel was discovered moments later, he felt one man lift him under the arms and heard another, reaching for his feet, shout in horror, "Where the fuck is the rest of this guy?"

A medic jammed a big needle in Hannas's chest, and the rescuers finally managed to get him aboard a medevac.

Fifteen brave Americans were placed in body bags. Fifty-four grunts were evacuated as wounded, a number of them, like Bob

Hannas, in very critical condition. Dust-offs took them to hospital facilities in the rear. Someone finally mentioned that it was Easter Sunday. No one felt like celebrating.

General Casey flew in shortly thereafter. He was greeted by sobering sights. Many men were slowly, as if drugged, trying to set things right, refilling sandbags, dusting off battered equipment, cleaning their weapons. A few others, thoroughly spent, simply sat on the ground or atop empty ammo boxes, their heads in their hands. A couple of men were walking around dazed and zombie-like. Many of the remaining men sported bandages.

The grunts had captured a handful of NVA prisoners. Interrogation revealed they were, indeed, part of the 95th NVA Regiment. The POWs also told Casey's intel men the location of the base in the jungle from whence they had commenced their attack. It was very likely that was where the retreating battalion had gone—except for these men, of course, and seventy-four dead comrades then lying scattered on or about FSB Jay. Casey wanted to gather up all the remaining effectives from the 2/7 and chase down the NVA before they could sneak into Cambodia. He radioed General Roberts and told him of his intentions. Surprisingly, Roberts vetoed the plan. Casey argued with Roberts. Roberts stood firm: He wanted FSB Jay dismantled and moved immediately.

By midafternoon, FSB Jay was history—an abandoned blot on the landscape once more. Anything of value was stripped and moved. All that remained was spent casings, bits of metal, busted crates, blowing bits of paper, a pit with seventy-four enemy bodies, and one small sapling that had once proudly flown an American flag. Four kilometers away a new fire support base was hastily being constructed to replace Jay. Appropriately, it was christened FSB Hannas.

8

ILLINGWORTH IN THE CROSSHAIRS

Given what had just occurred at FSB Jay, and the fact that the NVA had some pretty detailed plans on Illingworth in their possession, Mike Conrad was convinced that General Roberts would finally let him pick up the marbles at Illingworth and move on. There was a protocol to follow, however. It started with Conrad's immediate boss, brigade commander Ochs. When Conrad discussed the situation and the request to move (again) with Ochs, Ochs demurred and kicked it up the chain of command to General Casey. Colonel Ochs was not about to stick his neck out another time; besides, he was still dealing with the mess that had been FSB Jay. Casey agreed with breaking down Illingworth and relocating, but when General Roberts got wind of it he said no to Casey—again. Conrad was dumbfounded.

It was crystal clear to Mike Conrad that he was being hung out to dry. FSB Jay had been the warm-up to what Roberts was then hoping would be another "main event." The NVA had thrown a regiment on the guns at FSB Jay, and the Americans had smashed it, albeit at a high price. Roberts wanted to pound another regiment he knew was out there lurking on the division's front. The NVA would certainly be encouraged by their near-victory at Jay, and the kill ratio they achieved there would probably indicate to them that another attempt—this time at Illingworth—would be more than worth the risk. Roberts was going fishing, and Conrad was the bait.

[Author's note: Interestingly, years later, a retired Lieutenant General Roberts remembered it differently. He indicated that if Casey and Ochs had made a strong argument for moving Illingworth, he would have agreed with them. He also recalled that Casey, ever the aggressive commander, was still in favor of going after the NVA. This, in Roberts's mind, argued for standing pat with Illingworth. Sadly, Ochs, Roberts, and Casey have all passed away, leaving Mike Conrad as the only reliable authority. Given Mike Conrad's subsequent brilliant career and sterling reputation, it would be hard to say that his version of events was incorrect.]

It was March 31: FSB Hannas was nearly complete. FSB St. Barbara was still close enough to FSB Illingworth to provide some cover, as was Camp Hazard. Conrad knew, absolutely, that an attack upon his base was just a matter of time, probably hours, and most likely it would come at night, as had been the habit of the NVA. A great deal of begging and pleading produced a few more half-culverts, some additional PSP, and lots of sandbags, flown in by Chinooks. The men went into a frenzy of activity filing the sandbags, stuffing empty ammo boxes with dirt, and rearranging their firing positions.

Midday on the 31st, Conrad's anxiety level took another giant leap into the stratosphere. More Chinooks started descending on

Illingworth, this time with pallet after pallet of ammo for the big 8-inch guns. There was tons of it. Mules (small motorized carts, not the braying, long-eared models) began hauling the shells and ammo inside the berm to a spot smack-dab in the middle of the compound.

[Author's note: The situation with the arrival of the 8-inch ammunition points up a very big flaw in the command-and-control scenario aboard FSB Illingworth. One might think that Lieutenant Colonel Conrad, as commanding officer of the fire base, would have had the authority to order the Chinooks to turn around and fly back to wherever they had come from and take the unwanted ammo with them. Conrad did not have that authority, however. The op con (operational command) of the cavalry and the artillery assets at Illingworth had not been given to Conrad. The cavalry—although virtually useless—was op con to the 11th ACR, which was, in turn, op con to the 1st Cav, but only at the very highest command level. The artillery assets all belonged to 2nd Field Force, Vietnam; but the units at Illingworth had been given op con to the division artillery commander who, at the time, was Col. Morris Brady. Only Brady could dictate the disposition of the artillery assets at Illingworth and how much ammunition they would have on hand.

Interestingly, just prior to the construction of Illingworth, Colonel Brady had convinced his boss, Brig. Gen. F. B. Roberts (no relation to division commander Maj. Gen. Elvy Roberts), commander of the 2nd Field Force, Vietnam, that even the large guns like the 8-inch howitzers needed to be moved up closer to the action and nearer to the Cambodian border. This was why the 2/32, with their big howitzers, had showed up unexpectedly at Illingworth on March 21. Conrad was not going to get the guns removed, because he was bucking a policy put in place and agreed to at the general officer level and implemented by a colonel senior to him who was outside of his chain of command. Conrad knew this, tried anyway, got rebuffed, and decided to just live with it and move on. The ammo piles that were arriving, however, were another story.]

Conrad got on the radios and protested vehemently to Ochs. Ochs, as was becoming his habit, did nothing but pass the buck. Conrad's comments went up the line to Casey, who kicked them over to Brady, who promised to "look into it." This meant that the piles and piles of explosives would sit inside Conrad's perimeter until an "investigation" as to who had sent the ammo and why could be conducted. After these unproductive conversations Conrad knew he was saddled with another potentially disastrous challenge. The bottom line was that he would not have enough hours, manpower, or equipment to properly site or bunker in this much ammo.

SP4 Ralph Jones, twenty-two, from Cincinnati, Ohio, an assistant gunner on one of the 8-inch howitzers, remembers the astonishment he and his fellow redlegs felt when they saw the mountains of ammo arriving. "There must have been 40 tons of the stuff—enough for 20 tons per gun. Normally, we might have 10 tons per gun on hand, and then call for more when we ran low. This was much, much more than we needed. Then, where to put it all? No time to dig it in; plus, even though it wasn't the rainy season, we weren't sure the soil was moisture-free, either. Putting that stuff in damp ground would make it useless."

The men frantically covered as much of the ammo as they could with sandbags and empty ammo boxes filled with dirt, but most of the arty guys saw it as an exercise in futility. The NVA had to be watching, and one redleg remarked, "They must be pissing in their pants with joy." Maj. Tom Magness, the officer in charge of the big guns, was heard to complain postbattle (after being severely wounded), "Whoever ordered that ammo to be sent to Illingworth ought to have been court-martialed."

The huge pile of ammo became like a big candle on the gift of a cake the Americans were handing the NVA. If someone lit that candle, there'd be hell to pay. To Conrad, it was all beginning to look like a comedy of errors. It was certainly one thing to be used as bait, but it seemed that General Roberts and his staff were giving the NVA more than just bait. They were giving them the rods, reels, lines, and nets as well.

SP4 Rick Hokenson had somehow managed to survive the worst that a tour in Vietnam could dish out. He felt he had seen it all in the 358 days he had been in country. On March 31, he was only seven days from being done and going home. He had never thought he would make it this far; in fact, even before he left the States, the young sniper had reconciled himself to the fact he would never see his beloved Cotton Lake in Minnesota or any of his family or friends again. That thought certainly didn't make him happy, but he wrapped it around himself as a psychic suit of armor, preparing for the inevitable. It was just the hand he been dealt, and that was it. There was nothing he could do about it. This had given Hokenson a certain amount of sangfroid that many of his comrades could not appreciate. It had even allowed him to do some pretty crazy things, such as "borrow" an NVA uniform off of a dead enemy soldier. His own army uniform was falling off his back from jungle rot, and the dead Communist had some new clothes he wouldn't need; so why not make use of what was at hand?

So what if the NVA caught me in one of their uniforms? he rationalized to himself. *By that time, I'll be dead anyway.*

As he worked on the fortifications around Illingworth on the afternoon of March 31, a little voice inside him began to grow louder. "Only seven days to go, friend. You might actually get out of this alive after all," it said. "If you survive what's out there in that jungle over there, that is."

This was the cruelest moment of Hokenson's war. Here he was, against all the odds he had stacked up in his own mind, six and a wake-up* away from making it. It had also become customary, but not codified, that if a soldier got close (loosely defined as between one and two weeks prior to rotation), he would be allowed to get off the line, go to the rear, and begin the winding-down and checking-out process. Hokenson was then inside that window of opportunity, but because of the horrendous casualties suffered by Charlie Company of late, he was told he had to stay until enough "cherries" were shipped out to Charlie to make them seem more like a company instead of a platoon.

On March 28, thirty newbies arrived. By then, however, it was too late for Hokenson to leave. Everyone knew the NVA were swarming in the tree line and Illingworth was in for a blow. No one was going to be leaving. The small voice in Hokenson's head began to mock him, and sadistically so: It reminded Hokenson that one of his best buddies, with seven days to go, had recently been blown away in a rocket attack on a nearby firebase.

All things considered, Sgt. Lee Weltha was feeling pretty smug. He was down to his last couple of weeks in country—in fact, in the army altogether—and he couldn't wait to get the hell out of Vietnam and get back home. Somehow, he had survived almost twelve

* When a soldier was "short;" as in very close to going home, the time remaining was usually expressed as *x* number of days and a "wake-up," the wake-up being the morning of the very last day.

months in the bush, gotten a Purple Heart (but not dinged badly enough to get out of the war altogether), and been given this cushy job in the Headquarters Company as a supply sergeant. He considered that his main job was to make sure his old buddies in D Company of the 2/8 got more "smokes and Cokes" than the system might normally allow.

Weltha wasn't thrilled with duty aboard a fire support base, especially a dump like Illingworth. It was filthy dirty, hot, miserable, uncomfortable, and dangerous. It wasn't as life-threatening as humping around in the bush, though, and even if it was a pigsty relative to being in the rear, he didn't have to wear a full uniform, stand inspections, and otherwise look like a "real soldier." He was tired of soldiering. He had, in fact, extended for two more months in country to avoid six months of duty stateside on some "parade ground" base where he'd have to train newbies about what it was like in Vietnam.

He and a buddy had spent the better portion of the last couple of days working a chain saw on the wood line, hacking down a couple of big trees and turning the trunks into logs. The sturdy timbers formed the sides of their revetment and sleeping bunker, augmented by piles of sandbags and dirt-filled ammo boxes. No gook was going to get Lee Weltha during the last few days of his Vietnam experience. The sturdiness of the bunker did have one unfortunate side effect: The first sergeant had dragged over a .50 cal and told Weltha and his bunker mate to mount it in their "fortress." Worse, the gun was busted. The men were told to "fix it" and get it into operating condition. Working all day on March 31, they field-stripped the weapon, cleaned it up, reassembled it, and test fired it noisily "a hundred times." When they were finally satisfied that it would work, they set it up in their position along the berm. The men linked it up with four boxes of ammo, ready to rock 'n' roll.

One of the very last helicopters that landed at FSB Illingworth on the evening of March 31 brought one more officer who would bring a great deal of comfort to the men during the hours ahead, division Catholic chaplain Capt. Patrick Boyle. The priest hopped off the bird along with his dog, No-Nuts. (When the grunts asked why his dog was so named, Father Boyle smiled and replied, "Why, son, it's 'cause he's got no nuts!" The men jokingly agreed that a Catholic priest could not have a more appropriately designated mutt.)

Father Boyle got right to work upon arriving. He set up a small makeshift altar of ammo boxes near the huge pile of 8-inch explosives. Among the handful of men who gathered to participate or who were otherwise excused from duty were SP4 George Burks and Sgt. Ken Hodge from the 11th Armored.

Burks wrote later, "Even though both Hodge and I were Protestant Southern boys, we decided it couldn't hurt—seeing what Father Boyle might have to say and all."

Boyle gave a short homily on the possibility of the battle ahead and asked for prayers from the men gathered around his open-air church. He then proceeded to perform the traditional rituals of the mass.

One of the men, another Protestant, spoke up, "Chaplain, sir, if you don't mind me saying this, some of us are Protestant and, well, you are Catholic. I don't know about all this stuff you're sayin'."

Father Boyle chuckled, then took the large silver crucifix he wore around his neck and stuffed it under his T-shirt.

"There," he said, "now I'm a Protestant, too. Is that better?"

The men all looked around at one another, broke out in grins, and admitted that it was.

Instead of useless artillery ammunition, Conrad needed more men. Other than the few replacements for Charlie Company and a priest, he didn't get any. He could have taken advantage of more claymores, machine guns, and grenades. He didn't get any of those items either. At the end of the day on March 31, all the men at Illingworth knew that something bad was "coming down." They felt as if they were at a shooting gallery at the county carnival. This time, however, they were not the shooters. They were the "sitting ducks," and they were right in the crosshairs.

9

"IT AIN'T NO LAUGHIN' MATTER"

All of the following action takes place on April 1, 1970, between 0001 and 0244.

No one really knows how April 1 of each year turned into April Fool's Day. Some scholars trace the tradition back to Chaucer's time, around 1392. Apparently the famous chronicler made some humorous reference to "March 32," which, of course, in truth would be April 1. After that it was "game on," and although April Fool's Day never became an official holiday anywhere, the tradition spread, and April 1 morphed into the day reserved each year for playing tricks on the unsuspecting.

For the men stationed at FSB Illingworth in the early morning hours of April 1, 1970, April Fool's Day would be no laughing matter. The North Vietnamese had probably not even considered the irony of the date since, from all indications, their calendar does not honor an April Fool's Day tradition. There would be, however, many tricks played that day on friend and foe alike. Unfortunately, they all would be deadly serious.

The hell that FSB Illingworth would become had a prelude just before midnight on the 31st of March. The ground surveillance radar team picked up some movement in the tree line outside the southwest corner of the base. Gunships swooped in and raked the jungle at the edges opposite Illingworth. Conrad called for artillery to fire on the aiming points that had been preplotted. He had every gun on the base open up in a "mad minute," wildly firing into the dark. Conrad had, however, relocated his machine guns to dummy positions prior to the mad minute. If the NVA were spotting his guns, and they undoubtedly were, he was not going to let them have easy targets. Right after the mad minute the gunners raced back to their former firing positions.

After several minutes, and no movement from the tree line, all the guns aboard Illingworth fell silent. An uneasy quiet ensued. Eventually, the normal night sounds returned; the crickets, lizards, and night animals resumed their nocturnal chatter. The jungle was never silent for very long. The men relaxed, but only a little. Quiet conversations resumed. Cigarettes and reefers blinked in the night. The harsh sting of marijuana smoke drifted over the berm. The normally strident senior noncoms let it pass. Secretly, a few beer cans popped. The officers said nothing. A few men wrapped themselves in ponchos or their dirty fatigues and tried to snooze. Rucksacks were used as pillows, but no one took off his boots. Even Colonel Conrad dropped onto his cot in the TOC to try to catch a few z's.

[Author's note: I carefully canvassed the veterans of Illingworth in regard to the use of "recreational drugs" while they were aboard the firebase. Marijuana and any more potent form of drugs were absolutely illegal—and if any man was caught using, it was a court-martial offense. These were, however, extremely difficult and stressful times, and strict adherence to the rule of military law was often dependent on the situation or, in many instances, the local commander. Recreational drugs were readily available throughout the various war zones, and impressionable young soldiers were particularly vulnerable.

Were recreational drugs a factor in this battle? Probably not. In all the interviews conducted for this book, the overwhelming opinion given by the grunts who were there was that "dope" was not a problem. That is not to say that a few reefers weren't smoked along the berm that nervous night of March 31; they were. The men were hyperaware, however, of the effects of drugs on combat, and almost all of them were very adamant that the vast majority of guys who were on the front lines, on jungle patrols, or facing imminent combat would not be "using." It could get you killed, or get your buddies killed, and for that reason alone, drug use was frowned upon in the fraternity of frontline grunts. The believability factor on this point seems high. The men who were at Illingworth during the times described herein had many other incredible stories to tell, both good and bad. There seems to be no reason why they would not also tell the truth about their use—or nonuse—of drugs in combat. As one veteran relayed, "Only the guys who wanted to die were gettin' high." Mike Conrad tells a story about Peter Lemon in this regard:

> I nominated Pete Lemon for his Medal of Honor. These things usually take some time to process, of course. It was about a year and a half after Illingworth—I was already back stateside and well into my next tour, at the Pentagon. Some researcher—I can't remember his name, if I ever even knew it—from DoD calls me up and says, "Look, we're about ready to go forward with processing Lemon for the Medal; but, I hate to say this, there's a lot of stories going around."

"About what?" I asked.

"People say he was high on dope when he did what he did."

"Really?" I laughed. "I didn't know that. If I had known, I would have asked him what kind he had. Then I would have had the sergeants round up a couple of kilos, and give it to all of 'em."

Lemon got his Medal. Pete Lemon denies, by the way, that dope of any kind had anything to do with what happened that night, and those who were interviewed, and who knew Lemon, back him up completely.]

0200, the TOC

All military campaigns have tipping points, those moments in time when the outcome hangs in the balance and the ultimate fate of the engagement depends on which way the scales tilt. Sometimes the tipping points are grand and obvious: the arrival of Blucher on the fields of Waterloo; Theodore Roosevelt Jr. saving the landings at Omaha Beach (for which he would win the Medal of Honor); Longstreet failing to advance the right of Lee's army on the second day of Gettysburg. Sometimes the differences are very small, and yet they end up starting a cascade of events in one direction or another. Maj. Michael Moore's five-dollar, wind-up, tabletop, very small Big Ben alarm clock would end up generating one of the biggest tipping points of all at FSB Illingworth:

After the excitement at midnight, when the antipersonnel radar detected movements in the tree line and the precautionary mad minute and artillery firings ensued, the jungle became quiet once again. The temporary silence allowed sleep-deprived soldiers to catch catnaps or otherwise relax their guard a bit. Colonel Conrad knew his men were exhausted and needed rest, but he didn't want anyone to get too complacent. He told Major Moore he wanted everyone up and on alert again at 0200. Moore dutifully set his alarm clock for that exact hour. The tiny gears and springs whirred and clicked as they had been designed to do, and at exactly 0200 the alarm bells started chiming. This set off a series of jabs, pokes, punches, and whispered wake-up calls all over the camp. All the officers and noncoms were told to personally see to it that every man under their charge was awake, armed, and ready. Seventeen minutes after the alarm clock sounded off, the NVA assault began. The small difference between every man being awake and prepared when the attack commenced and half of them being asleep or distracted was thanks to Major Moore's little wind-up sentinel.

0217, the tree line, opposite the southwest corner of the berm

Colonel Nguyen Tuong Lai nodded to his captains and senior lieutenants. They were as ready as they would ever be. His regimental officers raced away to join their companies. They knew the colonel's plan by heart, and they were anxious to get the operation under way. They wanted to sweep forward and overcome the Americans, but mostly they wanted to get out of the woods. The American aviators could come back at any moment and pummel their lines again. Two hours before this, the regiment had sustained a number of casualties as the gunships rained death upon the waiting cohorts. The men were nervous and edgy, and they needed to either move forward or get back to their sanctuaries in Cambodia. It would be madness to stand in the tree line any longer.

The NVA colonel glanced up and down his lines. He could not see very much in the dark, but the few men near him had their eyes locked on their leader. They stared at him, waiting for his signal. He placed his whistle to his lips and blew three sharp blasts. This signal was repeated by his officers up and down the lines. This was the announcement to the grenadiers, mortar teams, and artillerymen to commence fire. The first artillery and mortar rounds arced skyward, and RPGs sizzled out of the trees and flew toward the enemy camp.

The men gripped their individual weapons, their SKSs and AK-47s, tighter. The sappers, with their satchel charges and Chicom grenades, crept closer to the front of the lines. Five minutes after the initial barrage, the bugles would sound and the men would be off, racing toward the American fire base, some 200 yards away.

0218, at the TOC

Once you hear the raspy cough of a round leaving the bottom of a mortar tube, you never forget it—especially if you know it's not one of yours. At 0218 in the morning of April 1, the first of about three hundred mortar, artillery, and rocket rounds barked into the night sky. The munitions flew heavenward, their trajectories taking them first up and finally over, falling toward preplotted targets somewhere inside the perimeter of FSB Illingworth. Lighter RPGs and B-40s took a more direct path, bursting out of the tree line and flying straight at the berm.

It soon became clear that the first artillery and mortar rounds had been aimed squarely at the TOC. Just as they had done at FSB Jay, the NVA wanted to rip the head off the snake before it could get coiled and ready to lead a defense. It nearly worked.

The communications antennas toppled over immediately. In a strange but fortunate quirk of fate they fell in the direction of the brigade headquarters in Tay Ninh. Minimal but weak comms would still be available. An Air Force Forward Air Controller (FAC) was in the area, and he was pressed into service to relay radio traffic from Illingworth.

Mike Conrad knew his base was going to take a pounding. They would just have to endure it. He also knew that when the shelling stopped, whatever was left of his men and his resources would be subject to a direct assault. He believed he had done all he could with the resources he had been given. It was time to hunker down, try to stay alive, and wait. He wouldn't have to wait long.

0220, Echo Company, 2/8, mortar platoon, along the berm

First Lt. Mike Russell was the CO of the Echo 2/8 mortar platoon. He had three 81 mm mortars at his disposal and had set up his guns in three pits along the southwest corner of the berm. This was the expected closest point of approach for any attempt to storm the base. The pits were dubbed Blue I, 2, and 3. Russell had chosen the locations to be as near as possible to the enemy so that the mortars would get on the NVA quickly. It turned out that he was, indeed, very close—too close, perhaps.

Even before the bombardment stopped, in the dim light from the paraflares floating down from above, Russell and the others could see a gathering crowd of enemy soldiers plunging through the wind-blown dirt. Russell's mortar teams immediately got to work. Machine guns and M-16s opened up all along the firing line.

Sgt. Randall Richards, the senior NCO of the mortar platoon, had been in the nearby command post bunker when the attack began. As soon as he heard the first *whoomps* of the enemy mortars he was out of the CP and dashed to each of his three gun pits to be sure his crews were firing. Between the flashes of the guns he could see the NVA sprinting for the berm, bent low and racing ahead, as if charging into a stiff wind.

The incoming rounds kept falling, and in mere minutes the accumulated dust and airborne debris was so thick the enemy soldiers started disappearing behind the clouds of battle. Russell's men could no longer see their targets. He told his teams to keep firing anyway—just fire at the noise. Russell and Sergeant Richards ended up together in Blue 3. As they prepped the rounds they set them at "charge zero," which meant, essentially, the rounds would come right back down almost immediately after being fired. As they twisted the rounds to the lowest setting, Russell and Richards worked the tube as fast as they could.

Russell remembers, "Each time I would reach up to drop another round in the tube I could hear the sounds of the enemy bullets, *rip-rip-rip,* as they passed my hand."

Richards aimed the gun, and Russell hung the rounds. Richards told Russell he was worried that the azimuth was so near to vertical that he'd soon fire a round that would come back down right on top of them.

Russell replied, "At this point, I don't think it'll make a shitload of difference."

Moments later a satchel charge sailed out of the murk and landed right on top of the Blue 1 mortar. The gun tube was blown apart by the shattering roar of the pack as it detonated. The crew barely escaped being killed, but two men were wounded. The rounds that had been prepped and placed nearby started cooking off.

A bizarre event then befell the crew of Blue 2: Some sort of round or satchel charge hit the platoon's kitchen tent. It had been set up to the rear of the gun pits, right behind a small, secondary berm consisting of sandbags and empty ammunition boxes also filled with sand. The cookstove flew through the air, trailing burning gas, and landed right on the Blue 2 mortar. The crew scrambled over the berm before the stove blew itself up along with the gun.

Russell was running out of firepower, and more enemy soldiers were gathering steam, ready to rush over their section of the inconsequential dirt barrier. He knew some of the enemy were already close enough to toss the heavy satchel charges on top of his men, so he yelled at his troops to grab their personal weapons and scramble back. They dove behind the second berm, clutching their M-16s. Russell told them to get out their bayonets and attach them.

0221, the TOC, artillery liaison

Capt. John Ahearn had been assigned to Colonel Conrad as the LNO, or liaison officer, between Conrad's battalion and the artillery. The North Carolina native and former forward observer for the 1/77 Artillery was in charge of coordinating all the guns aboard Illingworth as well as communicating with the batteries at the nearby FSBs and Tay Ninh. Ahearn was very skilled at his job, but without radio communication to the outside world he wasn't going to do much good—and that's exactly the position Ahearn found himself in right at the outset of the battle. It was certainly not a surprise that the NVA had sent their first rounds in the direction of the TOC and its radio antennas. It still came as a bit of a surprise that their aim had been so good. The antennas came crashing down in the first moments of the bombardment. After that, Ahearn was flying blind until the radiomen could get a makeshift antenna rigged. That would take some time and a respite in the shelling. Somewhat miraculously, Ahearn found a PRC-25 handheld radio lying in the dirt. The PRC-25 was line-of-sight only, however, and wasn't going to be much good inside a heavily sandbagged, underground bunker.

Amid all the choking dirt, booming explosions, and flying metal, Ahearn had to stand in the doorway of the TOC, braving the firestorm, hoping he could get someone—anyone—on the line. He finally hooked up with one of the Blue Max pilots circling above the base. Mercifully, this aviator was willing, and more importantly able, to act as a relay between the besieged TOC and division artillery in Tay Ninh. While the radiomen frantically tried to restore comms on the big sets and rig some sort of antennas, Ahearn would have to be a lightning rod in the middle of the storm.

0222, Echo Company, 2/8, recon platoon, southwest sector of the perimeter

Echo Company's recon platoon, commanded by 1st Lt. Greg Peters, had been rushed to Illingworth by Colonel Conrad to bolster the understrength infantry presence—and they had arrived just in time. Although they numbered only twenty-two men, the recon platoon consisted of some of the toughest and best soldiers in the brigade. Peters was known as "Rooster" for both his bright red hair and his cocksure manner. His confidence and his physical abilities as a former college football star would be very valuable assets in the hours ahead.

Peters had placed his men along the southwest "wall" of the base, along the bulge that had been created to accommodate the huge 8-inch howitzers. This was also the spot where a trail led from the jungle directly to the berm. The Americans had been using the trail as their departure point for patrols moving into the bush. The NVA would use the well-worn path as an arrow guiding them to what could be Illingworth's jugular.

Echo Recon was stretched very thin. All in all, they had fortified five bunkers at this portion of the line: three to the right of the trail, two to the left. Lieutenant Peters commanded the right-hand bunkers; S. Sgt. James Taylor supervised the two on the left. As the dust and explosions continued to swirl, the bulk of the NVA attack could be seen plunging down the trail, headed straight toward Echo Recon.

0223, Alpha Troop, 11th ACR, northwest sector of the perimeter

Over on the opposite side of the perimeter, S. Sgt. J. C. Hughes, the senior man present from the 11th Cav, was having a hell of a night. He had missed the festivities in the jungle on March 26 due to enjoying R&R in Sydney. He had made it back just in time to get shuttled out to Illingworth on March 31. It was there that he found his Sheridan, A-18, the one he commanded, all but a useless wreck. His buddy, Sgt. Pete Cavieaux, had been the acting TC (track commander) while Hughes was away, and Pete had banged the old girl up pretty good in the firefight on March 26. Hughes was waiting for parts for his tank plus the spares required for Sheridans A-19 and A-37. He was also a bit steamed—his .50 cal was missing. Someone had "commandeered" it from the tank's turret. According to what he was being told by a couple of his guys, it was at that moment out "somewhere" along the berm, probably with Echo Recon. Yes,

Hughes was pissed—doubly pissed with mortars raining down on his head.

As ranking noncom, Hughes found himself in charge of three immobile Sheridans, an unarmed command track, a busted ACAV, and a truck full of tools and spare parts. They were being attacked (he could hear other men shouting about the NVA "coming up"), and all he and his men had between them was their personal side arms and a few grenades. His most fervent hope was that the NVA, seeing the usually powerful tanks, would figure they were armed and dangerous and avoid his part of the line.

[Author's note: Given the configuration and layout of FSB Illingworth, it is probable that the main thrust of the NVA attack would have come at the point closest to the jungle and tree lines; indeed, that is what happened. If, however, the 11th Armored units that ended up at Illingworth had been parked on the southwest corner of the base and not the northeast corner, would the NVA have gone around to attack the far side of the outpost instead? Possibly. What we can infer, based on the guarded comments of the NVA commander, and his respect for the power of the cavalry's guns, is that commencing his attack at the point where the defense of Illingworth could be backed by the Sheridan tanks and ACAVs was probably something he would not have chosen to do. A single beehive round from one tank's main gun could decimate an entire company of massed attackers. The NVA also knew that the Sheridans carried a powerful .50 cal in the cupola and that the ACAVs also had .50 cals and dual M-60s. The NVA had no way of knowing, of course, that the Alpha Troop assets at FSB Illingworth were practically useless; but, like an ICBM in a silo, they were a powerful deterrent. The NVA spearheaded their attack at what they believed was Illingworth's weakest point. It wasn't, as we know, and the presence of the cavalry most likely had some influence over the choice.]

Sgt. Greg Steege was in charge of the M-577, the command track ACAV. He and his crew had been sent to Illingworth by 1st Lt. Paul Baerman, XO (executive officer) and temporary CO of Alpha Troop. After the fight on March 26, and the wounding of the troop's CO, Captain Poindexter, Baerman had been ordered by Colonel Conrad to police up the site of the confrontation, which Alpha Troop did, on March 28. On March 30, Alpha Troop was released from their temporary duty with Colonel Conrad and returned to their rightful commander, Lt. Col. Jim Reed, CO of 1st Squadron, 11th ACR. Reed assigned Baerman to get right back out in the bush and chase down the NVA. Since the jungle Alpha Troop had been assigned to "bust" was really nasty stuff, Baerman had told Steege to take the command track to Illingworth. Its ungainly bulk and lack of firepower would only be a hindrance to the rest of the troop. Sergeant Steege had considered himself lucky to get out of the long, hot, dangerous patrol. Not anymore.

Hughes was everywhere, racing all over the berm. He was trying to coordinate with the infantry guys nearby and looking for more grenades and any additional weapons or ammo he could scrounge. He was also burning with a guilty rage.

Immediately prior to midnight, as Illingworth fidgeted and waited, he had specifically told the two mechanics not to sleep in the deuce-and-a-half, where they normally sacked out for the night. The truck had a canvas top and would certainly not offer much protection during a barrage. Hughes told both Sgt. Ken Hodge and Cpl. John Lee Smith to "get out and get under" the truck or one of the Sheridans if all hell broke loose.

Both Hodge and Smith either forgot or decided to ignore Hughes or fell asleep in the truck anyway. One of the first enemy rounds lobbed into Illingworth was a direct hit on the truck. Hodge was blown in half and bent back on himself, folded up like a blanket, killed instantly. Smith was blasted from the truck, mortally wounded, sustaining multiple punctures in several vital organs. The medics arrived quickly, but there was little they could do for him except pump him full of morphine and let him die as painlessly as possible (which he did several hours later, after being dusted off the base).

0224, 2nd Battalion, 32nd Field Artillery, 8-inch howitzer battery position

When Maj. Tom Magness, operations officer for the 2/32 Field Artillery, had rolled up to Illingworth with his two 8-inch howitzers on the afternoon of March 21, Colonel Conrad had nearly had a coronary. The last thing he needed was these two huge mechanical dinosaurs (though effective weapons, they were leftovers from the Korean Conflict). It was nothing personal against Major Magness, who was, indeed, a very fine artillery officer, it was just that Conrad had no place to put the guns, and they would be virtually useless in any direct-fire role in defense of the base. Spitting tacks, Conrad had called Colonel Ochs, who was no help. Magness had his orders, and Conrad was being given his. The guns would stay.

As the attack opened, Major Magness, an experienced West Pointer, was sleeping under a culvert near his guns. Donning his helmet and flak jacket, he raced toward his FDC, which he had set up in a CONEX box. As he neared the FDC, his heart sank. It had taken a direct hit. Although partially dug in and surrounded by sandbags, it was a mess, and at least two torn and lifeless bodies were scattered about in the darkness. The survivors were madly trying to restore some sense of order.

The A 2/32 redlegs assigned to the 8-inch guns could not possibly work the weapons in the kind of maelstrom that was swirling around them, so many of them were manning a section of the berm between Echo Recon and Charlie Company. Magness scuttled along that section of the line banging on the culverts and pumping up his troops.

Magness scrambled to one culvert where he could see the outline of an M-60 muzzle pointing toward the enemy but not firing.

"How could this man not be firing his weapon?" Magness practically yelled out loud.

As he poked around the edge of the culvert he was astonished to find it devoid of personnel. He whipped his head around, grabbed the nearest soldier, pushed him into the culvert, and told him to start firing. Magness spotted a pile of M-60 ammo at the mouth of a nearby bunker and lurched over to grab some. He threw several of the heavy bandoliers over his shoulder and loped back to the gun. When he got there, the soldier he had grabbed, whoever he was, had fled. Magness plunked himself down and started firing the gun himself. He could see little, between the darkness and swirling dust clouds in front of him. He did make out a few dim shadows running back and forth. He fired at them. He kept firing until the gun jammed. When he couldn't clear it he jumped up, intending to run back to the FDC and check on its progress. As he did so, he felt himself slammed to the ground by a crushing explosion that erupted very close by.

0225, Headquarters and Headquarters Company bunker

Sgt. Lee Weltha had been on guard duty at the .50 cal when the first rounds from the NVA started dropping into the compound. He had been sitting on top of his log fortress reading a trashy paperback by moonlight when steel rain stated falling. He immediately dove into the bunker underneath his butt.

The volume and number of rounds crashing down on his position seemed out of context with what was going on elsewhere, and Weltha couldn't help but wonder, *Why us? Why are we getting so much attention?*

Then it dawned on him—he and his buddy had been "playing" all day, in plain sight of the enemy. As they tinkered with and periodically fired the .50 cal they had been fixing, they had inadvertently attracted the attention of the NVA. As a result, Weltha's bunker was dialed into the firing plans of his watchful opponents.

0226, RTO sleeping bunker, near the TOC

SP4 Tim Hall, one of Colonel Conrad's RTOs, was on fire—at least that's what his back felt like. He, along with another RTO, SP4 David Dragosavac, and Father Boyle, had been awake but hunkered down in the RTO sleeping bunker next to the TOC when the NVA bombardment commenced. Powerful explosions were erupting all around them, and it was obvious that the NVA had the TOC squarely in their sights. Hall heard the big comm antenna topple over and crash to the ground. The blasts were coming uncomfortably close, but the three men, squeezed inside the small space, would be reasonably safe unless they received a direct hit. The sleeping culvert was covered in a steel shell and three layers of sandbags and closed on three sides. The trio pulled back as far as they could from the single half-moon-shaped opening—and prayed, which was a lot easier to do with Father Boyle present.

As Hall turned to adjust his position and pull back farther from the front of the cramped hooch, a mortar round landed close to the front of the opening. Hall's back was peppered with bits of hot, searing shrapnel.

"In the army, I had worked myself up to a long list of colorful curse words," Hall related, "and as soon as I got hit with that shrapnel, I let loose every single one of them. It hurt like hell and it felt like my back was burning up."

Father Boyle grabbed Hall and pushed him down on his belly. He yanked up Hall's shirt and, while the hot pieces of metal were still sizzling, pulled out as many as he could see, using his bare hands.

"While I was lying there screaming and cursing, Father Boyle was telling me, 'Now Tim, you ought not to be taking the name of the Lord in vain like that.' I stopped swearing. That was Father Boyle. He was one of the coolest, calmest, bravest men I ever saw," Hall states.

0227, "Blue Max," above the fray, circling Illingworth

"Blue Max" always took great pride in getting to the heart of the action as rapidly as possible. To do this, A Battery of the 2nd Battalion, 20th Artillery, ARA (Aerial Rocket Artillery), had a hot team on a two-minute reaction time, 24/7. A second team could be in the air five minutes after the hot team was told to "go!"

The battery had been briefed, earlier in the day, that "something was going to happen" at Illingworth, and soon; so it came as no surprise when the hot team was bounced shortly after the first NVA rounds began streaking toward the base. From that moment, until the end of the battle, at least one Cobra, and most often two, from Blue Max (call sign that day "Silver Dagger") would be circling the defenders. They would respond to targets as directed by the fire control officers at the TOC while dodging bullets and antiaircraft rounds fired by the enemy.

0228, B Battery, 1/77 Field Artillery, the 105 mm howitzers

It was a rude welcome to the war. Capt. Arnold Laidig, with only a one-week tenure as CO of B Battery behind him, was sitting on his cot, reading quietly, when he was blown off his rickety bed and slammed to the deck by the first incoming rounds. He scrambled to his feet, scooped up his M-16, and headed for his FDC, which was near the 105 mm howitzer gun pits. His six guns had been silent for some two hours, by his watch, but they needed to get going again, and as he neared the FDC he was pleased to hear that one or two of them had already started blasting away.

He was horrified, however, as he watched an incoming round land squarely on top of one of the battery's sleeping positions and blow it to bits. Everyone had been awakened minutes before and told to stand by, and he desperately hoped that no one had decided to sneak back into the culvert for a quick snooze.

His men had been given preplanned targets and specific responsibilities. By the time he reached the FDC, all the guns were in action. His number-six howitzer was firing illumination rounds, as prebriefed, and the other five guns were pumping out a mixture of "killer junior"* and direct-fire rounds. Two guns were aiming squarely at the B-40 and RPG flashes and the green automatic weapons tracers coming from the tree line closest to the pits.

With his men on task, Laidig ducked inside the FDC and got on the radio with Captain Ahearn at the TOC. No sooner had he gotten in contact than an artillery round slammed into his number-one gun, knocking it out of action. Thankfully, no one in the gun crew was badly injured. The gunners jumped away from the damaged piece and spread out among the remaining guns to help the other redlegs. It was instinctual behavior born of necessity, but Laidig was still mighty proud of the way his new outfit was responding.

0229, Headquarters, 1st Squadron, 11th Armored Cavalry, March 31 NDP

From 8 kilometers away, Lt. Col. Jim Reed, CO of 1st Squadron, the 11th Armored, could see the fires and hear the roars of a battle shaking FSB Illingworth. Reed, his headquarters unit, and D Company were south of Illingworth, bivouacked in an NDP. They were very close to the fire support base dubbed Camp Hazard.

Reed was only hearing some of the radio traffic being relayed by Blue Max, but he had heard enough to know that bad things were happening over there. The guns at Camp Hazard, behind Reed, had opened up to support Illingworth, and he felt he should be doing something, too. He knew that a small detachment of his

* "Killer junior": is a term of art for the artillery, referring to the lighter guns (105s and 155s) firing air-burst rounds at predetermined ranges and altitudes. As opposed to direct-fire rounds, aimed dead-on, killer junior rounds are designed to explode above the enemy, raining down shrapnel. "Killer senior" refers to the use of the larger 8-inch howitzers.

own men was aboard Illingworth, although he wasn't exactly sure how many were there and what equipment they possessed.

Alpha Troop, the heroes of the battle in Tay Ninh on March 26, was out in the boonies, chasing the NVA up to the Cambodian border. With Captain Poindexter still in the hospital, the XO, Lieutenant Baerman, was in temporary command.

Good man, Baerman, Reed reasoned, but he was probably too far away to do any good for the men at Illingworth.

Reed got hold of his current operational commander, the 1st Brigade's Colonel Ochs. Ochs, aware that something disastrous had happened at Illingworth, and unable to gain direct contact with Lieutenant Colonel Conrad, quickly agreed with Reed that he should dispatch whatever elements he had at hand. It wouldn't be easy, though. There were no roads leading to Illingworth from where Reed's men were positioned.

Reed radioed Capt. Jerry Hensley, CO of D Company, who was parked nearby. D Company, unlike Reed's other three troops, was equipped with the M-48 Patton medium tanks, not the Sheridans. The Pattons had a smaller main gun (90 mm vs. the Sheridan's 152 mm), but they were made of sturdier stuff (steel vs. aluminum), and though older than the Sheridans (early 1950s vintage) they had proven they could hold up very well in the Vietnam environment.

Hensley hustled right over to Reed, and they discussed the situation. "I remember Colonel Reed asking me—not ordering me—about busting jungle during the middle of the night," Hensley recalls. "That is something we would not normally do. Smashing through the brush at night was not conducive to your health."

Hensley told Reed he'd give it a go, but he wanted access to a flare ship. Reed said he'd try to get him one. Hensley was also worried about water and marshes. Although it was not the rainy season, there were still many ponds and lakes in the area, and the jungle was dotted with swamps and muddy sinkholes. That sort of terrain, if the tank drivers were not careful, could bog down a Patton tank in a heartbeat.

It looked to be about a two- to three-hour slog, working off just a compass heading, and could only succeed if there were no water hazards, unknown arroyos, or invisible ditches in their line of travel—or enemy troops. If they ran across any suspicious activity the company would conduct "recon by fire," that is, blast away with their .50 cals, straight ahead, knocking aside any opposition. This was going to be pure guesswork and a dangerous mad dash, just like the cavalry rescues of John Wayne in the Old West.

Hensley got his men saddled up quickly, and off they charged. The relief column consisted of three tank platoons of five tanks each; the two headquarters tanks (one sporting a bulldozer blade in case any heavy clearing work or digging was required); and assorted ACAVs for fuel, maintenance, and forward air control. General Patton would have been proud—as would his son, George, who, as a colonel, had recently commanded the 11th Armored.

0230, 2nd Battalion, 272nd NVA Regiment Position, in the jungle

Colonel Nguyen Tuong Lai stared through his binoculars at the battle unfolding in front of him. He wished he possessed a pair of those magical night-vision glasses. He had peered through a Starlight rifle scope once. His men had found it on a dead American sniper. He'd even settle for that.

His troops were moving forward, as he had commanded. From what he could tell, they were very near the perimeter of the base. He hoped with all his heart they had enough momentum to carry them over the top. Colonel Lai knew he had numerical superiority.

The monitoring of the American fire base over the past week indicated there could be no more than 200 soldiers in the compound. He had 440 men to commit to the attack, and he would push them all forward if this initial assault gained any momentum.

The Americans had moved in a couple of big guns—prize guns—and then, incredibly, just yesterday, they had flown in tons of ammunition and stacked it right in the middle of the compound. What an utterly stupid mistake! Colonel Lai wanted to destroy those big guns very badly—and capture the base, of course. He couldn't believe his good fortune. These cavalry "cowboys" had left this isolated and vulnerable fire base in place too long. His men had been able to measure and lay in exact coordinates for the enemy command post, each of their artillery pieces, every bunker. His rocket teams and mortar troops were blasting each of those positions with impunity—and deadly accuracy. His RPG teams would soon be on top of the berm and adding their firepower to the fight. He had sent two squads of his best sappers with the vanguard, each man with two satchel charges. Their mission was to blow the big guns and the stacks of ammunition the Americans had been so foolhardy as to leave in the open. His only real worry was the three tanks sitting in the back of the perimeter. They could break up and decimate his attack in no time, if they were put into play.

As he thought about those—what were they called? Sheridans?—his mind slipped back five days to the last time he had seen those damned tanks. He and his men had been guarding an important supply base, which they had hidden deeply in the jungle, when a small company of Americans had wandered into the area. Although they had been very quiet, for Americans, and had moved carefully, they still made lots of noise, compared to his skilled jungle fighters. His scouts could also smell the Americans anytime they got close. Their cigarette smoke was different, and it drifted for miles. They used odorous liquids in futile attempts to kill the native bugs and leeches that his men had learned to ignore. Their food had distinct smells, and those odors wafted through the jungle even if they didn't heat their rations. Then, of course, most of these men just plain reeked from days of not bathing. Americans smelled different than Asians. Colonel Lai had often mused that it must have something to do with their rich diets. Their fatty food and its stink seemed to ooze out of their pores.

This group had killed one of his best officers with a booby trap but in so doing had revealed their position. From that point on, it was a simple matter of leaving a few subtle signs here and there, markers that would pique the curiosity of whoever was leading the American patrol. Lai and his men knew which branches to twist, which footprints to leave, what communications wires to expose on purpose to fool the traitorous scouts—what did they call them? "KCs," whatever that meant?—men who had turned against the rightful cause and worked for the Americans. As surely as if leaving them bread crumbs, they had walked the Americans right into their trap.

Colonel Lai had been in the first series of bunkers as the American company tried to slide silently by. He had instructed his men to wait until the entire column had passed before opening fire. He did note that whoever was in charge of these men was no novice. Unlike many other patrols he and his men had ambushed, this group was not in the typical single-file column. The American commander, whoever he was, had been prudent; he had his men patrolling in two parallel columns about 20 yards apart. This would normally have made them harder to attack, but Colonel Lai's base and bunker complex was so large that four parallel lines would have been able to walk through its throat and still not touch the sides.

Colonel Lai counted the GIs as they slid by. He was less than 20 feet away. The American patrol had 87 men. He had 686. This would be over quickly. As the last of the Americans went by, Lai had a company of his soldiers silently fall across the rear of the American column, thus blocking their avenue of retreat. The Americans were surrounded before they even knew the NVA were there.

On his signal, his men opened fire, hitting the head of each line first. He expected the Americans to pull back immediately, which would place them directly on the guns of his waiting troops. Surprisingly, they did not do as he expected. In fact, they did something he had never seen before. The front and rear of each line halted, and the soldiers in the middle fanned out, forming a circle. It created an instant perimeter defense. Lai was impressed by the ingenuity.

No matter, he thought to himself, *these men will be overwhelmed quickly.* He told his men to pour it on.

The defense put up by these Americans was surprisingly stubborn. The battle went back and forth all afternoon. Then, of course, the tanks had shown up. That was a different matter. Lai still elected to hold his ground. Even with their superior firepower he outnumbered the Americans, and he and his men were dug into highly defensible positions. He also knew he could not retreat. He had been given orders to hold and guard this supply base at all costs. What he protected was too valuable for the NVA to lose; plus, the Americans had their damned air assets in the area. They could not be used on him and his men as long as the Americans were tangled up with his troops, but if he broke off and fled, their attack helicopters and fighter planes would decimate his fleeing troops. He could do worse than to stay in place.

Inexplicably, the Americans finally broke off the engagement themselves. Neither side had gained any clear advantage, but at least the Americans had been able to save the men they had undoubtedly been sent to rescue. Colonel Lai thought about pursuing the column as it pulled back, but then decided against it. Given that he and his storage site had been discovered, he would need every one of his men and all the nighttime hours available. They would pack up and move as much of the valuable supplies and equipment as possible, back across the Cambodian border, where the Americans could not touch them. Lai knew that by first light, American air forces would be pounding this position into oblivion.

Those damn tanks. He had lost nearly two hundred of his men to those tanks and their guns five days ago, and here they were again, three of those beasts sitting at this fire base. Would they move against him? Could they? If they did, he would have to call off the attack. Then again, as his men had observed, they had not moved in five days. He desperately hoped these tanks were broken down. It could make all the difference.

0232, Echo Recon position on the berm

The NVA were dropping everything they had on Illingworth, and it was an impressive array. Somehow, the NVA had been able to muscle some heavy firepower into positions around the base even though Blue Max, TACAIR, and all sorts of artillery and mortar assets had blasted the tree line on numerous occasions.

Illingworth, by several estimates, absorbed well over three hundred well-aimed hits in a very short period of time. The barrage consisted of 107 mm and 122 mm artillery shells, 240 mm rockets, 82 mm and 120 mm mortars, 75 mm recoilless rifle rounds, and a couple dozen RPGs. Once this initial bombardment ceased, everyone still alive inside the perimeter knew what was coming next.

SP4 Peter Lemon was out on the berm with Echo Recon. He was relatively new to the platoon but not to Vietnam—or combat. Canadian by birth, and an American citizen since age twelve, the nineteen-year-old from Michigan had signed up as soon as he had finished high school. He had reported to basic training with some 200 pounds on his large, 6'2" frame, but the army and four months in Vietnam had stripped 30 of those pounds right off him. Lemon was originally assigned to the 75th Infantry (Rangers) of the 1st Infantry Division, but when the "Big Red One" got orders to redeploy back home, he had only finished a third of his Vietnam tour. He was shuttled back to the replacement center, where he just happened to hook up with some veterans from the 2/8 Echo Recon Company. Impressed with their demeanor and swagger, and having at least some minimal say in where he might want to complete his tour, Lemon said, "Send me to those guys," and the army did. Fate placed him along the berm at Illingworth.

As soon as the shelling stopped, Lemon and the other men of Echo Recon quickly scrambled out of their shelters. They knew what the next phase of the attack would entail. Lemon was an assistant machine gunner assigned to Sgt. Lou Vaca's M-60 machine gun. Lemon spotted Vaca, who was already on the gun, and raced over to get to work. As Vaca fired, Lemon fed him the ammo; then, in the thick dust from all the explosions, the gun jammed. Lemon glanced up. Despite the poor visibility he could still see, outlined in the shadows thrown off by the flares, a wave of NVA racing toward the berm. He guessed they were no more than 50 feet away, and they were lined up thirty to forty men across. It was eerily like the war movies he had seen as a kid, but this film was becoming all too real, and it looked like he would have a starring role.

As Vaca furiously worked to clear the jam, Lemon raised his M-16 and fired at the first of the advancing enemy soldiers. He had the presence of mind to fire short bursts, just as he had been taught. Five NVA went down, and then his rifle jammed, too. Fortuitously, each gun position had set out supplies of frags. There was a box of them at Lemon's feet, so he threw down the useless rifle and began pitching grenades as fast as he could. More NVA disappeared in the billowing blasts.

"C'mon, Vaca! We need that gun!" Lemon shouted.

Lou Vaca, from Galveston, Texas, dropped out of high school at age seventeen, while in the tenth grade, the week after he learned that one of his best buddies from home had been killed in Vietnam. It was not right, and he was going to join the army and get revenge. He lied about his age, the recruiter looked the other way, or both, and Vaca was off to basic training. He also got into the paratroops, and after he was shipped to Vietnam he was sent to the 101st Airborne. He served a complete tour and volunteered for another one. The Army gave him thirty days of home leave first, however, and so Vaca went home to party—and party he did. So much so, in fact, that he missed his scheduled flight back to Vietnam. Not wanting to be put on report for failing to catch his flight, he reached deep into his own pocket and paid for a commercial flight back to the war.

"Can you believe I actually did that?" Vaca asks laughingly these days.

By the time Vaca got back, the 101st was going home, so Vaca was reassigned to the 2/8 Cavalry, Echo Recon. That's how this second-tour but seasoned nineteen-year-old veteran ended up struggling with a malfunctioning M-60 at FSB Illingworth during the early stages of the escalating fight.

As he worked furiously to clear the jam, Vaca glanced up once or twice to see Pete Lemon flailing away with an M-16 and frags. Out of the corner of his eye he also caught sight of the enemy tide about to crest upon the berm.

"It looked like a solid wall of men," Vaca says. "All of them wearing shorts and sandals and humping all sorts of bad-looking weapons."

At that moment, a grenade landed nearby. The explosion knocked the M-60 from Vaca's hands and spun it back behind him. Thinking only of the need for that gun, he reached for it and accidentally grabbed the hot barrel. He burned his hand—badly—but retrieved the piece. It would only fire one round at a time, continuing to jam. Vaca saw a stream of green tracers race by his left side, between himself and Lemon. As if in slow motion, the tracers inexorably tracked right and directly into his leg. He went down on a knee. Another grenade went off. This one was very close. A piece of shrapnel sliced right across Vaca's midsection. As Vaca looked down, he could see his innards beginning to ooze through his shirt. He quickly wrapped his left arm around the mess and began pushing the organs back inside.

"They felt squishy and sticky," Vaca recalled with clinical dispassion.

Another grenade flew out of the night. This one blew him into the air and slammed him down a few feet behind the berm. Amazingly, he managed to keep a tight hold on his ruptured midsection.

"Two guys grabbed me and pulled me back," Vaca knows, but he does not remember who they were.

Lemon saw Vaca get hit and fall backward, writhing in agony. Lemon moved to help, but a few steps away—the enemy. Four soldiers were ready to jump the berm. Lemon threw the grenade he had in his hand, and three of the four were ripped apart. The fourth was wounded but still alive. Lemon leapt over the barrier and landed on the man, full force, his hands around the enemy's throat, squeezing the remaining life out of him. He grabbed the dead soldier's AK-47, whirled around, and fired a full clip into the next line of the onrushing NVA.

As he fumbled for more ammo, an enemy grenade landed nearby and exploded. Hot shards of metal pierced Lemon's scalp and neck.

Enough of this shit, he told himself, and he jumped back over the berm. A couple of grunts from recon were beginning to take up the slack nearby and were pouring effective fire into the attackers. Lemon wasn't sure about his own wounds, but he could see Vaca was in desperate trouble. He was going to die without some immediate help. Lemon reached down, scooped up Vaca as if he were nothing more than a big sack of flour, and loped off to the aid station, which was about 25 meters away.

Lemon laid Vaca down with the medics, and they began to tear at Vaca's shirt, desperately trying to get the blood to stop gushing and the guts to stop moving. They pumped some morphine into him. One of the medics glanced at Lemon. Blood was coursing down Lemon's chest and side from the head and neck wounds. Lemon could feel a couple of the metal shards grinding under his skin.

"Lemon!" the medic shouted. "Get down here. Lemme take a look."

Lemon stood there. "Nah. I'm good. Take care of Lou."

The medic ignored him, stood, poked around Lemon's face and neck for a minute, pulled out a couple of obvious pieces of metal, and dosed the cuts with antiseptic. He slapped a bandage on Lemon, then went back to work on Vaca.

With that, the big kid from Michigan spun around and humped back to the berm.

0233, FDC, B Battery, 1st Battalion, 77th Field Artillery

They called him "Polar Bear." He was, indeed, a big bear of a man, well over six feet, stocky and sturdy. His naturally blond hair had been bleached white by the Southeast Asian sun. All this combined with his fair complexion led to the nickname. His given name was

Cleaveland Bridgman and he was from the small coastal town of South Dartmouth, Massachusetts, a stone's throw from the famous New England seaport of New Bedford. Bridgman was a first lieutenant and had come into the army via the ROTC program at Knox College in Galesburg, Illinois. He graduated in 1968, married his college sweetheart, and was quickly ordered to Fort Riley, Kansas, for initial artillery training. Shortly after finishing the course at Fort Riley, he was given orders to Vietnam.

By the end of March 1970, Bridgman had completed half of his one-year tour and had soldiered well. His first months were spent with Charlie Company, 1/5 (1st Battalion, 5th Cavalry), as a forward observer. He was then detailed to the same position with Charlie 2/8 and worked with the soldiers of that company as they slogged through the terrible months of February and March. As the last half of his tour commenced, he was brought in from the field. This was pretty typical of arty guys like Bridgman who had endured—and survived—months of tough frontline duty. His experience and well-honed combat skills would be put to use in positions of more responsibility. He was attached to B Battery of the 1/77. At Illingworth, he would be their artillery liaison officer and work in the battery's FDC.

Capt. John Ahearn didn't want any more friends. He had made too many friends already, and most of them were dead or wounded so badly they had been shipped home. Making friends was just a painful exercise in frustration. You get close to someone at breakfast and by chow time that night they're being dusted off or zipped into a body bag. He couldn't help it, though, with Cleave Bridgman. The guy was just too nice, too friendly, too hard to turn away from.

They had arrived aboard FSB Illingworth at about the same time. Ahearn, as the battalion's LNO and the senior artillery officer on the base, would have to know—would want to know—all his artillery counterparts. Bridgman, as the FDC director for the six 105s of 1/77, would play an important role in any engagement. It was natural for them to interact, but that didn't mean they had to be friends.

"He was just impossible to dislike," Ahearn remembers. "He was a bigger-than-life individual with a bigger-than-life personality."

As night came upon Illingworth on the evening before the battle, Ahearn and Bridgman met out along the berm, close to the 105s of the 1/77. They plunked themselves down atop the sandbags and popped open a couple of warm beers.

"We were both apprehensive about the coming hours," Ahearn recalls, "but it wasn't out of fear. We were all exhausted and worried, that's all. We both talked about our families, back home. That always helped calm us down—the talk of home and families. Cleave was always a great guy to talk with. He was never 'down,' he was always upbeat and smiling. If he had any concerns about life and making it out of that hellhole, he never said anything about it to me."

By 0233 the barrage thrown out by the NVA had started to abate, but not completely. Hundreds of rounds of various types had fallen on Illingworth, and with the accurate prebattle spotting conducted by the enemy gunners, considerable damage had been done to the base's infrastructure. The TOC was all but radio silent and struggling. All the mortar positions had been knocked out of action. The FDC for the 2/32 had been destroyed, and the big 8-inchers weren't firing.

In terms of the artillery on the base, the 1/77 and their six 105s were shouldering the load and blasting away fast and furiously. The direction these critical guns were receiving was from their own FDC and Lieutenant Bridgman. Standing right by Bridgman's side was Sgt. Bobby Lane, his RTO.

The NVA gunners wanted desperately to knock out the 105s. They were throwing dozens of rounds at the gun emplacements, but they knew that if they could knock out the FDC, the guns themselves would be "blind" and forced to fire only at what the gunners themselves could see or guess at. The FDC itself wasn't much to write home about in terms of its construction; it was nothing better than a hole scooped out of the ground by a bulldozer and covered with planks, PSP, and lots of sandbags. The center had an L-shaped entryway constructed of more sandbags. It was dug in enough to shelter someone standing in its protective L from direct gunfire, but not much more. The interior was poorly lit, barely deep enough to allow men to stand, and, when in action, very crowded if more than three or four men were in it. It could, however, withstand just about everything but a direct hit—and what were the chances of that? Unless the NVA gunners were very good or very lucky or both, the odds were deemed to be in favor of the FDC's occupants.

On this night, however, the NVA gunners got lucky. The FDC did, indeed, take a direct hit, right in the doorway, from a munition that fell squarely into it from above. No one knows if it was a mortar round or an artillery shell. All we do know is that it was deadly. Lieutenant Bridgman was standing in that entranceway so that he could communicate better with the gunners. Radio reception inside the FDC, with all the dirt, dust, noise, and firing, had been poor. That decision sealed his fate, along with that of Sergeant Lane. The concussive force of the round apparently killed Lane instantly. He may have, in fact, absorbed the majority of the impact. Bridgman was wounded, mortally, but managed to keep hold of the radio he was clutching.

All the other men inside the FDC were stunned and wounded. It was utter confusion, pain, and screaming. Bleeding profusely, Bridgman staggered from the doorway. It is not known if he appreciated the extent of his injuries. What is known is that he somehow managed to keep talking on the radio, continuing to direct the fire from the 105s for a few minutes more. Another NVA round slammed into the earth a few yards away. Bridgman's exposed position could not withstand another blast. The radio and the Polar Bear were silent for good.

0234, B Battery, 5th Battalion, 2nd Field Artillery position

The quad .50 gun truck sported a battery of four .50 caliber machine guns in a single mount placed in the flatbed of a 2½-ton truck. The truck made this asset highly maneuverable, and the four machine guns, linked and fired as one, made the battery quite lethal. At Illingworth, the truck was placed in close proximity to the 8-inch guns, which it was detailed to protect. The quad's sole employment, apparently, was as a stationery gun platform. This was probably a fatal error, as far as the destiny of the truck was concerned. It was clear, very early in the battle, that the big howitzers were a primary target for the NVA—and so was the gun truck. The bulk of the NVA attack came straight at the 8-inch howitzers and the troops manning the southwest portion of the berm. The quad .50 started firing immediately but quickly used up so much ammunition (approximately nine thousand rounds) that the barrels became red-hot; in fact, they started to melt, which made their barrels warp, and the ammunition started to fly in all directions, not necessarily where the guns were aimed. The gun truck crew was forced to abandon the truck, grab their personal weapons, and take up positions with the infantry along the berm.

Likewise, the crew from I Battery, 2/29 Artillery, and their searchlight jeep, found that their best avenue of defense was to take their M-60 and personal weapons and get on the berm. In a situation like this, searchlights were not going to be of any help. As it turned out, both the quad .50 and the searchlight jeep would be rendered into junk by NVA rockets and grenades during the course of the battle.

0235, Headquarters and Headquarters Company .50 cal gun position

Lee Weltha had huddled in his bunker with about a half-dozen other men in a space designed for two, maybe three. The stout log redoubt had attracted a couple of the "cherries," the new men.

When the shelling stopped, Weltha started yelling at everyone to get out. The newbies didn't want to move.

"Get out or die, you stupid fuckers!" Weltha screamed at them.

Even in the darkness, with dirt choking and covering all of them, their pink faces and clean green fatigues stood out.

"Why, Sarge?" one of the newbies wailed.

"Because Charlie will be here soon, you idiot, and he's goin' to be tossing satchel charges and frags into all these bunkers, now *move out*!"

The men stumbled out of the bunker and into the night. Weltha noticed right away that the .50 cal they had so carefully restored would be worthless in their defense. "It looked like a bad piece of modern art," he wrote later.

One rookie gasped, "Sarge, are we gonna die?"

"If you think like that, you're already dead," Weltha said, trying to calm the man.

He shouted to all of them, "Take it moment by moment. Stick together and stay cool. It gets weird."

"What do we do if we see gooks coming at us?" another man asked.

"Say 'Trick or Treat,' then shoot them," Weltha smirked, trying to sound nonchalant.

The new men stared at Weltha dumbfounded. "That's right. This is it, but go easy, keep your spirits up, stay alert. Take it one gook at a time. Protect each other first, and you all can make it. Now, grab your weapons!"

0236, A Battery, 2nd Battalion, 32nd Field Artillery, 8-inch howitzer gun position

SP4 Ralph Jones was pinned down and feeling as if his life were about to be ripped from his soul. He had spent fourteen months in Vietnam so far and had never been that close to an actual firefight. As a gunner on one of the large 8-inch howitzers, it wasn't his job to be this close. He and his crewmates were typically stationed miles behind the front lines. Recently, however, someone "up the chain" had decreed that the big guns were no longer going to hang back; they were going to get up close and personal with the NVA. Jones did not know what SOB had decided on this new policy, but at that moment Jones wanted to strangle the bastard.

Jones was far beyond the normal time for rotation back to the States, but his sergeant had told him that if he got off the line and went home, he'd likely end up at some spit-and-polish post to serve out the remaining six months of his obligation to Uncle Sam. Jones had gotten used to wearing grimy, hydraulic-fluid-stained pants and going around in the jungle mostly bare chested. He could not bear the thought of putting on a shirt, tie, and army blouse again.

"I felt that if I had to salute one more asshole with a brown bar on his shoulder, I would just crack," Jones related. "I just couldn't do it, so I decided I'd stay with my buddies in A Battery, 2/32. They were really good guys."

He landed in country in January 1969 and immediately gravitated to the men and the work in A-2/32. Most of his time had been spent in the jungle taking on targets for the 1st Cav and firing his big gun with its 200-pound shells at coordinates many miles downrange. "Sometimes," Jones admitted, "even firing into Cambodia."

On January 31, 1970, Jones and his crew, under the "new directives," were sent for "a few days" from their large, hardened base at FSB St. Barbara, to the smaller, less well hardened FSB Carolyn. Those "few days" turned into six weeks, and then they were shuttled again, closer to the front, from FSB Carolyn to FSB Beverly. On March 21 they were told to move again, this time to a Special Forces Camp farther up the line. When the battery arrived at the camp they discovered, much to their chagrin, there were no fortifications for them to occupy and no plans to make any; so they were directed to move even farther down the road to FSB Illingworth.

Illingworth proved to be no artillery paradise either, and the base commander was not happy to see them, but at least he was willing to expand his perimeter to accommodate the guns. Jones and his battery mates settled in and waited.

Like everyone else aboard the base, the men of A-2/32 began

to get itchy about moving again after five days at Illingworth. No orders to move were received, however. By the evening of the 31st, Jones and his pals knew they were "in for it." Jones went to his sergeant and begged him to allow the gunners to preload a round. They wanted to get off at least one good shot if the "shit hit the fan." The sergeant refused, calling it "a safety issue."

"Can you imagine?" Jones laughed. "We're about to get clobbered by the NVA and this guy's worried about 'a safety issue'?"*

Jones had taken shelter in a culvert near his 8-inch howitzer as the NVA firestorm of rockets and artillery commenced, but when that portion of the fight was over, he crawled out, grabbed an M-16, and threw himself on the berm. He was amazed by the tracers, red and green, flying everywhere. Dimly, in the swirling dust and darkness, he saw a form trying to climb up on his gun. The man put a foot on the gunner's seat to lever himself up. Jones thought the grunt must either be crazy or have a death wish; then, as light from a descending paraflare danced across the gun pit, Jones froze. The climber was an NVA soldier, clutching a satchel charge. He obviously wanted to destroy the gun.

Forgetting the danger, acting purely out of concern for his beloved cannon, Jones popped up, snapped the M-16 to his shoulder, and fired a burst. Jones watched a hot red tracer bury itself in the enemy soldier's back. The man turned slightly, glancing at Jones over his shoulder, staring at Jones with pure hatred before crumpling to the ground dead, mission unfulfilled.

"It was the first time I ever killed someone directly," Jones said sadly, "and that man sure hated me in his last living seconds."

---

* The "safety issue" in question turned out to be real. The base plate of the big 8-inch rounds, when fired at flat elevations, could come blowing back toward the gun crews and become a deadly missile in its own right.

0240, the TOC

RTO Hall's back had been bandaged, and the stinging sensations had begun to subside. He and RTO Dragosavac had evacuated their bunker and were back at the TOC, which was their normal duty assignment. Both men had their back-pack radios at the ready. Major Moore came over to where the two were waiting.

"Men, we're shit for comms. I need to know what's happening. One of you needs to report to Lieutenant Peters's area, with Echo Recon, and stay by him and relay traffic. One of you needs to come with me, to the do the same over by the 8-inch guns. You decide who goes where."

"Dragosavac and me, we flipped a coin, to see who would decide," Hall reported. "I won and I picked E-Recon. No particular reason. I just knew some of those guys. Dave, he went with Major Moore. I never saw him again. He was blown away. Pretty lucky toss of the coin, if you ask me," Hall said wistfully.

0244, Tay Ninh, Capt Joe Hogg's Blue Max Cobra

Capt. Joe Hogg, a native of the Black Hills of South Dakota, would be the number-four Blue Max Cobra to fly into the firestorms of Illingworth that night. His two hours on station would be some of the most tense and eventful moments of his life.

Hogg's Cobra, fully loaded with ammo and fuel, labored skyward into the thick, humid air of Tay Ninh. Even from a distance of about 8 miles, Hogg could see the flares and flashes from Illingworth as soon as he got airborne. It took only a few minutes to cover the klicks between his ARA base and the beleaguered compound. Hogg checked in with the artillery liaison at the TOC at Illingworth, Capt. John Ahearn.

"I was amazed, given all that was happening, how utterly cool, calm, and collected Ahearn seemed," Hogg reported. "As I rolled in along the berm to the southwest, he immediately started giving me targets."

The flares were falling all around Illingworth, offering Hogg and the other Blue Max pilots some light with which to work. One of the first visions Hogg remembers after reporting on station was something he saw in the vicinity of the E-Recon and Charlie Company positions. At first it seemed as if a large black plastic sheet was blowing on the wind, lazily moving toward the outer positions along the southwest corner. Hogg banked his Cobra in order to get a better look. The next flare revealed that what he had seen was the collected shadows of a large mass of NVA running toward the berm. He yanked the collective and shoved the stick forward, rolling in on the wave of men spread before him. Before he could fire his rockets, the flare blinked out and the target went back to black. He fired anyway, using the last visual he had had on the enemy. Several rockets ripped the ground beneath the Cobra. Hogg didn't know if he had hit anyone or anything. He pulled up to come around again.

One isolated NVA 51 mm antiaircraft battery was lobbing a few desultory shots at Hogg's Cobra. There had been several other AA batteries banging away at the beginning of the fight, but the previous Cobra pilots had neutralized all but this one lonely battery.

Hogg fired off a couple of rockets in the direction of the enemy gun, "just to let him know that I knew he was there. He wasn't really much of a threat."

From his cockpit, Hogg had a perfect view of the dance of death that was unfolding below him. He could see each of the artillery crews working their guns. Five of the 105s were firing directly into the tree line or at the onrushing NVA; one was tossing illumination rounds into the sky. The quad .50 was blasting away, but the big 8-inch guns appeared to be silent. Tracers were flying everywhere. The red ones of the Americans flew out from the berm; the green ones of the NVA guns arched inward.

It was Hogg that Captain Ahearn had managed to contact with his handheld radio. Soon Hogg, in addition to attacking targets as directed, found himself in the role of airborne radio relay station. Ahearn would radio reports and requests to Hogg, and Hogg would pass the info on to the artillery in Tay Ninh.

After a prolonged spate of furious calls back and forth, Hogg realized that things had gone quiet for a few minutes. As his brain was registering that fact, he rolled over the southwest sector of the berm again and was shocked to see another large wave of men stacking up to rush the perimeter. At that very moment the eerily calm voice of Captain Ahearn came back on the net.

"Max, this is Midland Notcher [Ahearn's call sign for the day]. I need you to do me a favor."

"Roger Midland Notcher, this is Max. Go!"

"Get on the battalion frequency. For God's sake, tell them if they don't send help, and now, we are going to be overrun."

Hogg's blood froze. *Oh my God . . . could it be possible?*

"Roger that," Hogg clicked back.

Hogg furiously dialed in the battalion frequency and keyed his mike.

"Tay Ninh, this is Silver Dagger. Midland Notcher says if you don't get them some help ASAP they are going to be overrun, over."

Hogg said he could hear muffled shouting and voices in his

headset, as if several people on the other end were in a heated discussion about what to do. After a moment, a loud and irritated voice he did not recognize shouted into his radio, "We know that! Out!"

10

"I THOUGHT IT WAS THE END OF THE WORLD"

All of the following takes place on April 1, 1970, between 0245 and 0318.

0245, Echo 2/8 mortar platoon position

They'll be on top of us any second, Sgt. Randall Richards told himself, as he gripped his M-16 a little more tightly. He, Lieutenant Russell, and the remaining men of the mortar platoon were hunkered down on the interior side of their secondary berm, waiting for the tidal wave to flow over them. All their mortars were out of action, so these grunts were infantrymen again.

Through the darkness and choking dust Richards saw Cpl. Bobby Barker jump up and start running.

"Barker," he shouted above the din, "where the fuck you goin'?"

Barker yelled back, "Don't have no rifle, Sarge. I'm goin' to the FDC to get one!"

Another loud explosion. Richards screamed at Barker, "Don't

go in there, Bobby!" Too late. Barker disappeared into the night. He hadn't heard.

Dumb sonofabitch . . . Well, that's Barker, Richards mused. Memories of his friend flashed through his mind, even in the midst of battle.

Shouldn't even be here, Richards grumbled to himself.

Barker was eight days shy of his twenty-first birthday. A few days ago he had come to Richards with a request. He wanted to go to the rear for a couple of days to see a dentist—get his teeth fixed so he could show off his new smile to his mother back in Harvey, Illinois, when it came time for him to go home. Bobby had been a decent soldier, if a bit of a "scam artist," but Richards decided to cut him a break. He wrote a note to the first sergeant, who approved the request. Richards told Barker to get his teeth fixed and take some R&R. He hadn't expected to see Barker for a couple more days. Then, there he was, in the middle of the battle.

"What the hell are you doing back here, Barker?"

"Sarge, I just wanted to show you my new choppers! See?" Barker smiled, revealing a lovely new set of front teeth.

Richards tried to raise the FDC on his handheld radio. He had talked to them earlier, but the radio was dead. He wanted to warn them Bobby was coming in. He was afraid the guys in the FDC would blow Barker away.

The grunts inside the FDC knew the NVA were trying to storm the base. They were given specific instructions to shoot anyone who tried to get inside the FDC without the password. Bobby Barker had been away for the last few days. He didn't have the password.

0250, Charlie Company's interior lines

It was three days and a hundred years ago that SFC Charles Beauchamp had stepped off the Huey into the madness of FSB Illingworth. Beauchamp, a career army NCO, was on his second tour in Vietnam. Previously, in 1966, he had served in country with the 25th Infantry, "Tropic Lightning." Seriously wounded, he was evacuated to Japan, then the States, and when he had recovered, he was assigned to the 5th Infantry in Germany. Promoted to sergeant first class in 1969, he was reassigned to the "Big Red One," the 1st Infantry Division, and back to Vietnam. When that division was ordered home, Beauchamp was shunted over to the 1st Cav. He had less than ninety days to go on this tour. He figured he'd be assigned to some rear echelon duties and be done with it. Awaiting orders in Phuoc Vinh, Beauchamp was awakened in the middle of the night on March 27 and told he was urgently needed: A company from the 2/8 had been decimated in a jungle firefight, and they needed a first sergeant desperately—along with a planeload of replacements.

Sergeant Beauchamp flew into FSB Illingworth with thirty replacements, most of them newbies, on the afternoon of March 28. He reported immediately to Captain Hobson, who had been made CO of the fire base security forces by Colonel Conrad. Beauchamp and Hobson got right to work reorganizing the company, setting up fire teams, assigning gun placements, shoring up the culverts, packing empty ammo boxes with dirt (they had run out of sandbags), and digging in the command post.

Later on, during the evening of the 28th, Beauchamp had a chance to meet the lieutenant colonel commanding, Mike Conrad. Beauchamp recalls the conversation something like this (after pleasantries had been exchanged):

"Sir, the compound looks mighty light in terms of fortifications."

"It is, First Sergeant. That's because we intended to be here only a couple of days."

"But sir, the base has been here better than two weeks."

"Yes it has, Sergeant. Yes it has." End of conversation.

Beauchamp drilled the new men very hard, for two straight days, outside the berm. They practiced responding to an initial attack of mortars and rockets, then sprinting toward the correct positions along the lines where they had been assigned. They fired rounds at imaginary targets in the tree line and trained with the company's veterans, setting up new firing teams.

Each night, the "Pipsy-5" radar reported movement in the jungle areas the men had been using as mock targets. Apparently, the woods truly were becoming dangerous. The first night the range was 1,800 meters, shrinking to 1,500 meters. The second night the range was 800 meters, then 500 meters. Beauchamp knew the enemy was drawing closer and sizing up his men and the camp. He hoped the frantic pace of his instruction would be enough to keep some of these men alive.

By midnight on the 31st, practice was definitely over. By 0250, the entire company, new men and old, were on the hot seat again, and the NVA was turning up the flames.

0251, Echo recon platoon, along the berm

Lieutenant Peters and Staff Sergeant Taylor had been flailing away like madmen. Peters figured that his twenty men were trying to hold off the bulk of each NVA charge—they had probably thrown two hundred troops or more at them already. Ten-to-one odds were not good. Peters did wonder why they just didn't all charge at once, but he was mighty glad they hadn't—at least not so far.

Fires were erupting everywhere, and somewhere in the recesses of his mind Peters knew that there was a huge stockpile of exposed artillery rounds right behind his back. It would only take one determined enemy sapper to get through his lines with one satchel charge and it would all be over.

He could only worry about what was in front of him and his men at the moment, however, and that scenario was bad enough. Over to his right he could see that big kid, Lemon, acting like a one-man wrecking crew. Another grunt, SP4 Casey Waller, was right beside Lemon, and it looked like they were doing the job of a whole platoon, just the two of them. Then again, weren't they all doing the same?

Peters kept ranging up and down, making himself visible, firing as he went, encouraging the men assigned to the three bunkers he controlled. On the left, Taylor was doing the same for his grunts and his two bunkers. The line was holding, but Peters was not sure how much longer they could stand the pressure. Ammunition was dwindling, and grenades were running low. The NVA, by individual soldiers and then by squads, were beginning to gain footholds all along the line. The American artillery and gunships were still raking the enemy as they plunged across the open spaces, but more and more of them seemed to be making it through. Soon both opposing forces would be completely entangled, at which point in time the guns and aircraft outside the base would no longer have any value. It was a favorite tactic of the NVA, something they called "danger close." Simply described, it was a maneuver designed to negate the superior firepower of American arms. If the NVA could somehow dash in and mingle with their opponents, the powerful artillery and air assets of the American forces would be forced to back off lest they endanger friend as well as foe.

Peters watched in horror as a couple of satchel charges were tossed over their heads landing near the stockpiled 8-inch ammo. Then—was it possible?—was that an enemy sapper streaking by?

"Get that man! Shoot him!" Peters bellowed to no one in particular.

But was there anyone there? Or was it just a shadow? He couldn't be sure. Then he was. A sickening *whoomp* erupted behind Peters, and the ammo pile, or at least a portion of it, was on fire.

Oh, shit! This is bad . . .

0252, 2nd Battalion, 32nd Field Artillery, 8-inch howitzer battery position

Major Magness was badly hurt—and he knew it. His left arm was a bloody mess, his left leg shredded. He couldn't feel any extensive pain—yet—but he knew he would soon enough. He hollered for a medic. Amazingly, right at that moment, one was running by. The man stopped and rolled Magness over. Then the pain shot through his body like fire and knives. He couldn't help it—he screamed in agony. The severed artery in his left leg shot out a fountain of blood, so the medic got a tourniquet on that immediately, then slapped some bandages on the mangled arm. Magness refused the morphine offered. He needed to think.

Once he was stable, Magness told the medic to move on—there were other men who needed him, no doubt. Magness could not stand up but probably wouldn't have wanted to anyway. Bullets and other deadly missiles were zipping in all directions immediately above his head. He managed to crawl to the nearest culvert. It was empty, but at least there was a cot inside. He rolled onto the temporary bed and lay there, hoping his men would find him quickly and get him to a dust-off—if there were any, that is. Given the extent of his injuries, he knew his war was over, but he would not be out of it completely until the battle abated. He hoped he could hold on long enough. He prayed that by the time he could be evacuated there would still be more blood inside his body than in the growing pool on the stretcher underneath him.

0253, E-Recon position, along the berm

RTO Hall was crouched down, behind the berm, trying to make sense of the carnage and accelerating destruction. Lieutenant Peters and his men were too busy fending off the NVA to pay much attention to the radios. Major Moore kept asking for updates, and Hall relayed back what he could see and understand, which wasn't much more than "we're still here."

Four men from E-Recon were blasting away at the enemy from inside a bunker nearby. Hall watched in horror as a satchel charge sailed over the berm and landed right on top of their position. The bunker disappeared in a ball of fire. The blast also sent Hall flying through the air. He landed a dozen feet away. This time his face, not his back, was on fire, his eyes and cheeks full of bits of debris and shrapnel from the explosion.

As Hall picked himself up off the ground he looked back toward where the E-Recon men had been. He was sure they were dead, but he couldn't tell.

"I did see, before my eyes swelled shut, the most bizarre thing I ever saw while I was in Vietnam, though," Hall declared. "It was an arm, a human arm, standing straight up, dancing. It jumped a couple of times before it finally flopped on the ground. Must have been the severed nerves, or something. I still see that arm in my nightmares, which are pretty frequent, forty years later."

0258, 272nd NVA Regiment forward lines, FSB Illingworth

Colonel Lai was running through the trees, trying to gain the best perspective on the battle his men were pressing forward. He was also trying to avoid the American gunships that were raking the jungle all around him. A C-130 "Spooky" had come within feet of ripping him apart a few minutes back as the aircraft worked over his forward positions. Several of his men simply disappeared in puffs of bloody mist as the miniguns sawed back and forth through the trees. The firepower in those planes was truly savage, and very frightening.

Lai, thirty-one, had been a soldier since he was fifteen. He had started as a raw recruit in the Viet Minh, signing up to fight the French. Later, he had joined the Vietcong to battle the Americans and the South Vietnamese. He had risen steadily in the ranks and was, for several years, an intelligence officer and propaganda chief in the southern provinces. He estimated that he had spent the better part of the last eight years living in the jungle.

By the end of the Tet Offensive, in 1968, the Vietcong had been decimated, all but wiped out as an effective fighting force. Lai had managed to survive somehow, but not without a few wounds and many close calls. When the People's Army of Vietnam had moved in from the North and taken over after Tet, many of the old Vietcong units, the men and their leaders, like Lai, had been absorbed into the NVA. By early 1970, Nguyen Tuong Lai was in charge of a frontline regiment, the 272nd.

On April 1, 1970, that regiment was being torn to pieces, and Colonel Lai was watching it happen right in front of his eyes. The attack that he had so carefully planned was starting to falter. It was essential, and he had stressed this to all his men, that once the bombardment stopped, they go forward resolutely and get over the flimsy walls the Americans had erected as quickly as possible. It was also vital to get to that big mound of exposed ammunition. It must be blown, no matter the cost. Once that happened, Colonel Lai was convinced, the battle would be over. The Americans would all either be dead or ready to surrender. He would achieve what no other regimental commander in the long history of the war against the Americans had done: a clear-cut, outright victory against an opposing force of similar size and capabilities. He wanted to taste that victory—and hasten the peace talks he knew were already going on half a world away.

He saw—at last!—a number of his men go over the enemy's berm. At least a squad, maybe a platoon, was inside the compound. He wished he was among them, firing, running, bayoneting the Americans, but he knew he couldn't. Those days were behind him. He was a senior commander, and his job was to tell his men to die, not to die himself. His men were tough. They were veterans. He knew them well, and he believed they could succeed. Just a little longer . . .

0229, Echo recon platoon, along the berm

Aching, sweaty, covered in blood and dust, Pete Lemon was painfully jogging back to the berm when another RPG slammed into the ground nearby. Lemon was hurled through the air and thrown down, hard. New pains. He didn't know exactly where, and decided not to look. As long as he could get up—and he did—he'd move on. Pulling himself out of the dirt once more, he continued his jog.

He returned to the site where he and Vaca had been firing the M-60. To his horror, he saw the gun was in the hands of several NVA. One of them was tugging at the bolt, trying to get the gun working. Clearly, they intended to turn the weapon on the Americans and give back some of what they had been getting.

Lemon still had a couple of frags. He pulled the pins, flicked the spoons away, and held them for a couple of seconds before tossing them at the NVA—who had not yet noticed Lemon materializing out of the storm of dirt and dust. He kept the grenades for those brief moments so the NVA couldn't scoop them up and toss them back at him. He finally let them fly. All but one of the enemy soldiers went down. The one NVA remaining was the man trying to work the bolt. Somehow, he had escaped the blasts. Lemon dove for the man, bowling him over and sprawling the two of them across the top of the berm. Lemon was too powerful for the soldier to resist, and for the second time that morning, Pete Lemon choked the life out of a man.

Lemon popped back up, and right beside him was SP4 Casey Waller, a pal from Echo Recon. The M-60 was apparently useless, so Lemon grabbed an M-16 lying nearby. He and Waller proceeded to hose down the next line of NVA storming the perimeter. The line behind that—they were still coming in waves—pitched several grenades at the two Americans. Lemon saw one coming in and screamed for Waller to duck. They both dove back behind the berm and pulled themselves into a culvert. The grenades landed and—*whump*—*whump*—*whump*—went off all around them.

Jumping back out of the culvert, Waller and Lemon heard Lieutenant Peters, who was only a few feet away, hollering and furiously pointing at—something. There was an unmanned .50 cal a few feet away from Lemon and Waller. Peters was trying to get the two of them on that gun. The men went for the powerful machine gun only to find it, too, wasn't functioning properly, firing only one round at a time. That would be pretty useless against the onrushing attack, so both Waller and Lemon went back to work with their M-16s. Their red tracers flew outward in the night, and the NVAs green tracers zipped inward. Lemon felt several rounds rip the air near his head.

Lemon heard it more than saw it—the RPG that roared into their position. It smacked into something. Lemon, for the third time in less than an hour, was hit and down on the ground. More wounds. Punctures on his right side, as far as he could tell, but the rocket hadn't ripped off any appendages, apparently, or penetrated any vital organs. Getting woozy from the loss of blood, he staggered to his feet. He glanced around for Waller. He was not there. It was at that moment Lemon realized that the "something" the RPG had hit was Waller. It had completely obliterated him. There wasn't enough of Waller left to stick in a tin cup.

Lemon looked ahead. It seemed to him that the enemy waves were waning, but the world was losing its color. Everything functioned in black and white only. There was a tunnel in front of his eyes, and it was narrowing, collapsing inward. He realized then that he was passing out. He dropped to his knees and then flopped into the dirt, the night folding over him.

0300, Charlie Company position, along the berm

SP4 Cliff Rhodes, twenty, from Collins, Mississippi, had landed in Vietnam in November 1969 and had been posted to Charlie Company almost immediately. He was one of the very few men from the November rolls who had somehow made it through the gauntlet of tragedies experienced by Charlie over the next four months. Rhodes had done so without sustaining so much as a combat scratch. It was a minor miracle. This night, of course, was looking like it was going to be very different.

Unexpectedly, there would be another "good old boy" from back home in Mississippi to share the "fun." Much to Rhodes's delight, Billy Pat Carlisle had shown up at Illingworth a couple of days prior. Carlisle was from the tiny town of Pelahatchie, right off of Interstate 20, east of Jackson. He was actually a replacement, assigned to Alpha 2/8, but Alpha Company was already out on patrol, so Carlisle was told to cool his heels at Illingworth until the company got back. They would not return for at least a few more days. Carlisle fell in with his fellow Mississippian and decided to bunk with Rhodes until he could join up with his own unit.

Also in the same tiny culvert was one of the FNGs—fucking new guys—assigned to Charlie Company. Neither Carlisle nor Rhodes had gotten to know the kid's name yet and, frankly, didn't much want to. The way Charlie Company was losing men, it didn't pay many dividends to get to know too many FNGs. They were usually dead or wounded before very long, and it was just too painful.

It was good to have companionship from "home," but Rhodes had pretty much given up on life. His days were stretches of pure terror and the constant threat of death. His nights were spent mostly crying quietly. Recently, though, he had experienced an incredibly vivid dream. In it, he was in his uniform, stepping off a bus, right in front of Pickering's General Store, at the intersection of routes 588 and 84, suitcase in one hand, rifle in the other. Was it the dream of a walking dead man, who would never see his home again, or a hopeful sign that he might actually make it through this hell he was going through? He did not know, but the dream had given him a strange kind of hope.

Once the bombardment stopped, Rhodes, an M-60 machine-gun team leader, scrambled out of the culvert to man his weapon. Carlisle did likewise, M-16 in one hand and dragging a case of grenades with the other. The FNG, however, was useless. No amount of shouting and cursing at the wretch could get him to pick up his rifle. The best Rhodes could get him to do was to help him load the ammo for his M-60.

Rhodes and Carlisle kept firing, and firing. When the M-60's barrel started glowing red, Carlisle would cease firing it and pick up the useless FNG's M-16 and start blasting away with it. Carlisle was shooting and lobbing frags like a madman, screaming at the "fucking gooks," daring them to kill him. They did. A B-40 rocket slammed into the ground right in front of the culvert. The FNG was curled up in the fetal position but caught a few hot shards of steel, wounding him slightly. Hot metal spewed over the entire position. It tore Billy Carlisle to shreds, but once again Cliff Rhodes went miraculously unscathed.

0305, Near the 8-inch howitzer positions

Tired of stumbling around in the dark, Sergeant Weltha ran over to a nearby bunker where he thought he had seen a "thump gun." The M-79 was still there with a four-pack of illumination rounds beside it. Weltha grabbed it, ran back outside, and loaded up. Firing one round at a time, about 100 yards out and 50 yards apart, everything around the position and out into the field in front of the berm was lit up like daylight.

Weltha later wrote, "My heart froze!" Enemy soldiers were swarming toward the 8-inch guns. Some were running, others were crawling, but all were firing their weapons or throwing grenades.

Weltha frantically looked around for help. A case of frags he had set aside was gone. He had stored a couple dozen more in the bunker, so he dove back in to retrieve them. Dashing back out again, he began pitching them at the NVA. Several that landed among the enemy soldiers created secondary explosions, no doubt from the munitions the NVA were carrying.

When Weltha ran out of grenades, he picked up his M-16 and started firing. Something was wrong, however. His many months in the war instinctively told him something was missing. It took him a few seconds to realize what it was. It was too quiet on his side of the line. The American mortars had gone silent. They weren't firing. The quad .50 gun truck, which had been putting out a steady stream of lead, was likewise mute. All machine-gun fire had slackened, and the artillery was slowing down. It could only mean that the human wave was on them, about to wash over them. It was mano-a-mano time, bayonets and gun butts.

Jesus, we're fucked . . .

0307, 272nd NVA Regiment forward lines, FSB Illingworth

Colonel Lai could no longer spot his men—the ones who were still alive, that is. He could see dozens of bodies: his soldiers, scattered across the approach to the fire base. Several were attempting to crawl back to the jungle, but the vast majority of the forms were inert and undoubtedly dead. How many of his men remained? How many of them were inside the base? Any? Something was happening within the base, he just knew it. Less fire was flowing outward, and more gunfire was swirling within. He hoped with all his being that his men had made it inside and were slaughtering the Americans.

A "Blue Max" AH-1 Cobra, Vietnam, 1970: Note four rocket pods, two under each wing, and the muzzle of the machine gun under the nose of the aircraft. *(Photo courtesy of Captain John Ahearn)*

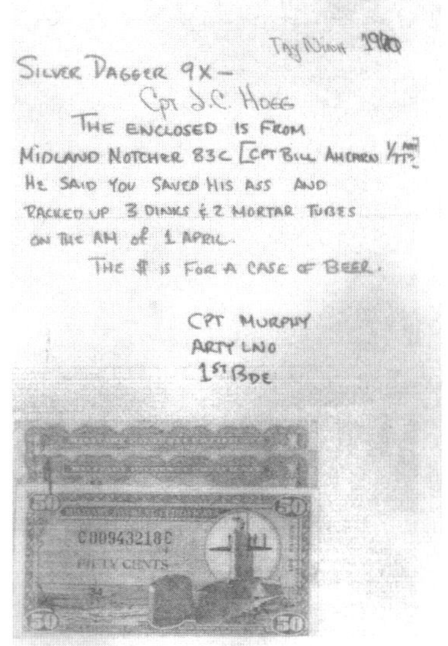

Tay Ninh 1970

SILVER DAGGER 9X—
CPT J.C. HOGG
THE ENCLOSED IS FROM
MIDLAND NOTCHER 83C [CPT BILL AHEARN
HE SAID YOU SAVED HIS ASS AND
RACKED UP 3 DINKS & 2 MORTAR TUBES
ON THE AM of 1 APRIL.
THE $ IS FOR A CASE OF BEER.

CPT MURPHY
ARTY LNO
1ST BDE

C00943218C
FIFTY CENTS

This note was delivered to Captain Joe Hogg from Captain John Ahearn (mistakenly called "Bill Ahearn" in the note) via Captain Murphy, and included $2.50 in MPC (Military Payment Certificates) to buy a case of beer. *(Copy courtesy of Captain John Ahearn)*

Damaged 8-inch howitzer, FSB Illingworth, April 1, 1970. *(Photo courtesy of Ralph Jones)*

FSB Illingworth ammo stacking, March 31, 1970. *(Photo courtesy of Captain John Ahearn)*

FSB Illingworth, March 31, 1970. *(Photo courtesy of Captain John Ahearn)*

FSB Illingworth—the cavalry drives by. *(Photo courtesy of Captain John Ahearn)*

FSB Illingworth Battery A, 2/32 Artillery sleeping positions, post-battle. Note the damaged 8-inch gun in the background, and how close it was to the living quarters. *(Photo courtesy of Ralph Jones)*

SP4 Peter Lemon, Vietnam, 1970 *(left and center)*, and Pete Lemon, 2012 *(right)*. *(Photos [l-r] courtesy of Colorado State University Alumni, HomeofHeroes.com, and U.S. Department of Homeland Security)*

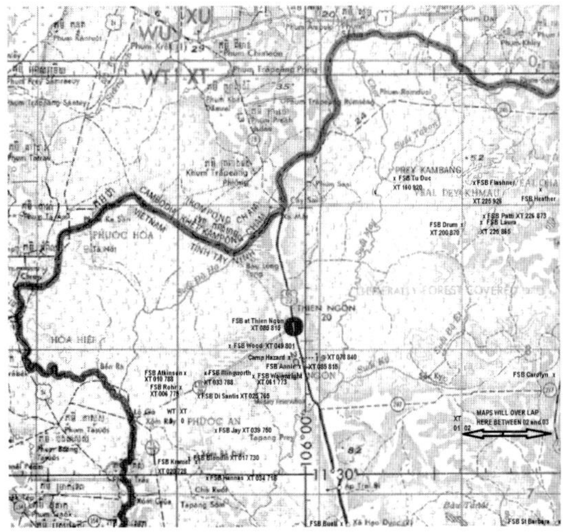

"The Dog's Head" area of War Zone C and the primary operations area of this book. *(Copy courtesy of Captain Joe Hogg)*

SP4 Jack Illingworth *(foreground),* March 14, 1970, three days before his death. *(Photo courtesy of Sergeant Randall Richards)*

Alpha Troop, 11th ACR, Illingworth Detachment, March 31, 1970. *(Photo courtesy of George Burks)*

Former NVA Battalion Commander Nguyen Tuong Lai, in exile, 1982. *(Photo courtesy of Parade Magazine)*

The 11th ACR Position, inside the berm, FSB Illingworth, March 31, 1970 (note the profile of the Sheridan tank behind the tent). *(Photo courtesy of Captain John Ahearn)*

FSB Illingworth, postbattle (note small shell crater in foreground). Behind the three soldiers that are seated on ammo crates is a tall pole, another pile of ammo boxes, and sandbags: This is the FDC where Lieutenant Bridgman and RTO Lane were killed. *(Photo courtesy of Captain John Ahearn)*

FSB Illingworth, postbattle, scattered ammunition. *(Photo courtesy of Captain John Ahearn)*

Damaged ammo carrier. This is taken from the side of the vehicle. Notice the oil leaks on the wheels. The ammo dump explosion caused all of the seals to break. On the right edge of the photo, you can see the other overturned vehicle from the 32nd Artillery. *(Photo courtesy of Captain John Ahearn)*

Taken from the side of the photo above. You can see the ammo carrier in the center of the vehicle. Notice the vehicle markings at the top—IIFF 32FA, and, at bottom right, the number is 2A38. *(Photo courtesy of Captain John Ahearn)*

Area of FSB Illingworth today: View is from what was the area of the southwest corner of the berm, where Charlie Company and E-Recon defended the base. Note the closeness of the tree line, which is still pretty much what it was in 1970. *(Photo courtesy of Ralph Jones)*

Former 8-inch gunner from the 2/32 Artillery Ralph Jones places soil from former FSB Illingworth at the 2/32 FSB Jay and FSB Illingworth Memorial at Ft. Sill, Oklahoma, 2008. *(Photo courtesy of Ralph Jones)*

Members of the 2/32 Battery A prebattle, FSB Illingworth, March 27, 1970. *(Photo courtesy of Ralph Jones)*

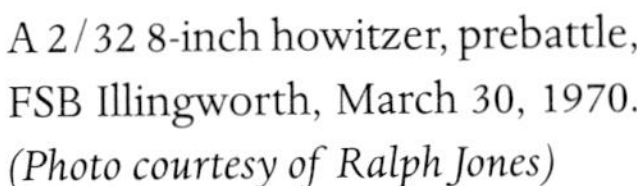

A 2/32 8-inch howitzer, prebattle, FSB Illingworth, March 30, 1970. *(Photo courtesy of Ralph Jones)*

Soldier life at FSB Illingworth (note the "height" of the berm behind the soldiers). *(Photos courtesy of Rick Hokenson)*

A 105 mm howitzer: postbattle, showing rocket damage to one gun. *(Photo courtesy of Captain John Ahearn)*

He hated the Americans with a passion greater than he had hated the French. The French, at least, had tried to make his country into an Asian economic center, even as they raped its resources and its women with equal colonial impunity. The Americans, on the other hand, had simply come to kill them, and to support the puppet regimes in Saigon that were pillaging the country even more than the French had ever dared to do. He also loathed the arrogance and the power of the Americans, interlopers who thought they could impose their will and politics on this ancient land. How stupid they were. How little they truly knew about "winning the hearts and minds" of the Vietnamese people, as they ignorantly called their strategy. Lai and his forebears had been in combat over their nationhood for hundreds of years. What made these overfed, pompous, patronizing foreigners think they were any better—or different?

Before he had taken command of this regiment, Lai had been the chief of intelligence in the region. As such, he was also the area's chief interrogator. He and his men had captured more than a few Americans. He had even snagged some helicopter pilots and air crewmen who had been shot down in his sector. Two navy pilots, forced to eject from their crippled plane, had also ended up in Lai's custody. Most of the prisoners were passed on, transported through Cambodia, destined for the POW camps in the north. A few, especially the officers, Lai liked to single out for his personal attention before handing them over.

Little of what Lai wrested from his prisoners was of any great value. The captured Americans often knew less than his superiors already did about American dispositions and operations. He played with their minds and their fears. It was a balm to him, to make up for all the insults and the indignities he and his country had suffered. Lai was hoping desperately that he would be able to get his hands on the commander of this fire base. He would particularly enjoy questioning that officer. Nguyen Tuong Lai was, without doubt, a talented and capable leader, but he had a distinctly dark side, too.

0310, A Battery, 2nd Battalion, 32nd Field Artillery, 8-inch howitzer gun position

Specialist Jones was lying on his belly, firing at the enemy. They were less than 20 yards away. If something didn't change soon, his position was going to be overrun. The NVA were in the base, no question, and the American response, as far as Jones could tell, was slacking off. Worse, there were fires in and near the piles of 8-inch ammo, and the flames were even closer to Jones than the enemy.

A few weeks back, at FSB Carolyn, Jones had seen and experienced the explosion of a stockpile of 155 ammo. The blast was horrendous and had torn a hole in the ground 20 yards across and 10 feet deep. That pile of ammo was nothing compared to what Jones was staring down.

If that ammo goes up, there is no way in hell anyone nearby is going to survive, Jones told himself.

Years after the fight Jones remembered, "I started yelling, screaming at everyone to get away. With the roar of battle, no one heard me. I started praying."

0311, D Company, 1st Squadron, 11th ACR, busting jungle toward FSB Illingworth

So far, no flare ship had shown up to light the way. Jungle that would probably have taken a little more than an hour to bust through in daylight was proving to be much more difficult to navigate on a dark Southeast Asian night. There was a moon, but the triple-canopy jungle overhead was so thick, moonlight had no value to the tracks.

Capt. Jerry Hensley was utterly frustrated. He wanted to get to Illingworth very badly. First and foremost, he wanted to help those men. Second, however, was the cavalryman's esprit de corps that told him he and his men must "ride to the guns" and "save the day." Also in the back of his mind was the recent tale of his regimental counterpart, Capt. John Poindexter and Alpha Troop, men who had courageously smashed through these same woods five days ago and pulled off the amazing rescue of Charlie 2/8. Hensley wanted a piece of glory like that for his troopers, too. Secretly, he also wanted to show that tall, skinny, cocksure ninety-day-wonder bastard Poindexter that he was no slouch at this kind of warfare, either.

Goddamn woods! Goddamn darkness! Hensley grumbled to himself.

Hensley had started his trek with an Air Force FAC circling overhead. The FAC was supposed to give him guidance and direction, from above, and help speed D Company to Illingworth. It wasn't working. The FAC couldn't see much of anything in the darkness and the thick jungle below completely hid the movement of the tanks.

Hensley got on the radio to Colonel Reed and asked him if he could hurry along the flare ship. Reed told Hensley he believed one was on the way, but TACAIR was busy at the moment sorting out the dire situation that FSB Illingworth had become. Apparently, the only flare ship in the area was illuminating the battle and didn't have the time or the sense of urgency to help light up the jungle for a column of struggling tanks and ACAVs.

Then Reed had a flash of inspiration. It was a brilliant one, pun intended, and an idea born out of the brain of one of the very few men in the entire army who could have thought of it at that moment. Lt. Col. Jim Reed, as a young tank commander in Korea, had led the very first platoon in the Armor Branch to be equipped with coaxially mounted searchlights, or big, powerful beams of light that were mounted in line with a tank's main gun. Wherever a big tank gun pointed, searchlight welded to its base plate, it would have instant and accurate illumination. Reed never forgot that experience.

Some of the Pattons had been equipped with coaxially mounted million-candlepower searchlights; not all of them, but, on average, one per platoon. Reed seemed to recall that Hensley had, maybe, two or three tanks with these searchlights. Reed radioed Hensley and told him to turn them on. Hensley was hesitant about lighting up his tanks in enemy territory, but Reed told him, "Just do it." He did.

Immediately, the FAC could see where the tanks were and which direction they needed to head. The jungle didn't get any easier to bust, but at least Hensley was being given a better chance to get where he needed to be.

0312, Capt. Joe Hogg, Blue Max, above Illingworth

The Cobra was becoming more nimble the lighter it got, but in this case, lighter didn't mean better. The powerful attack helicopter was shedding weight because Captain Hogg was firing off his seventy-eight rockets (which weighed 17 pounds each, including the booster) at a rapid clip. His fuel was more than half expended, and he had very few bullets left in his minigun. At this rate he'd be out of ammo and fuel very soon.

What the hell? Something caught Hogg's eye as he spun around the northern part of the berm, just outside the tree line.

It looked to him like a shower of sparklers from a 4th of July parade. Best he could tell, it was definitely inside the perimeter and very near the area where the 8-inch ammo had been piled. As the sparklers died down, small fires erupted, casting flickering lights on the ammunition boxes.

Shit, this is not good, Hogg said to himself as he banked away.

0313, Alpha Troop Detachment, 11th ACR, northeast corner of the berm

Much of the view that SP4 George Burks had of the battle, so far, was at boot level. Sergeant Hughes had told his men to take cover as soon as the rockets and artillery had started raining down, and Burks, along with several other troopers, had wisely elected to get under some of the best cover on the entire base—beneath the underbelly of a Sheridan. From this vantage point, all Burks was able to see was feet running by. So far, the only ones he had seen were clad in "boondockers," the army's ubiquitous combat boots. If any feet came by wearing sandals, they would be in real trouble.

Burks knew that a lot of rounds had landed nearby. The *whumps* in the dirt and the billowing clouds of dirt they threw into the air were constant. Once or twice he had heard the loud *bwang* of metal on metal, and he knew that could not be good. One of those blasts had been very close, and he thought it had probably had hit the mechanic's truck. Nothing had pranged off his Sheridan yet, but he was confident that if something did, the aluminum shell of the tank and the armor plate above his head would protect him.

It did grate on him that he was doing nothing to help. There wasn't much he could do, however. The infantry had taken away their only working machine gun, and the few M-16s the cavalry guys had possessed had already been confiscated by the artillery guys and were out on the berm. The big gun on the Sheridan above his head and the other two Sheridan cannons were silent, too. His gun was damaged and inoperable. The other two guns couldn't be cranked without power, and both those tanks had blown power packs.

He knew Sergeant Hughes had a .45. That was about the only weapon among all the cavalry troopers that was workable. Burks knew that Hughes wasn't going to fire it in anger, though, unless he absolutely had to do so. As the assault had begun, Hughes and Burks had looked at each other and agreed that if the "world went to shit" they were not going to be taken alive. Neither man wanted to go, as the phrase went, "down the rabbit hole;" i.e., disappearing into a POW camp. They were going to save the last rounds in Hughes's pistol for themselves.

0314, Charlie Company, Bunker 3

SP4 Rick Hokenson was about ready to snap. When the shelling had begun he, like everyone else out on the berm, had gone diving for shelter. He had been assigned to Charlie Company's bunker 2; in fact, that's where he'd been sleeping of late, head toward the enemy. As the mortars and rockets rained down in a seemingly never-ending succession, another grunt had jumped into his normal spot, feet toward the enemy. Rather than stand out in the open in a shower of hot steel and debate the issue, Hokenson flung himself into bunker 3. Moments later, a mortar round dropped in front of bunker 2, practically on top of the sandbagged culvert. The man in Hokenson's place had both legs riddled with shrapnel. Had Hokenson been in his place, his head would have shredded into hamburger instead of the other American's extremities. It was another sign from that mocking little imp bouncing around in Hokenson's brain.

"It was the worst pounding I ever experienced," Hokenson said later. "They kept hammering us mercilessly, and as the incoming grew louder and more intense, our outgoing started to slacken as more and more of the guns and mortars were being hit. That's when I knew we were in real trouble."

Hokenson and his culvert mates were three bunkers away from the 8-inch guns. The big howitzers were totally defenseless and seemed to be getting the lion's share of the incoming. Hokenson had a good buddy over there, a pal who had just come back that day from R&R in Hong Kong. The two of them had been sharing some C-rats a few hours ago, and Hokenson's friend had been bragging about his leave and some beautiful new suits he had ordered from Ricky's Special Hong Kong Tailors. As the blasts around the howitzers grew in fury, Hokenson wondered if his friend would survive the shelling—and if he didn't, where would Ricky mail the finished suits?

0318, the TOC, FSB Illingworth

Artillery was the key to defending Illingworth. Without the 105s, the 155s, the mortars, and the redlegs acting as infantrymen, the base would have been overwhelmed and picked clean. On the other hand, the artillery almost doomed Illingworth to utter destruction.

Colonel Conrad had been concerned about the exposed artillery stockpiles since the very first moments the mules started hauling the pallets inside his perimeter. The artillerymen themselves were worried about the tons of powder and shells that had been heaped inside the berm, near the southwest corner. Working like demons, the redlegs and a number of the grunts had done everything they could, before nightfall on March 31, to protect this monstrous pile of potentially hazardous ammo. It would not be enough.

Part of the stockpile had started to burn soon after the NVA bombardment began. Many of the redlegs—especially those from A Battery of the 2/32, the men physically closest to the trove—were well aware of the danger. As the battle ramped up, the fires burned untended. No one could be spared to fight the flames, so the men kept a wary eye on the danger and fought on, desperately hoping they could conclude their defense before the fires worsened. It was not to be.

Some of the survivors of the battle on April 1 swear, to this day, that they viewed one or more NVA sappers get inside the berm. Official army documents specifically state that "no enemy made it inside the lines." Those who say they actually saw the successful penetration of the base by the enemy also say they witnessed satchel charges—or possibly Chicom grenades—being tossed by the enemy into the standing pile of powder and projectiles. There has never been any absolute confirmation of this allegation, nor, at this late date, can there be. It is at least probable and likely possible that the assertions are correct. At the very least there are documented photos of NVA bodies inside the perimeter, postbattle.

Whether it was the smoldering fires finally reaching the powder bags or an NVA sapper making it to the 8-inch ammunition storage point, there is certainly no doubt that at 0318 most of the poorly sequestered ammunition finally blew up. There was a titanic roar that threw men, equipment, and tons of dust and dirt into the air. The blast lit up the night sky, flames reaching up over 100 feet. A gigantic crater was gouged out of the earth where the ammunition had been.

Colonel Conrad, who was back in the TOC at the moment of the explosion, later said, "I thought it was the end of the world."

11

WHEN DEATH RAINED DOWN

All of the following takes place on April 1, 1970, between 0319 and 0500.

Records have yet to surface as to who, specifically, ordered the 40 tons of extra 8-inch ammunition placed aboard FSB Illingworth on the afternoon of March 31. The (then) newly revised 2nd Field Force (Artillery) strategy of moving the guns forward, to take them out of hardened positions far behind the front lines and get them up with the troops, certainly had something to do with it. A June 1970 debriefing report written (or at least signed) by Brig. Gen. F. J. Roberts, commanding general of the 2nd Field Force, Vietnam (Artillery) from November 21, 1969, to May 9, 1970, addresses this. In the report, Brigadier General Roberts speaks to the perceived need to get his artillerists out from behind the lines and into more forward positions, up with the frontline troops. He sees this as a way to better train his men and as a tactic to improve the accuracy and effectiveness of his artillery.

The man who would execute this new strategy within the 1st Cavalry would be the division's chief of artillery, the universally feared Col. Morris Brady.* Did someone on his staff issue the orders to stockpile the 8-inch ammo at FSB Illingworth? Was all that ammo intended solely for Illingworth, or was it to be distributed to other forward bases? Did some supply clerk in the rear misinterpret or confuse a supply order for the ammo? It is impossible to determine. It is telling, however, that once the ammunition started to arrive, Colonel Conrad could not succeed in getting his boss, Colonel Ochs, to divert it, or at least some of it. Why would Colonel Ochs not listen to the sound advice of his best battalion commander?

0319, FSB Illingworth

The southwest corner of the fire base was obliterated. There was no more berm in that quadrant, not that it was much to begin with. The earth shook beneath the entire base, and the plume of fire and smoke could be seen several miles away. The concussion from the blast spread outward in a wide circle. What the detonation did not hurl into the air it slammed into the earth. There was so much dirt and dust in the air that paraflares, dropped from above, could not be seen from the ground. Raw earth swirled everywhere, and it continued to fall like dirty rain for several minutes. The air was so thick that men could barely breathe, and the atmosphere was so occluded that weapons ceased to function. Filth clogged every rifle and machine gun as if buckets of grime had been poured in every

* Col. Brady had a reputation for being tough, unforgiving, and inflexible.

breech. Pieces of equipment, shredded sandbags, chunks of wood, shards of metal, unexploded ammunition, and pieces of bodies came tumbling down all over the base in an unholy storm of death and destruction.

Of those who died, some were ripped to shreds, including several Americans and an unknown number of NVA. Others who perished were literally pounded into the earth, punched deeply into the soil, every bone shattered, every orifice packed solid with dirt. Of those who survived, many were tossed into the air, some landing well, others not. Most men near the explosion had one or both eardrums blown out. Everyone still left alive was choking, fighting for breath, stunned, and stumbling in the dark.

After the last echoes of the blast reverberated away, the entire base and the surrounding jungle fell deeply, eerily quiet for almost ten minutes.

In a curiously ironic way, the detonation was the critical tipping point of the battle, and it tipped the scales in favor of the Americans. The huge blast stopped all combat activity cold. Certainly, the shock of the explosion itself was enough to get everyone's attention and freeze them in place. The choking dust and dirt turned the simple, unconscious act of breathing into a major effort, forcing friend and foe alike to focus on survival instead of trying to kill each other. Weapons jammed all over the field of action. Guns simply would not function, AK-47s and M-16s alike. The momentum of the NVA attack was stalled. The ten to fifteen minutes of shock and awe after the explosion broke the back of the NVA attack. After this point in time, the fight devolved into clashes between isolated pockets of men and scattered attempts to reignite the action. The main thrust of the assault was over, however, and the bulk of the NVA began to withdraw. Stupid mistake or dumb luck, grievous tragedy or unintended consequence, the presence of that pile of 8-inch ammunition was a determining factor in the outcome of the fight.

0320, the TOC

Moments before the blast, Mike Conrad had finished a dash around the perimeter of the base, inspecting his lines. He had just ducked back into the TOC, intending to get on the radios and ask for more help, when the ammunition blew. The inside of the TOC turned into a giant blender, with radios and equipment flung in every direction. The single, puny incandescent bulb lighting the interior was instantly extinguished, plunging everything and everyone into total darkness. The space filled with choking clouds of dirt so thick it coated the insides of mouths and made breathing feel like being waterboarded. What antennas had remained above the TOC were turned into useless shreds of wire and twisted aluminum. Conrad figured the TOC had taken a direct hit, and he was amazed he was still alive. He and the radiomen groped for the exit. The atmosphere outside wasn't much better, but at least they could get small lungfuls of filthy oxygen.

0321, Charlie Company's lines, along the berm

The Charlie Company command bunker—a hollow dug out of the ground and hastily covered with dirt-filled ammunition boxes, a few sandbags, and some spare pieces of PSP—had collapsed on top of Sergeant Beauchamp, Captain Hobson, and their radiomen. It had, nonetheless, probably saved their lives. Beauchamp and the radiomen frantically pushed the debris aside, clawing to escape their tomb. Captain Hobson was pinned in the wreckage. A heavy, dirt-filled ammo box had fallen across his chest. He was soon freed by his men, none the worse for wear except a few more scratches and bruises.

Beauchamp had his bell rung—badly—and one of his eardrums was definitely blown. He wasn't sure yet about the other. As he stumbled out into the darkness, a group of redlegs tumbled down into the hole and piled on top of Beauchamp.

"What the fuck!" Beauchamp shouted, his good ear ringing loudly

One of the frightened artillerymen stared wide-eyed at the sergeant and said, "Gun's gone, Sarge! Fucker blew up!"

Beauchamp recognized the man as one of the soldiers manning a 105 mm howitzer.

"Well, then, you bastards are infantry now."

Beauchamp began pushing and shoving the men into position along the shattered berm, grabbing M-16s and thrusting them into their hands as he went.

Someone shouted, "Look, Sarge! Somebody's out there!"

Through the swirling dust, Beauchamp could see a prone form, outside the berm, trying to crawl toward safety. The man must have been blown over the wall and wounded. Beauchamp ordered the two men closest to the soldier to scramble over the barrier and pull the guy back in. Beauchamp himself hopped over the berm to help—then suddenly froze. Twisting around, he grabbed an M-16 from the nearest grunt, aimed it at the figure on the ground, and fired a burst into his back. The man stopped moving.

"Sarge! What the . . . !"

"Not one of ours. Fuckin' gook," and he was right.

Beauchamp spun around and jumped back over the berm, secretly amazed the enemy soldier had come so close to penetrating his lines.

0322, Alpha Troop, 11th ACR Detachment, northwest corner

Sgt. J. C. Hughes figured the crater left by the thunderous detonation had to be 100 feet across. It was certainly impressive. He could dimly see figures running through the clouds of dirt and dust, and he hoped they were grunts and not the enemy.

When the blast erupted, Hughes and his men were hunkered down under their armored vehicles. No one wanted to repeat the unfortunate and fatal error committed by Hodge and Smith when they got trapped and blown away in their canvas-topped track.

Hughes was frustrated. There was little he could do to help. His vehicles were useless as fighting machines, and even at that they were low on fuel. What little ammunition the tanks had couldn't be fired without power from the busted engines. The best he could do, and he was prepared to do it, was place his men somewhere along the berm with the infantry—if he could find them some serviceable weapons.

Hughes and his men cautiously crawled out from underneath their mechanized shelters. Out of the shadows, Hughes saw two figures dart by. He raised his .45 but was uncertain of what he was seeing. Were they grunts running for cover or NVA sappers headed for the center of the base? To this day, Hughes feels fairly certain that at least a handful of the enemy penetrated their lines. Nervously, the cavalrymen waited for the hammer to finally fall on their positions or for dawn to break, whichever came first.

0323, Capt. Joe Hogg, Blue Max, above Illingworth

When the 8-inch ammunition exploded, Capt. Joe Hogg was still circling above the base, about a half mile away, preparing for one more firing run. It would probably be his final pass. He was down to the last of his rockets, and his bullets were about gone as well.

"Just as I was lining up my run, that pile of ammo blew," Hogg stated later. "The aircraft shook violently, and I felt as if the air had been sucked right out of my lungs. There was a huge ball of fire. As I glanced at it over my shoulder my first thought was, *Oh my God, somebody dropped a nuke.* It looked just like an atomic bomb. My very next thought was *I hope I'm upwind. I don't want to get caught in the radioactive fallout.*"

As the fireball ebbed Hogg noted two very strange phenomena. It was weirdly quiet. He couldn't even hear the usual *whop-whop* of the rotor blades a few inches above his head. Then it started to snow; at least, at first it looked like snow. The dust was so thick that it was obscuring pretty much everything, but flares were still trying to punch some light into the gloom—and it was snowing. As Hogg urged his craft in a little closer he realized that what he was looking at wasn't snow after all. The blast had taken out the field kitchen. It was "snowing" glittery utensils and bits of pots and pans, thousands of pieces of shiny metal.

0325, Echo Recon, along the former berm

Lieutenant Peters had not joined the U.S. Army to fly in combat—but he did that night, through the air, along with a number of his men. He guessed he was tossed 30 to 40 feet, landing hard. He wasn't sure if he had broken any bones, but he knew he was in rough shape. He did sustain a number of shrapnel punctures and more aches and bruises than he could count.

Before the explosion disrupted everything, Peters had been all too aware that they were in a bad spot. The redlegs of 2/32 had been yelling at him and his men to move, to get away, abandon their position because their ammo pit was on fire. Looking over his shoulder, Peters could see that plainly enough, but he could not order his men to fall back. The NVA were still there, right in front of them, and still coming in waves. If he and his men pulled back, the entire line would collapse, and whether the ammunition erupted or not, it would all be over.

Waller, he knew was dead; so was Brent Street. Cpl. Nathan Mann was missing, and someone said he had been killed. Lemon, after a heroic, superhuman effort, was somewhere back at the aid station. Lemon's day was done. Sergeant Taylor was wounded but still at his post. The medics had Vaca stabilized, but he was in very bad shape and might not make it. Sergeant Richards was nearby, as was PFC Ken Vall de Juli.

Peters's tough platoon of pros had been wrecked, and the battle still wasn't over. Groggily, painfully, Peters shouted at his men to clear their weapons and get back on the line—wherever the line was.

0326, A Battery, 2nd Battalion, 32nd Field Artillery, forward positions

Ralph Jones was shaking—not from fear, but from the dehydration and the pounding his body had taken. He couldn't believe he was still alive—not after all that. His CO, Major Magness, was missing. He hadn't seen him since the beginning of the attacks. Someone had said they thought he was dead. Lassen and Schell, two of Jones's buddies, certainly were. Torn apart—blown to bits. Gone.

Trying to wipe the dirt from his eyes, Jones crawled up and out of the hole he had been thrown down and into. He was sure if one of the big ammo carriers hadn't been between him and the blast he would have become, like his dead battery mates, literal cannon fodder. One of the 10-ton ammo trucks had been blown on its side; the other was riddled with shrapnel holes. One of the big 8-inch howitzers looked to be mangled, maybe beyond repair. The rest of the men in A Battery who were still alive were nursing a variety of cuts, bruises, and broken bones. The few remaining men who could be remotely called effectives were being pushed and shoved by the sergeants onto what remained of the perimeter. The area used to be part of the berm but had become only a ragged mess of scattered bits of detritus, blowing bits of paper, and piles of sand. If the NVA had one more push within their capabilities, Jones believed, it would be the end.

0327, Charlie Company's lines

After the gigantic explosion, Sergeant Beauchamp immediately realized that if the NVA had not quit the fight, they had a wide open space, off to his right, to pour through. He got to work plugging the holes with survivors, some of them wounded but still able to function.

Glancing to his left, Beauchamp was desperate to see what was going on with Echo Recon. *If those guys collapsed,* he thought with dread, *we're doomed.*

It didn't seem like there were many of them left, but they were holding. Beauchamp spotted Lieutenant Peters. He was bloodied, but Beauchamp couldn't tell if the blood was Peters's own or the blood of others. Peters's shocking red hair was matted and dust colored, but his eyes were still gleaming bright. At that moment, Peters reminded Beauchamp of a young Errol Flynn, the swashbuckling actor, all grinning, wide-eyed motion. Beauchamp had only known Peters for a couple of days, but the veteran first sergeant could spot a "natural," and Peters was all of that. His men idolized him—and emulated him. If Peters was a little irreverent with army protocol, so, too, were his men. If Peters was a little out of uniform any particular day, his men were out of uniform in the same fashion. All that mattered at that point, however, was that Peters fought like a demon; so his men, even though they went down one by one, fought like madmen, too.

Beauchamp could only hope that his grunts, especially the newbies, would hold up half as well. Refocusing on his own lines, he spotted two of the new men. One had taken shrapnel in the eyes and was blinded. Beauchamp didn't know if it was temporary or permanent. The other had been wounded in both hands and couldn't hold a weapon. The soldier with eyes shouted directions and firing orders for the man who had hands. Working as a team they continued to point and shoot.

Hell of a way to start your war, men, Beauchamp marveled to himself.

0328, near the 8-inch howitzers

When the ammo blew, Sergeant Weltha, just like many other men, found himself sailing through the air, then landing with a thump. His ears were ringing, his whole body was quivering, and he could still feel the ground shaking. His first thought was that somehow the NVA had unleashed one of their big cannons on Illingworth, probably from the safety of a Cambodian sanctuary a few miles away.

He looked up. "The sky [was] lit with white smoke and cluttered with thousands of flying objects; a jeep, ammo boxes, junk, dirt, clothing . . . and people, all floating up, apart, and away. Everything was dancing in the sky, dismembering in slow motion right before my eyes—bodies into limbs, into parts and beyond. I froze, unable to take my eyes away from this shockingly grotesque aerial ballet."

Although it seemed like hours, Weltha's spell was broken quickly as all the material spiraling above his head started to succumb to the laws of gravity. He dove beneath a deuce-and-a-half parked nearby. A very loud *CLANG* announced an object landing on the hood of the truck. There was a softer thud in the dirt a few feet away from Weltha's face: It was a severed left hand, palm up. Horrifyingly, the fingers of the dead hand curled into a ball, revealing that the ring finger held a wedding band. Weltha had to turn away. As he did so, he found himself nose to nose with—a North Vietnamese!

Yelling, "Holy shit!" Weltha rolled out from underneath the truck, although objects of all types continued to rain down from the sky.

Weltha shouted at the man, *"Lai dei!"* Come out! *"Lai dei* right fucking now!"

The man, shaking both hands in a gesture of "don't shoot," did so, yelling back, *"Chieu hoi! Chieu hoi!"* I surrender!

Weltha was strung out on adrenaline and ready to shoot the gook anyway, but something gave him pause, and then he recognized the man. It was one of the battalion Kit Carson Scouts and not an enemy soldier. The man stood up, still holding his arms aloft. That was when Weltha realized that the man was seriously wounded. There was a large piece of shrapnel sticking out of the scout's right foot, still sizzling hot.

Out of the corner of his eye Weltha also noticed what had landed so loudly on the hood of the truck. It was a 200-pound projectile used by the 8-inch guns. It could still be live, for all Weltha knew. Weltha slung his rifle over a shoulder and grabbed the scout around the waist and frog-walked him to the medical bunker as fast as he could.

"The medic's bunker," Weltha wrote years later, "was a surreal salvation army of carnage. The types of wounds were staggering. One medic's face was covered with blood from his own scalp wound as he frantically bandaged a deep puncture wound pouring forth dark blood, the victim's eyes glazed over. Many were crying, moaning, convulsing or lying still, staring at infinity. One guy sat against the bunker holding his own arm, his bandaged stump still twitching. The aroma of fresh lethal injuries remains with you forever. I put down the Kit Carson, and he hopped over and sat on some sandbags. I gave him a thumbs-up and he did the same and then I noticed the huge pile of bodies directly behind him. 'Don't even think about that now,' I told myself. Only the living can identify the dead."

Weltha noticed Father Boyle among the men. He, too, was frantically working the medical bunker. He had procured a waterproof cardboard container and filled it. He dipped his fingers in the water and anointed each wounded forehead as he went from man to man. Weltha noticed the .45 caliber pistol Boyle had sticking out of a hip pocket, thinking it both strange and appropriate.

Boyle glanced up, saw Weltha, recognized him, smiled, and said, "Bless you, too, my son."

"Thanks, Father," Weltha replied, "but sure is hell tonight, eh?"

"God is with us," the priest reassured him.

"Yeah? Where?"

0330, 272nd NVA Regiment, forward lines facing FSB Illingworth

Colonel Lai was as shocked as anyone aboard FSB Illingworth when the tremendous explosion went off. He was half a klick away but still knocked to the ground by its power. Surprise turned to delight as he realized that probably one of his men had finally gotten through and had been responsible for the blast.

The gunships continued to circle the base, and their dreadful weapons constantly raked the edges of his jungle positions, but they were a minor annoyance to him. He was far more interested in what was happening after the explosion. Taking a huge risk, he ran to the very forward portion of the tree line just opposite the spot where the explosion had occurred. The trees there had been stripped to skeletons, but it was still dark, and he was desperate to see what was happening. If the destruction had been bad enough, maybe his men could finally take the base. He wished he had more troops, but there were none. He had no reserves. He had finally committed all his men, winner take all or die trying.

He peered through his field glasses. A pall of dust and smoke covered everything. He could see no movement. He stood rooted to the spot. Several minutes passed. Finally, men were stirring. His?

It took some time, but Lai finally began to see that the shapes were moving—backward. Toward him. His troops, what was left of them, were streaming back toward the jungle. Some carried other wounded men over their shoulders or between two men. Some fell to the ground again before they could get very far. A few were crawling. Small pops of renewed gunfire. Obviously, the Americans, some of them, had survived. The attack had failed.

Damn!

0345, FSB Illingworth Trash Pit

For reasons that will never be known—there were no survivors—about a dozen of the NVA who had charged the base near Charlie Company's lines veered off to the left after the ammunition disaster and took refuge in the trash pit. Unfortunately for these survivors, the trash pit was very near where 1/77 had positioned its howitzers. The NVA began taking potshots at the surviving Americans, and it didn't take long for the redlegs to figure out where the firing was coming from. With three of their five surviving guns, the artillerymen quickly slewed their weapons around and took dead aim, at zero elevation, on the trash pit. They blasted the bits of refuse and discarded junk into even smaller pieces, along with the unfortunate NVA.

Another small group of three NVA dove into the latrine area. They tried to hide behind the 55-gallon drums that were currently serving as makeshift toilets. They didn't offer much cover, and they surely must have been foul-smelling shelters. Several of the Americans spied the enemy soldiers and opened up on the barrels with their M-16s and an M-60. This was one time when the phrase "shit flew everywhere" was pungently accurate. The unfortunate NVA infantrymen were soon stilled. In typical battle-hardened and pun-loving American soldier style, the men who had done the killing were instantly dubbed the "Crapper Zappers."

0350, the crater

Right after Sergeant Weltha deposited the wounded Kit Carson Scout at the medic bunker, he walked over to the crater caused by the ammunition explosion. Even though the battle was still moving forward, in fits and starts, Weltha couldn't help himself. He had to see the huge hole.

What kind of enemy round could have dug this monstrous pit? he wondered. It looked to him like the craters he had seen left behind by the blockbuster 1,000-pound bombs the air force used.

He then asked himself, *Where's that huge pile of ammo that was sitting here yesterday? They couldn't have used it up already, could they?*

Finally, his shell-shocked brain was able to put it all together. *Oh, no . . .*

He stepped up to the lip of the crater and crouched down. Bullets were, after all, still flying around. At his feet he found a flak jacket. It took a couple of seconds for him to realize that there was something in the flak jacket. When he did, he jumped back in revulsion. The flak jacket contained a torso, and only that; no head, arms, or legs.

Someone started yelling, "Gooks! Gooks!" Dirt flicked up around Weltha's feet. He spun around to find four NVA rushing toward him. Weltha dropped to his knees to present a smaller target and raised his weapon, carefully squeezing off several bursts. Three of the enemy went down, but the fourth kept rushing forward.

This man, for some reason, did not have a gun, only a machete, and it was already raised over his head, in the hopes that he could make it come down on Weltha's skull.

Weltha's clip was empty. The man lunged, but Weltha rolled to his left, already grasping for another clip. As the NVA scrambled to his feet again, Weltha, in record time, ejected the empty clip, slammed a fresh one home, raised his weapon, and fired. The enemy soldier's head exploded, his lifeless body slamming to the ground, still clutching the machete.

Weltha decided that the lip of the crater was not a safe place to be. He turned away from it and started to move toward some of his wounded comrades. At that second, a large piece of shrapnel struck the stock of his M-16 and blew him backward. He found himself on his back and sliding down the inside wall of the slippery crater.

He checked his slide and sat up. He was stunned but otherwise unhurt. His M-16 was almost sliced in half and useless. An NVA soldier came racing over the lip of the crater. This man had a metal engineering stake in his hands, and his intent, apparently, was to drive it through Weltha. The sergeant scrambled to his feet just as the man lunged at him, the ugly spike being aimed for Weltha's face. Weltha drove the barrel of his gun into the man's throat just as the spike hit Weltha's scalp and shoulder a glancing blow.

The enemy soldier went down in a heap, gurgling, choking for breath, mortally wounded, his throat smashed. Warm blood poured down Weltha's back and neck. His shoulder started to throb from the pain of the blow. Enraged, Weltha used his rifle as a club, repeatedly smashing the dying soldier in the head and neck, although it was hardly necessary.

Moments later, Weltha sank to the ground, spent. He knew he couldn't fight anymore. "So, I opened a can of pecan roll and prepared to enjoy my final meal for this lifetime."

0400, FSB Illingworth

The first, dull rays of incipient dawn began to loom on the horizon. It was far from light, but the deepest, darkest part of the night was finally over, figuratively and literally. A number of the enemy were still outside the perimeter, and firing at the Americans, but there was no longer any great substance or consistency to their attacks.

Two Blue Max Cobras still circled overhead, protectively. All flights were being carefully choreographed so that refueling cycles would not leave the base unprotected for even a minute. The controllers had also crafted an approach toward the base, a flight corridor where enemy antiaircraft activity was nonexistent and the chances of friendly fire were very low.

The artillery fire programmed to support Illingworth from FSB Hannas, FSB St. Barbara, and Camp Hazard began to ebb. After the night was finally over, someone calculated that the off-site artillery pieces had pumped well over 3,300 rounds of fire into the environs surrounding Illingworth—and not a single one of those rounds had been errant or turned into a friendly fire incident.

0410, Echo Recon, original position on the berm

The first one was already detached, probably due to some explosive shard of hot metal flying through the air, or the disruptive force of a hand grenade. Lieutenant Peters picked up the severed head of the enemy soldier and plopped it on top of a pile of sand, near the platoon's original position along the berm, twisting the skull around to face the man's former regimental mates. Peters wanted the skull's dead but still-open eyes to warn the other NVA that doom lay ahead. That's when the idea probably came to him, and he decided more heads might be a fitting touch. He pulled out the razor sharp Ka-bar he carried strapped to his hip.

Peters found another mangled NVA soldier, his head still attached. He grabbed the dead man's hair and jerked the body up, Ka-bar at the man's throat. An iron vise grabbed the forearm of Peters's knife-wielding hand before the young officer could hack away at the corpse.

"Lieutenant," Staff Sergeant Taylor shouted above the din, directly into Peters's ear, "not a good idea, sir."

Peters looked up into the big sergeant's face. Taylor saw Peters grinning like a jack-o'-lantern, a bit of madness in his eyes. The two men stood there, locked together, for a few seconds until Taylor felt the tenseness in the other man's arm relax. The spell was broken. Peters yanked his arm away and sheathed his blade. He said nothing to Taylor, but the veteran noncom knew, in that moment, that something very dark and disturbing had taken hold of his lieutenant during that hellacious and deeply troubled night.

0415, Echo Recon, new position, on the firing line

Someone shouted, "There's one! There's one!"

PFC Ken Vall de Juli leapt up from behind Echo Recon's secondary line, swiftly putting his M-16's stock to his right shoulder. In the strengthening light of the new day, he aimed and squeezed off a shot. The running figure flopped to the ground.

The attack had finally petered out. The once superbly coordinated and well-executed dash toward the American lines had devolved into a few pockets of resistance and desultory firing.

Vall de Juli lowered his weapon. He looked around. There were five men left standing, all that was left of Echo Recon platoon. Five. All the others were dead or being treated for their wounds back at the aid station. Lieutenant Peters was among the wounded. Staff Sergeant Taylor was in command of what was barely a squad.

0422, Capt. Joe Hogg, Blue Max, circling above Illingworth

The alarm was about ready to explode in his ears, the Klaxon that would tell him he was dangerously close to being out of fuel. His gauge was bouncing on empty. He'd been out of bullets and rockets for some time, but he was still useful as a radio relay station, so he had stayed. It was clearly time to go.

Hogg signed off with Ahearn and headed for home plate. He was looking forward to the hot breakfast he knew was waiting. Then he thought about the poor bastards he had just left behind. He doubted they were looking at bacon, eggs, and toast anytime soon.

0430, Charlie Company positions

SP4 Cliff Rhodes was still digging the dirt out of his mouth as dawn broke. Ever since the 8-inch ammo dump had gone up he had been trying to clear the filth from his eyes, ears, nostrils, and weapons. It had been a constant battle. The cowering FNG had disappeared. Rhodes didn't know if he was dead or had simply di di maued to the rear—wherever the rear might be. His buddy Billy Carlisle was still there, what was left of him. There was another body a few feet away, too. Rhodes stared at the corpse. It was clearly inside the berm; in fact, it was partially draped over his bunker. It was a dead NVA soldier, dressed only in his underwear and sandals. Rhodes started to laugh—and cry at the same time.

0440, the tree line, 272nd NVA Regiment

Colonel Lai was apoplectic, yet at the same time drained. His men had come so close to capturing the detested American compound. They had given it their all, but they had failed. All he could do was gather up what remained of his shattered regiment and slink away into the jungle once more, dash across the border and into

Cambodia. He could already hear the rumble of tanks in the trees not far away. He felt like screaming at his men, berating them for their failure, but it was not all their fault. He had failed as well, and he knew it.

Col. Nguyen Tuong Lai's dispositions at Illingworth totaled somewhere in the vicinity of 450 troops under his command. Some of these troops were used in support roles, manning the antiaircraft guns, the mortars, and the artillery field pieces. The balance of the regiment was available to charge the fortifications. The 272nd Regiment was a battle-tested and experienced force. Similar to the typical American company, an NVA company had roughly one hundred men, was commanded by a senior lieutenant or a captain, and had two or three platoons. Not all companies were at their full complement due to casualties (just like the American companies they faced), and there were eyewitness reports from the Illingworth survivors that not all the NVA were fit to be in the fight to begin with. At least one dead NVA soldier who charged with his comrades was discovered, after the fight, to have lost an arm at the shoulder in a previous battle (possibly the tangle with the 11th Armored on March 26). His horrific wound had been stanched and bandaged for several days.

[Author's note: There has been some speculation that Colonel Lai's forces were augmented by an unknown number of Chinese Communist regular army soldiers. One or two of the NVA KIA at FSB Illingworth seemed "bigger" than the "normal" skinny, underfed, poorly nourished ethnic PAVN warriors. Some veterans even recall that, postbattle, "some of the G-2 [intelligence] types" were actually measuring and examining the "unusual" casualties. If so, and if the assertions were accurate, none of this intel ever made it into any of the postbattle reports that have surfaced to date. It would not be totally unusual or even surprising if the Chinese had inserted some men in the regiment; after all, they, like the Americans and the Russians, had a constant stream of advisers filtering in and out of the fighting forces. It's also possible that some of the NVA troops were ethnic Chinese from the North; if so, they would have a different physiognomy than some of their ethnic Vietnamese counterparts. If Colonel Lai is to be believed, however, he has denied that any Chinese Army troops were in his regiment at the time of these events.]

The NVA came at the base in waves, probably a platoon or two in each wave, or roughly thirty to forty men at a time. Each wave had a different objective, apparently, but most of the attacks came at the western and southwestern areas of the berm. Colonel Lai did not commit his forces to one all-out, sustained charge; he fed his men into the fight one group at a time. This was, in all likelihood, a fatal mistake. Each time a group of thirty to forty men assaulted the strong points of Illingworth they were faced with about an equal number of determined defenders.

If, on the other hand, Colonel Lai had sent one hundred or two hundred troops at once at a single point of concentration along the berm, it is possible, though not certain, of course, that his men could have been successful in cracking the American lines and getting a real foothold inside the base. The reasons why Lai did not rush his entire force forward at once seem to have been focused on the following circumstances: (a) He was still unsure of the actual dispositions of his opponents from a manpower standpoint. He was looking for a weak spot in the initial stages of the battle. If he found one, he would pour it on. He never did find a weak spot. (b) Colonel Lai's regiment was only at two-thirds strength and had not been reconstituted after the March 26 battle. He had no reserve. He needed to make a good choice about where to totally focus his forces before committing them. (c) Before he could decide where to pile on, the 8-inch ammunition blew, changing everything. Lai's ultimate caution, as he hinted at during the course of the interviews conducted, was part of the undoing of the NVA attack.

0458, D Company, 1st Squadron, 11th ACR, on the perimeter

After two and a half hours of hard-charging and tough jungle busting, Capt. Jerry Hensley and his tracks finally blew through the jungle's perimeter opposite Illingworth. Hensley immediately ordered his Pattons to throw a perimeter around the base.

First Lt. Tim Brooks, CO of 2nd Platoon, less than a month in country, recalls the macabre sights greeting his men. "We had been hearing the sounds of the battle the entire time we were busting through the jungle. By the time we got there, it was pretty much winding down, however. Dawn was breaking and there was still a great deal of smoke and dirt lingering in the air. As our tanks began to encircle the base, I saw them, the bodies, in the early morning light. Lots of dead NVA hung up in the wire atop the berm, especially in the southwest corner where the attack had been the heaviest. That really got my attention."

Brooks also saw many blood trails snaking off into the jungle. Whether the blood was from the wounded or the NVA hauling off their dead could not be ascertained, but Brooks speculated it was probably some of each. It seemed pretty obvious to Brooks that it had been a hell of a fight.

Brooks's tank drove up to a spindly little tree—the only one still standing in the middle of the clearing, stark in its loneliness. An NVA soldier sat at the base of the tree, his back up against the trunk. He was not showing any obvious signs of trauma: no blood-soaked clothing, no distinctive wounds. He was just sitting there, rifle on the ground by his side. He did not move. Brooks could not tell if he was dead or alive.

"I told my gunner to put a round in him if he moved or reached for his weapon. Apparently the man did because as soon as I said it, my gunner fired squarely into the man's chest."

0458, Alpha Troop detachment, on the perimeter

They might be a little late, but they sure are a beautiful sight, S. Sgt. J. C. Hughes said to himself.

Hughes was standing atop the berm watching D Company charge out of the jungle. His cavalry heart swelled with pride as the tanks came storming up to the fire base, in a column of twos. As the columns peeled apart, left and right, to establish a protective circle around Illingworth, he knew that he and his men were finally safe. Their long night of darkness and terror was over.

A few feet away SP4 George Burks stood shakily by the side of his Sheridan watching the parade of tanks course into view. His ears were still ringing, and he was quaking all over. He couldn't help it—nor could he stop it. He was there . . . and he wasn't. He was watching himself from somewhere else, maybe above, and then he was standing there, looking at the wreckage. He could talk . . . then he couldn't. He realized he was in deep, serious trouble.

[Author's note: Years later, and after much counseling, Burks realized that the moments described above were the beginning of the rest of his life with PTSD. It would be a life wherein, as he says today, "no amount of therapy will ever take Fire Support Base

Illingworth away from me." He has, however, decided to live with it; actually, he no longer wants Illingworth taken from him. "It's just too much a part of me." Other former soldiers told me pretty much the same thing.]

0459, the crater

The pecan roll stuck in Sergeant Weltha's throat. From the tree line he could hear the throaty rumbling of very big engines. The trees along the perimeter started shaking.

No . . . no . . . no . . . Weltha moaned to himself. *To come all this way . . . to survive this night . . . to be finally blown away by Chinese tanks!*

They weren't Chinese, of course. "The first track lurched into view, and it was the 11th Armored Cav! I jumped up and screamed, 'Fuckin' A!' Others were yelling and jumping for joy as more than twenty tracks thunderously emerged from the wood line, bouncing and rocking at high speed, and proceeded to surround the entire [base]. When they had completed the circle, they came to a stop and each turret slowly slewed outward, their barrels facing the jungle. We were safe! I stood there and wept the deepest, hottest tears of my life."

0500, FSB Illingworth

By 0500, the battle was over. Those NVA still mobile enough to get away had slipped back into the jungle. They had left dozens of their dead behind, which was something the NVA tried hard to avoid. Just like the Americans, the NVA preferred to take their dead off the field—no man left behind. With Americans this dictum was a matter of honor. With the NVA it was more likely a matter of not allowing the Americans to know how much damage they had inflicted. Once the NVA had realized the American commanders were obsessed with body counts they had started making a concerted effort to deny the Americans this gruesome measure of achievement.

With the first light of dawn, the dust-offs had begun. Those that could help were making every possible effort to get the wounded to the rear for medical attention. The worst cases went out first, as prioritized by the medics. A handful with minor wounds slipped aboard the slicks (the unarmed medevac helicopters), these men more concerned about getting the hell away from that scary cauldron of death and destruction than any taint of shame.

Peter Lemon was not one of those men. He was seriously banged up and had more wounds than just about any other man, but he insisted that all those more seriously wounded than he were going to get aboard first. No amount of cajoling would dissuade him.

Ralph Jones and his comrades managed to cut down a sapling that had survived the bombardment. They stuck a small American flag atop the makeshift flagpole and raised it, just like the survivors of FSB Jay had done several days prior. Many of the veterans of this battle remarked later that this tiny pennant was not only a symbol of perseverance but also one of the few stark bits of color remaining in the drab and shattered landscape.

The destruction was nearly total, biblical in scope, as in the passage from the Book of Matthew, chapter 24, verses 12: " "Not one stone here will be left on another; every one will be thrown down." Culverts were blasted, the TOC was a smoking mess, and the berm was flattened in several places, obliterated in others. The quad .50 truck was destroyed, the searchlight jeep was a burned-out hulk, a

10-ton ammo carrier was blown over on its side, and a 30,000-pound howitzer was damaged. Dust and dirt particles were still stubbornly clinging to the air, and bits of paper skittered across the ground everywhere, fleeing on the breeze.

Many men were in shock. Some could no longer function. A small handful were discovered hiding in deep recesses or the remaining culverts, still too frightened to emerge. Several asses were kicked. A dozen or so men wandered the compound aimlessly.

The other survivors began to return to reality. Urged on by the remaining NCOs and officers, who understood the need to get the men refocused, the effectives started policing up what was left. Some began cleaning their weapons. Others moved to assist with the wounded. The artillerymen began to attend to their weapons and assess the damage. After all, no one was altogether convinced that the NVA wouldn't try to mount another attack.

Then the parade began. Soon after dawn, a steady stream of visitors descended on Illingworth. The arrivals became more and more senior in rank as the morning progressed. Assessments would begin immediately. Some would involve recognition for valor; others would allocate criticism or blame. Illingworth had been either an unmitigated disaster or a brilliant success depending on who was speaking and what sort of skin they had in the game. What could not be disputed was that twenty-five Americans were dead and another fifty-eight wounded seriously enough to require evacuation. The enemy body count was eighty-eight; at least that was the number of corpses or partial corpses recovered on-site. No one knew how many more KIAs had been spirited away by the NVA as they retreated.

[On this point, former SP4 George Burks tells a remarkable tale of something he observed as he crossed the base seeking treatment from the medics. Several of the newly arriving soldiers, directed by a couple of newly arrived officers, were pulling bodies of the dead NVA back across the berm, from the inside to the outside. At the time, he viewed that as curious, but he had other things on his mind and didn't really dwell on that observation until many years later.]

The Americans had held, and overcome, but there was no question that the ratios of friendly and enemy KIAs were badly skewed, and not in favor of the Americans. When added to the KIAs at FSB Jay, the total of 1st Cav killed over the last five days in one small corner of the operations area was going to raise a few eyebrows, a passel of questions, and a lot of ire higher up the chain of command. One general's aide, walking the compound and shaking his head, was overheard to say, "Someone is going to catch some serious shit for this." By 0530 on April 1, 1970, the scramble to avoid the excrement was already under way.

12

JUDGMENT DAY

Early Morning, FSB Illingworth, April 1, 1970

Two of Illingworth's first visitors on the morning of April 1 were Lt. Col. Tom Fitzgerald and Maj. Bart Furey, from the 2nd Battalion, 19th Field Artillery. Both men had been instrumental in directing thousands of protective artillery rounds from other fire bases at Illingworth during the previous night. They arrived by Loach, anxious to see what condition the base was in and to find their friends, many of who were scattered among the artillery assets aboard Illingworth.

Furey was most anxious to find Major Magness. A couple of redlegs told Furey they thought Magness was dead. He wasn't, but not by much. Furey discovered Magness, still languishing on his bloodied cot, in a half-buried culvert. A medic was working furiously to stabilize Magness's serious wounds. The loss of blood was appalling, but the medic had finally gotten some morphine into him to dull the pain.

Magness was able to tell his friend Furey a few bits of information, including the tale of the tremendous blast that had nearly wiped out the base. Magness also related that shortly thereafter he had heard several voices just outside his culvert. They had been speaking Vietnamese, a language he knew well. Magness pulled out his .45 and got off a shot before the gun slipped from his blood-soaked grip. He didn't know if he had hit anyone, and he didn't know why the Vietnamese hadn't simply finished him off—but he knew, without question, that the enemy had been just a few feet away. That was significant to Furey because it meant, unless his friend was already delirious, the NVA had made it inside the base.

Stretcher bearers scooped up Major Magness and raced him to the next dust-off. Furey and Fitzgerald turned their attentions to the other artillery survivors, the equipment that could be salvaged, and the wreckage. They could see that the quad .50 gun truck was utterly destroyed, along with the searchlight jeep. One of the big 8-inch howitzers was covered in dirt and debris. It was hard to tell if it was irreparably damaged or just a mess from the explosion. The ammo carriers, one blown on its side, could probably be salvaged. All but one of the 105 mm howitzers had survived, as had all of the 155s.

Slowly but steadily the surviving redlegs began to pull themselves together. Fitzgerald and Furey went about getting the men to reorganize their ammunition supplies, replace their aiming stakes, reset their batteries, and police up their areas. One squad was organized to recover the dead and body parts.

Capt. Arnold Laidig, B Battery of the 1/77, had expended tremendous effort during the previous night to keep his batteries working and on task. By dawn, however, he was spent. There were murmurs among his men, who were just beginning to get to know their new CO, that he should be designated the hero of the moment—worthy of at least a Silver Star if not a DSC.

Unfortunately for Laidig, another visitor flew in: Col. Morris Brady, the notoriously tough CO of the division's artillery. Brady was a brilliant artillerist but a harsh taskmaster. He was rough on his men, and not many of his subordinates liked him, but, as Brady believed, command was not a popularity contest. He was an SOB for a reason: this was war, and there were no "do-overs." Brady was ambitious (he would later become, as he had always wished, a general officer), and he was quick to weed out those who worked for him if they did not meet his exacting standards.

Moments after Brady landed at Illingworth he was "kicking ass and taking names." Many of the men still standing thought it was overly cruel and unnecessary, but Brady felt otherwise. He believed that the only way to get these men functioning again was to make them mad and get them moving. Brady knew that many of the survivors needed to focus on something other than what they had just been through. If that meant thinking that he, Brady, was the meanest bastard in their valley, that was OK with him.

Brady spotted Captain Laidig, who was still shaking and barely able to speak. Hero or not, Brady relieved him of his command on the spot and got him on the next slick out of Illingworth.

Colonel Ochs flew in next. The first person Ochs wanted to see was Illingworth's commanding officer. Mike Conrad walked up to Ochs covered in so much dust he looked like a ghostly apparition, which, during the previous night, Conrad had come very close to becoming. His throat was still raw from the dirt and sand he had inhaled, and his voice was barely audible after all the shouting he had done over the past few hours.

If anyone on Illingworth had the right to say, "See? I told you so!" it was Mike Conrad, but good soldier that he was, he simply stood there and delivered to Ochs as much of a sitrep as his larynx and his fatigue would allow. Ochs then gave Conrad the stunning and unwelcome news that he would have to stay on Illingworth one more night, after which he and his men would be rotated out, to Phuoc Vinh. Conrad could hardly believe what he was hearing, but after the battering he and his men had taken over the past few hours, he was too stunned to protest.

A herd of slicks, dust-offs, and command helicopters kept coming and going from Illingworth all morning. Totally unnoticed in all the frantic activity was that one lonely replacement flew into Illingworth shortly after 0800. He had hopped aboard the first Huey headed out of Tay Ninh, a flight destined for Illingworth to pick up a load of dead or wounded.

SP4 Dave Nicholson was his name, and he figured that he had missed being in the battle at Illingworth by two or three minutes, tops. On the previous day, March 31, he had spent many frustrating hours in an effort to get back to his unit, Charlie Company, 2/8.

For the better part of the last three weeks Nicholson had been convalescing, mostly at the massive field hospital in Cam Ranh Bay. On March 8, he had been in a big firefight near Tay Ninh, and during the action an NVA mortar had missed taking off his right arm by an inch or so. As it was, he had been banged up pretty good, and the medics spent several days sewing up his back and portions of his right bicep and picking shards of metal out of his neck and side. Unfortunately, it wasn't quite the "million-dollar wound"—

the one that got you a free pass back stateside and out of the war. It did generate an award for a Purple Heart, however.*

Right after the doctors released him as "fit for duty," Nicholson began tracking down his old unit. He stuffed his orders into a fatigue pocket, but it was anyone's guess how he would comply with them; no one had a clear Idea of where Charlie Company was at that moment. He decided to backtrack, using the bits of info and rumors he was able to gather. He started by hopping on a bus from the hospital to the airfield. To the best of his knowledge, his unit was still out in the boonies somewhere near Tay Ninh. He found a flight to Bien Hoa, the 1st Cav's big staging area. He figured that would be a good place to start or at least get him close.

Nicholson wasn't all that gung ho to get back. At one point, this college-educated former soccer player from Vermont had been very keen to sign up and go to Vietnam. He had, in fact, beaten back an army classification as "finance clerk" to change his designator to "rifleman." He had, at one idealistic point in his young life, declared that the burden for the war was falling disproportionately on "the Negros" and he wanted to show the world "white boys can fight, too." Being in Vietnam for several months had opened his eyes to the realities of life in the field; still, the pull of loyalty was strong. A little more whining, a bit more conniving, a tad more deceit might have gotten him on a plane home, or at least a softer assignment in the rear. He couldn't do it. He had left good friends on the field of battle, some of them forever, and he still had friends in Charlie Company. As he later wrote:

* Sadly, three decades later, Nicholson would discover that the blood transfusion he received at Cam Ranh was tainted with hepatitis C, a blood-borne disease that was not understood well at the time. The Hepatitis would silently eat away at his liver until it was, as he himself described it, "a gooey mess." Fortunately, a donor liver was made available in 2005 and Nicholson had a liver transplant.

I had learned a great deal about Vietnam, the Army, the NVA, and myself. I had learned that western Tay Ninh Province was a good place to get killed and that's where I was heading back to. It didn't really bother me, though. I'm not sure why. It seemed as though I hadn't quite gotten the Field out of my system. I still owed Uncle Sam 119 days—so the Dog's Head would be a good place to go, if I were still trying to uncover Vietnam's secrets, which I guess I was. I also didn't think I'd be making those 119 days. But Tay Ninh was where my comrades were, so it was going to be a homecoming of sorts.

Nicholson landed at Bien Hoa and quickly found another transport flight to Tay Ninh. At Tay Ninh, he got the discouraging news that it was no longer the 1st Cav's rear. It belonged, at that moment, to the 4th Infantry Division. The 1st Cav had moved their rear to Phuoc Vinh. Another grunt, who had just come out of the field, told Nicholson that Charlie Company was actually at a fire base called Illingworth. The safe choice would have been to head to Phuoc Vinh and let the REMFs sort it out, because that's what his orders allowed. The emotional choice, however, was to get back to his pals.

A sympathetic jeep driver took him all the way across the base to the heliport. Nicholson soon found the NCO in charge of the helipads and said he needed to get the next chopper out to Illingworth.

The grizzled old sergeant squinted at Nicholson and grunted, pointing skyward, "See that Huey?"

Nicholson looked up and saw a helicopter rapidly ascending. It was already about 500 feet in the air. "Yup."

"Well, that's the last bird headed out to Illingworth today," the sergeant chortled.

Nicholson had missed the flight by two or three minutes—no more. They were the few minutes that most probably saved his life.

Relief at not being in the previous night's battle should have been the dominant emotion in Nicholson's brain as he surveyed the incredible devastation of Illingworth the next morning; instead, utter despair had him in its grip. Where was his company? His platoon? His friends? None of them were in sight. Instead, he watched in horror as grunts filled body bag after body bag while other men tossed the bodies of the dead NVA into a gigantic pit.

The next feeling to swamp him was regret. Why couldn't he have made it back in time to save his friends? Could he have saved his friends? Would he have made any difference? Perhaps not, but at least he could have tried. Nicholson had no way of knowing it at the time, but he was suffering the universal shock and angst of soldiers, who, against all the normal logic of self-preservation, always seem to say, "Why not me? Why wasn't I the one?"

Brigadier General Casey arrived. He conferred with Ochs, then Conrad. Casey's demeanor was grim, as Conrad remembers. The general was a realist, and he knew this was war, but Casey had the reputation of caring deeply about his men. He seemed to feel the death of each of his troopers personally, and lurking in the back of his mind, very likely, was the thought that his eldest son and namesake was about to graduate from Georgetown University. George junior was a member of ROTC and would be commissioned a second lieutenant on graduation. Orders to Vietnam would likely follow. Would he end up at a hellhole like Illingworth, too?

As he continued to survey the destruction, Casey was solicitous but not apologetic. He couldn't be. This was part of the strategy he had worked hard to advance. The death toll and the woundings were horrible, regrettable, maybe even excessive, but "acceptable" if the action had destroyed the enemy's capability to conduct operations in this sector. Had it? That was the question for which Casey desperately sought an answer.

Sometimes the right man comes along at the right moment to make the difference. That was certainly the case with Mike Conrad and FSB Illingworth. Captain Ahearn, one of the many capable eyewitnesses to Conrad's leadership, had a chance to see the total man up close, how he handled tough situations, and how he related to his troops. In all instances, according to Ahearn, Mike Conrad more than measured up: He was liked by his men, viewed as tough but fair, smart, and very capable. Conrad had graduated from West Point, Class of '56 (the same class as future generals H. Norman Schwarzkopf and John C. "Doc" Bahnsen Jr.) and, in fact, still serves as his class president today. He had had one previous tour in Vietnam in 1963–64 as adviser to an ARVN battalion. He completed an MS in mathematics from Rensselaer Polytechnic Institute in 1965.

Commanding officer of the 2/8 was Conrad's second Vietnam tour, and it would be a very eventful one. He was in the circle of General Casey's favorite officers and was very instrumental in implementing Casey's successful strategy of base-hopping with the fire support installations. Conrad was a faithful subordinate, but he was not afraid to say what he thought if something did not look right to him. We know he fought hard to move FSB Illingworth when it became obvious that the base had been in place too long and the NVA were dialed in on his dispositions. He worked diligently to keep the base effective and properly fortified. He did not win the arguments to relocate the base or to get rid of the unwanted ammunition, but he did everything else in his power to make sure the pending attack was not going to overwhelm his men. His preparations, tactics, and the decisions during the course of the fight were, without question, responsible for the survival of his outpost. Mike Conrad received a Silver Star for his efforts on April 1, 1970, which is a high honor, indeed, but in the view of some, perhaps less than he deserved (the Distinguished Service Cross is the award a number of veterans mentioned as being more appropriate). The politics of the aftermath may have had something to do with this, but there is no blame to place on Mike Conrad for what happened at FSB Illingworth and only praise to give that he led such a successful defense.

SP4 Rick Hokenson has no clear memory of the huge blast that nearly swept away all of his comrades. One moment, after the NVA bombardment had stopped, he was looking over the berm at the onrushing NVA, and the next moment he was standing in the middle of a shattered compound and it was midmorning.

"I have absolutely no idea what happened to me, what I did or where I was from the time of the blast—which I learned about later—to like, maybe, nine or ten in the morning. That was when I 'woke up,'" Hokenson related. "All I remember was that when I regained consciousness I was on my feet, in the middle of the base, and I was watching some combat photographers taking pictures of the destruction. Then I felt something. I looked at my right hand and it had gotten all torn up by shrapnel. My right ear was also bleeding, and blood was leaking down into my collar."

Hokenson looked around and saw a number of men, none of whom he recognized, doing "the Thorazine shuffle."* A few others

* Thorazine is a powerful antipsychotic drug that was used in Vietnam—though not widely—to treat combat anxiety, among other mental and physical conditions. One of

were trying to clean or reload weapons. Nobody from his squad or Charlie Company was anywhere in sight. He decided to find a slick and get the hell off this nightmare of a base. He did, and was treated for his wounds in the rear at Tay Ninh. Six days later he was drinking wine on the beach in California. The little voice in his brain, the one teasing him about whether he would make it out alive, was finally quiet—or at least totally inebriated.

As General Casey surveyed what was left of FSB Illingworth, he sought out the commander of the tank company that had rolled up and surrounded the base. He had two tasks for Captain Hensley. Noticing that one of his Pattons was equipped with a dozer blade, he ordered Hensley to have a pit dug immediately so that the dead NVA could be tossed into a mass grave. After that, Casey wanted Hensley to take his tanks and make a run out to the Cambodian border and chase the NVA up and down, for 20 miles in each direction, trying to kill as many of them as he could.

Hensley, the former sergeant and career soldier said, "Yes, sir, I can do that, but I have no fuel with me and no supplies. We tried to get here as quickly as we could."

"I'll get some blivets out to you, and we'll log you from wherever you tell us,"* Casey responded.

"Yes, sir. Thank you, sir, but what you're asking me to do will take about two weeks."

Not pausing for a second, Casey came right back and said: "Well, I guess we'll see you in about two weeks, then."

---

its side effects could be a tendency to lose full motor control, so those given Thorazine were sometimes observed to shuffle along instead of walk normally.

* In Vietnam terminology a blivet was a heavy rubber bladder in which fuel or POL (petroleum, oil, and lubricants) was transported. Each blivet usually held about 500 gallons. To get "logged" was to get resupplied with food, water, and ammo.

When the soon-to-be commanding general of your division gives you a direct order, there is no argument to be made. Hensley rounded up his men and machines for a second time that morning and stormed off into the jungle to chase the bad guys.

Last but not least, in came General Roberts. Roberts had actually been aloft in his command helicopter for the past hour, monitoring the last moments of the battle and all the comms. By the time Roberts alit at Illingworth, several of the officers had scraped together a handful of survivors who could still stand erect and form a small honor guard. The group was gathered near the remnants of the TOC and told by a beaming General Roberts what a fantastic job they had done. Roberts then asked Captain Hobson, who was standing nearby with Sergeant Beauchamp, which of these men had done exceptional work. Hobson pointed out several. They were asked to step forward. Roberts's aide then produced, from somewhere aboard the general's helicopter, a box with a stash of Silver Stars. Roberts went down the line, pinning a medal to the fatigue pocket of each man, as the division combat photographers snapped away. Moments later, the general was back aboard his chopper and gone, leaving the devastated remnants of his Illingworth defenders to carry on as best they could. Roberts did, however, promise the men that hot chow would be on the way "soon." It arrived just before nightfall.

Dave Nicholson eventually located the spot along the berm that had been defended by his platoon. The March battles had already whittled Lonely Platoon down dramatically but after the April 1 debacle, there were only six men left—just three of whom Nicholson knew. Six total: two comrades, one good buddy, three total strangers, zero officers, zero noncoms.

Nicholson stared at the blackened landscape all around him, the destroyed bunkers, the blasted culverts, the dark red stains in the sand. He slumped to the ground in a funk. He wrote down the following years later:

> I sat there staring at the destroyed bunkers thinking I do not know what. Men were walking past me but I could neither see nor hear them. My body was there but I was numb and could neither think nor move. [Enemy] Bodies were still being thrown into the pit only 75 feet away, helicopters were taking off nearby, and smoke was still rising all around me, but I was aware of none of it. After a while, I once again became aware of the activity around me. I looked down at the ground and saw a helmet lying there, just about brand new, the cloth still bright green, with hardly any of the writings GIs loved to mark on them. Not even an FTA ["Fuck the Army"]. Whose helmet had this been? I didn't know, but now I needed it, and evidently he would not any longer. I stuck it on my head and it fit just right. It was only a couple of more minutes of looking around before I had an M-16, a bandolier full of clips, web belt, and canteen. I needed to gear up, because, after all, the NVA had staged an all-out attack that ended only about three and one-half hours earlier. Who could say what they were planning next?

Eventually, the shattered platoon began to function. No one told the men what to do, but no one needed to. They all knew what was required. They scrounged claymores, extra ammo, frags, better weapons, canteens, replacement gear. Interestingly, no one thought about food very much. Eventually, about dusk, General Roberts's promised "breakfast" finally arrived by chopper. The powdered eggs, chipped mystery meat, coffee, milk, and hot bread and butter all went down easily, but the men were focusing on the hours ahead. Everyone believed the NVA would be back to finish them off.

Sgt. Randall Richards could only stand there and sigh in bewilderment and sorrow. He was staring down at a long row of body bags awaiting dust-off. He wasn't sure which bag it was, but he had been told that one of them belonged to Bobby Barker. As Richards had feared, Barker had gotten blown away at the FDC. Someone told him another grunt had riddled Barker with bullets as he came running into the bunker without the right password. Someone else told him Barker was caught at the doorway in the same rocket blast that had killed Lt. Cleaveland Bridgman and Sgt. Bobby Lane. Richards wanted to open Barker's body bag to say one last good-bye—and to check Barker's wounds, to prove one way or another how he had died. He couldn't bring himself to do it, but he hoped that whatever had killed Barker didn't screw up his face. It would have been a shame to mess up the new teeth Barker had been bragging about.

[Author's note: There has been some controversy over the recording of Barker's death. In the original army casualty count of KIAs at FSB Illingworth, the number killed by enemy action was listed as twenty-four. Barker was the twenty-fifth casualty and initially listed as "other." On some occasions "other" was used to label friendly fire casualties. No one seems to know—today—why the clerk filling out Barker's forms checked the box for "other." It could have been a simple mistake, or it could be because someone told the clerk the death was "suspicious," in which case the "other" box would be checked until someone further down the line made a final determination. Over the years there have been lingering doubts. One Illingworth veteran, reportedly, has harbored agonizing nightmares believing that, possibly, he mistakenly killed Barker as he rushed into the FDC without the proper password. Those uncertainties can now be put to rest.

I petitioned for a copy of what is called an IDPF, standing for "Individual Deceased Personnel File," under a Freedom of Information Act request and received a copy of the complete file on Barker. The army pathologists (two doctors and a civilian mortuary specialist) who physically examined Barker's remains and prepared his body for return to his family officially listed the cause of death as "fragmentation wounds (two) upper left chest." The examiners who saw Barker's injuries would, in all likelihood, have been able to readily distinguish between a death by shrapnel fragments and a demise by bullet wounds. They went even further, describing the damage to Barker's body as "mutilations," which is not typical of contemporary pathology descriptions of through-and-through gunshot damage. Apparently, either one or both of the shell fragments tore apart Barker's heart, and he died instantly. The IDPF also clearly shows that Barker did, indeed, have that dental work he wanted.

On another note: If there had been any suspicion, even slight, that Barker's death had been due to friendly fire, the army would have convened what is called an Article 32 investigation. There is nothing in the records to suggest that this was ever done. Colonel Conrad would have known about any Article 32 proceeding and he is very clear, even today, that none was initiated in regard to Barker's death.

There is yet one more legend that needs to be put to bed about Barker's death: the story has been told (and written) over the years that Barker, at the time of the Illingworth events, was a "short-timer" and had been sent to the rear a couple of days before the battle to see the dentist and then "go home." The story continues that, illogically, Barker decided to return on the eve of the battle to show off his new teeth and to spend one more night in the field with his buddies before finally going back to "the world." His tragic death, then, might have made a poignant coda to the total story of Illingworth, but the facts do not bear this out: It turns out that Bobby Barker's "start tour" date in country was September 4, 1969. He would not have been eligible to return stateside until the beginning of September, 1970, at the earliest. On April 1, 1970, Barker's rotation date was at least five months away. Even with an "early out," which some men were receiving at the time, the best he could have hoped for was another three months in Vietnam. In the final analysis, Barker's death may not have the storybook-legend patina that some would like to bestow, but neither do the facts of his death diminish Barker's legacy as a true American hero who died bravely, fighting alongside his comrades.]

During the day on April 1, the survivors, amounting to fewer than half the number from twenty-four hours prior, spent considerable time picking up the pieces of those who had not made it. The NVA bodies were gathered and dumped in the hastily bulldozed pit. There was no ceremony or moment of silence. By nightfall, all the American casualties had been evacuated, but as the survivors went about getting ready for another evening in the jungle, they would occasionally stumble across a body part or a fragment that had been overlooked in the frenzy to get the wounded—and the dead—away from those who remained behind.

Dan Tyler was a Huey pilot assigned to the 1st Cav and flew many medevac and resupply missions among the fire support bases in War Zone C. He describes some of his experiences this way:

> Some of the Fire Support Bases—*Wood, Hannas,* and *Illingworth* are the ones I remember—were hit really hard in night attacks. It was

eerie watching such a fire fight from the flare ship or "Chuck-Chuck" (Command & Control). The red tracers going out from the inner concentric circle—the green tracers going in from the outer circle—the tracers from the Cobra's miniguns looking like a bright red stream of water from a hose spraying onto the ground and splashing up. Invariably, before dawn, the bad guys would break off and retreat back into Cambodia.

At *Hannas,* they pushed the dead bad guys up into a pile with a bulldozer and poured diesel over them and burned them. At *Illingworth,* I was flying "hash & trash" the day after and wound up carrying "Line-One's" (KIA's) all day. When it looked like we wouldn't get them all back to Tay Ninh before dark, we put the remainder into a cargo net and carried them on the sling.

They had so many dead, they ran out of body bags and had to cover them with poncho liners. I hovered my Huey up next to a pile of bodies and blew away most of the poncho liners. I stared at one poor kid—a red headed, freckled kid who looked barely eighteen—whose lifeless eyes were wide open and were rapidly filling with red dust moved by the rotor wash. I wanted to climb down from the cockpit and close them for him. I wanted to send a message back to Tay Ninh to say, "make sure you wash the dirt out of his eyes before you ship him home and his mother sees him." I guess what I really wanted to do was cry, but I didn't think officers were expected to do that. Nobody had cried in World War II—at least none of the characters in "Combat" or "Twelve O'Clock High" cried.

Everyone knew that Illingworth was finally going to be abandoned, but it could not happen soon enough as far as those who stayed behind were concerned. There was a significant amount of bitching about having to spend one more night in that hellhole, but at least they had the comfort of knowing the cavalry was nearby.

The artillery, too, had been reset and the guns resupplied with enough ammunition to defend what was left. Thankfully, no more 8-inch powder and shells arrived.

A disheveled group of survivors gathered, toward sundown, near the middle of the base. Father Boyle was going to render a blessing—and give thanks for those that had survived. The actual text of what he said was not written down, but several men remembered his words and say that they were pretty close to the following:

"You men went through hell on earth today. You will never forget the events of last night, and you will never forget your brothers who lost their lives last night and the ones who were wounded. You will never live your lives in the same manner as you did before. You must now live your own lives and a piece of each life that was lost. You have been changed. Your appreciation of life has been elevated to a new plane because no man can appreciate life as much as he who has come close to losing his life. God bless you all!"

As night fell again on April 1, the soldiers who remained at Illingworth were once again in a state of high anxiety and sleeplessness. Most of the men anticipated that the NVA would somehow avoid the cavalry and sneak back to complete the job. It did not happen, however, and by daybreak on April 2, the men finally started to believe that the hell that Illingworth had come to represent might finally be over.

A week after the battle at FSB Illingworth, there was no more FSB Illingworth. Lt. Col. Mike Conrad's shattered battalion was, indeed, able to stand down. The two companies that were not at FSB Illingworth, A and B, were pulled out of the jungle and reconstituted with the remnants of C, D, and E companies. It would be several weeks before the 2/8 was brought back up to strength, and that would be just in time for them to go plunging into Cambodia with most of the rest of the 1st Cav.

There wasn't much left to salvage, from a logistics standpoint, in the sand piles that still formed a shadowy outline of the former fire support base. The usable artillery was lifted off or towed away to the next fire base down the road. Any equipment that had been damaged beyond repair, like the quad .50 gun truck, was hauled off to the rear to be cannibalized for spare parts. Alpha Troop's busted Sheridans were finally repaired and driven away. The M-577 command track rejoined its unit, too. The engineers stacked any salvageable PSP, culverts, and planking, which was then airlifted out; the rest was left to the elements. Grunts from Division intel scoured the area for any classified materials that might have been scattered to the winds.

As the last soldiers departed, all they left behind was some shredded sandbags, busted ammo boxes, bits of twisted metal, crumpled beer cans, empty C-rats boxes, cigarette butts, shell casings by the thousands, and the ragged ends of the reefers that had been smoked as they waited for the NVA to come. Life moved on. Death stayed behind, as evidenced by one anonymous mound outside the former base containing what was left of the brave and nearly victorious soldiers of the 272nd NVA Regiment.

13

REPERCUSSIONS AND REVERBERATIONS

April 1, 1970, across South Vietnam

It was not as spectacular as the Tet Offensive of two years prior, but the April 1, 1970, attack on FSB Illingworth was only one of a number of engagements that the NVA initiated that day, all across South Vietnam. In something called "the April High Point," the COSVN (Central Office for South Vietnam) planned and carried out one hundred engagements on April 1—a real April Fool's Day for the Americans and their allies. The thrust at FSB Illingworth turned out to be the nastiest and most brutal battle of the day; indeed, it made the front pages of many domestic newspapers and was a highlight on the six o'clock news.

This was, after all, supposed to be a time when America was withdrawing its forces from South Vietnam—not engaging in more pitched battles and producing more significant casualties. For one brief moment, FSB Illingworth held an unwanted spotlight, and it didn't help that 60 percent of the casualties suffered during the April High Point occurred there.

April 2, 1970, MACV Headquarters, Saigon

On April 2, 1970, the Office of Information at the Military Assistance Command, Vietnam (MACV), issued a morning news release, number 92-70, that read as follows:

> *At approximately 0230 yesterday morning (1 April), an element of the 1st Brigade, 1st Cavalry Division (Airmobile), at a fire support base 34 km (22 miles) north-northwest of Tay Ninh City and five miles from the Cambodian border, received about 200 mixed 120 mm mortar and 82 mm mortar rounds, 15 mixed 107 mm and 122 mm rockets and a ground attack by an estimated two enemy companies. The enemy employed small arms, automatic weapons and rocket-grenade fire. The troopers returned fire with organic weapons supported by helicopter gunships and artillery. As action continued, an element of the 11th Armored Cavalry Regiment, in tanks and armored personnel carriers moved to the area and reinforced the troops in contact. Fighting continued until about 0430 when the remaining enemy withdrew. No enemy were reported to have penetrated the perimeter. In a search of the battle area, the bodies of 54 enemy soldiers were found. In addition, 28 individual weapons were captured. U.S. casualties were 24 killed [actually 25] and 54 wounded. Materiel damage was light to moderate. (The name of the fire support base was FSB Illingworth.)*

With these few words, the army made its official public disclosure on the battle at FSB Illingworth. Many at MACV hoped this would be the sum total record of the dust-up. The report failed to mention, of course, that the two hundred or so Americans at FSB

Illingworth were nearly overwhelmed by an enemy force better than twice their numbers.* Extolling the actions of the 11th Armored was gallant, but, in fact, though the cavalrymen tried very hard, they arrived after the battle was already decided and took no part in its outcome. The missive also failed to do the math: the Army sustained better than 10 percent KIA, a total casualty rate of almost 40 percent, and the all-important ratio of enemy dead to Americans killed was only slightly better than 2-to-1. In a command structure obsessed with "body counts" and "kill ratios" where 10-to-1 or better was the minimally accepted goal, the firefight at Illingworth was a bit of an embarrassment. Worse, it came on the heels of the attack on FSB Jay, five days earlier, where equally distressing casualty figures were experienced.

The two engagements did not escape the attention of the commanding general in Vietnam at the time, Gen. Creighton Abrams. They also received critical scrutiny at the Pentagon and ended up in the daily war briefings conducted for President Nixon. Nixon was very upset, and Abrams was furious. Someone was going to need to explain what had happened.

April 5, 1970, 1 Cavalry HQ, War Zone C

The hot potato landed right back in General Roberts's lap. On April 5, General Roberts issued a six-page report on the events at Jay and Illingworth (see appendix 1 for a complete copy of the report). In the missive he cited, right up front, the strategy he (and General

* Although release 92-70 mentioned "an estimated two enemy companies," which might normally be around two hundred men, the eyewitness accounts and statements from the NVA on-scene commander put the force at four hundred plus.

Casey) had put in place that purposefully put the two fire support bases in the path of the NVA. The strategy of drawing out the enemy, Roberts believed, had been highly successful. He made no apologies for using his forces as tantalizing targets. This was, after all, war.

Roberts then went on to state the obvious at several junctures. (1) The way that the bases were placed had undoubtedly allowed the NVA to zero in on specific targets within their perimeters. Roberts felt that could not be helped; it made the scenario more believable to the enemy. (2) Roberts also defended the tactic of not hardening the bases better than they had. Doing so would probably not, in his view, have done much to prevent the casualties. He wanted to maintain mobility, which meant sacrificing substance. Interestingly, he did not give any reasons, in writing, for not moving Illingworth sooner, as had been urged by both Conrad and Casey. (3) Roberts made mention that in future, all artillery ammunition should be sufficiently dug in, properly covered, and adequately dispersed so that there would not be too much in one spot. This, of course, should have been blazingly obvious from the get-go but was entirely overlooked—and even ignored after Conrad protested the situation he faced on the afternoon of March 31. Roberts did not place blame for this glaring failure on anyone.

In 1973, Lt. Gen. John H. Hay Jr. wrote an in-depth study for the Department of the Army in regard to FSBs in Vietnam.* General Hay's treatise, *Tactical and Materiel Innovations*, carefully points out some of the strategies and lessons learned in regard to FSBs and their uses by highlighting two engagements that occurred at FSB

* Vietnam Studies, Lt. Gen. John H. Hay Jr., *Tactical and Materiel Innovations* (Washington: Dept. of the Army, 1974).

Crook in June 1969 and FSB Floyd in August 1970. These clashes are bookends to the April 1, 1970, fight at FSB Illingworth, but unlike Illingworth they stand out as shining examples, as far as the army is concerned, of what could go right if the fire support base concept were used according to doctrine as it existed at the time. It is worth examining the differences between these encounters to get a better perspective on FSB Illingworth. Contrasting the battles at FSB Crook and FSB Illingworth is particularly instructive.

A reading of General Hay's description of the action that took place at FSB Crook, as well as the Operational Reports of the 25th Infantry Division for the same time period, presents an eerily similar scenario to FSB Illingworth. The NVA soldiers who attacked FSB Crook were even from the same 272nd Regiment that would attack FSB Illingworth nine months later. Like Illingworth, Crook was placed across a prime enemy infiltration route, planned so as to agitate the NVA into taking action, situated on a flat area near forested triple-canopy jungle, set up with interlocking fields of artillery fire from nearby FSBs, ringed by concentric aiming circles and the area around it was dotted with patches of potential concealment set up as traps for NVA recon parties and observers.

FSB Crook was manned by B Company, 3rd Battalion, 22nd Infantry, as well as elements of the medical, communications, and mortar platoons of the same battalion. There were six 105 mm howitzers, just as at Illingworth, but there were no 155 mm or 8-inch guns on-site. The firebase was protected from on high by the same types of gunships, aerial rocket artillery, and TACAIR that would be available to the defenders at Illingworth.

Late at night on the evening of June 5, 1969, the seismic sensors picked up signs of activity in the tree line; the commanding officer at Crook initiated the pre-planned artillery firing program; the fire base was placed on 100 percent alert; mad-minutes were conducted.

At 0255, the NVA commenced a bombardment of the base and shortly thereafter conducted a battalion-sized attack at the southwestern part of the berm, exactly as at Illingworth.

Where the two stories start to diverge is in the ultimate defense of the base and the casualties. The NVA did get inside the perimeter of FSB Crook, notably with Bangalore torpedoes, something they apparently did not use at Illingworth, opting for satchel charges instead. Considering the flimsy nature of the berm at FSB Illingworth, Bangalore's were unnecessary in terms of penetrating the perimeter. Satchel charges, which could be delivered more easily and in greater quantity, might be able to do more damage faster, and they apparently did so. The enemy was quickly overcome at Crook and the attacks blunted by a spirited and aggressive defense. Meanwhile, as the NVA were charging, artillery units off-site, including 8-inch guns stationed at other fire bases to the rear, were hammering the areas immediately around FSB Crook and the NVA positions in the tree lines. The artillery used a lethal combination of killer junior and killer senior in defending FSB Crook.

By 0400 the next morning, the NVA were pulling back, having suffered very heavy casualties. Seventy-six bodies were discovered. Only one American was killed and only one wounded.

Unlike at Illingworth, the NVA came at the base again the next evening and received an even worse pounding for their efforts. This time, the NVA attacked the northeast corner of the base but were immediately decimated by a furious barrage of killer junior as well as air assets. They did not even get close to penetrating the lines at FSB Crook during this attack. Three Americans were wounded, none killed. The next morning 323 enemy bodies were discovered.

This is a vastly different outcome from the battle at FSB Illingworth. Why?

The Operational Reports/Lessons Learned documents from the 25th Infantry Division for June 1969 were published and distributed soon after the events at FSB Crook. Copies were sent to the 1st Cavalry Division. They would have been read by the intel staff, at least, and probably by every senior officer in the division, so the facts and lessons learned would have been available. Whether the particulars were absorbed and included in future action plans within the 1st Cav would be, at this late date, only conjecture, but the historical record of General Casey would lead us to believe that this avid reader and excellent strategic thinker would have at least seen the material at some point.

We also know that FSB Crook had been in place for almost two months before it was attacked and that it was "hardened" to an extent that FSB Illingworth was not. For one thing, it had a more robust concertina wire barrier than Illingworth. FSB Crook was not designed to be a permanent installation at all, but it was constructed to parameters that were more robust than the flying forward base, "hit 'em and run" concept that General Casey was demanding of the FSBs like Illingworth.

FSB Crook received a barrage of NVA rockets and artillery prior to the ground assault, just like Illingworth, but at Crook very few of the rounds did any appreciable damage. That was not the situation at Illingworth, where the compound suffered extensively from the fusillade and several men were killed or wounded. The accuracy and effectiveness of the NVA bombardment at Illingworth has been attributed to the extensive time the NVA had to take the measure of the base prior to the attack. FSB Crook, however, was also in place for an extended period, so it's hard to explain the difference in the results of the two opening salvos. What we do know is that the first few minutes of the engagement made the defense of Illingworth much more problematic.

Illingworth's infantry defense was conducted by the remnants of one company—Charlie—that had been reduced to thirty-nine effectives augmented by twenty-two men from the battalion recon platoon and 30 or so newbies. Crook's infantry component was the full-strength and rested Bravo Company of the 3/22 Infantry. That had to have made a difference, and it says absolutely nothing about the innate bravery of the men of Charlie 2/8; it was just a question of numbers and the relative physical health of the two outfits. Bravo 3/22 was also backed up by elements of their own battalion for mortar, communications, and medical support and had had more time and experience in working together and coordinating with one another than the patchwork of units at Illingworth.

The mortar pits at Illingworth were removed from the fight soon after the battle commenced. The mortars at Crook were in place and operating throughout their two engagements. There was no cavalry component at Crook, but the cavalry units at Illingworth were there by accident and not design. They contributed little to the defense of Illingworth, but in fairness to the reputations of those men, they couldn't have due to the condition of their equipment. They did, however, provide an unintended but effective intimidation factor in the minds of the enemy.

The artillery units at Illingworth fought bravely and effectively—especially the 1/77 105 mm battery, whose six howitzers certainly made a big contribution. The 155 mm and 8-inch guns could hardly have been very effective, as organic artillery; it just wasn't their kind of fight. When you factor in the contributions of their crews, fighting along the berm, sometimes hand to hand, and the contributions of the men from the quad .50 and the searchlight unit, it certainly made a positive difference in the outcome.

The artillery assets at FSB Crook also figured heavily in the successful outcome of that action, but for different reasons. The artillery created the majority of the casualties and did so before the NVA could even get close to the perimeter of the base. The combination of killer junior from the fire base and killer senior from offsite compounds decimated the enemy before they could get near enough to execute their favorite "danger close" tactic.

In hindsight, placing the two big 8-inch guns from the 2/32 aboard Illingworth was certainly a useless and wasteful tactic insofar as their potential use in defending the base was concerned. That was not the main reason the guns were there, of course; they were intended to fire on other, longer-range targets, but they never did. It was also a miscalculation to think that the big guns could be well defended—or even defend themselves—in the confines of a lightly constructed and intentionally impermanent enclosure like FSB Illingworth.

There were certainly no huge piles of unprotected or unbunkered ammunition aboard FSB Crook as there were at Illingworth. As it turned out, the explosion of the 8-inch ammo at Illingworth was both a blessing and a curse, but mostly a blessing. All things considered, that ammo should not have been there in such quantities and in such an exposed condition. It was only dumb luck that the catastrophe didn't kill far more of the American defenders or blow away the base completely.

General Roberts's report on the actions at FSB Jay and FSB Illingworth seems to have been accepted without further comment. The focus on Jay and Illingworth swiftly receded into the background. This might seem unfortunate but was probably totally logical because all eyes, ears, and efforts were turning swiftly to a new dynamic: the planning for the invasion of Cambodia.

Cambodia had an urgency that was both political and practical. The governing regime in Phnom Penh was changing dramatically, and into one that was finally fed up with the constant interference within its borders by the government in Hanoi. It was also approaching the end of the dry season, and if a major push was not initiated before the end of May, there was a strong possibility that the tanks, tracks, and trucks needed for the drive into Cambodia would be mired in mud up to their axles, or worse.

In truth, many of those with responsibilities for Jay and Illingworth were just as happy to see affairs quickly swept under the carpet. As mentioned, the casualty ratios between the Americans and the NVA were embarrassingly poor—that is, decidedly in favor of the NVA, at least in regard to the "norm." Then again, since no one really knows how many NVA perished, it may be better than the record indicates.

There was a positive side, though. The 1st Cav unquestionably hurt the NVA—badly. The casualties suffered by the enemy were steep and devastating. At least two proud, experienced, frontline NVA regiments were wrecked during March and early April 1970. Several major supply bases were captured and destroyed. Important trails and interdiction routes were disrupted and uprooted. The actions of the entire 1st Cav in War Zone C during this period rocked the NVA back on their heels and unquestionably helped set the stage for an easier invasion of Cambodia.

Life is a constant series of choices. Thankfully, most of our options are not life threatening. Vanilla or chocolate? iPad or PC? There is, of course, that occasional decision with potentially life-changing consequences. Marry or stay single? Medical school or law school? For those in authority in combat, decisions are constantly demanded, and almost every choice affects a life—or ends one. It is a heavy burden.

The colonels and generals directing the American efforts in Vietnam in 1970 had a particularly difficult time of it. This was the first American war where technology allowed the Defense Department, the Pentagon, and the White House to look directly over the shoulders of the leaders prosecuting the conflict. Former Defense Secretary Robert McNamara (1961–1968) was always meddling in the process of the conduct of the war. Melvin Laird, who was Defense Secretary at the time of the battle at FSB Illingworth, even had a Vietnam Task Force that met nearly every morning when he was at the Pentagon.

Vietnam was also the first American conflict that had more political considerations than strategic ones. As a result, the senior officers on the front lines had to worry often about being second-guessed. They had to employ tactics based not on what might be strategically sound but on what might look politically correct on the six o'clock news. For a professional war fighter, especially the senior officers, many of whom were still steeped in their World War II combat experiences, it was a difficult, frustrating, and especially inept war to navigate.

Gen. Elvy Roberts was surely in this category. On the one hand, his orders were to clean out the nest of snakes in War Zone C represented by the PAVN and their infiltration activities. On the other hand, he was told he had to do it with caution while not incurring any unnecessary casualties. He was also tasked with doing it "economically," not spending any more money than absolutely necessary. His division even had its flight hours cut back in the middle of March 1970 in an effort to save on the budget.

Roberts also knew that his command tour was winding down. He faced leaving the greatest position of combat authority he would ever hold in his long career, and it was happening just as the big push into Cambodia was about to begin. The old warrior would not be around to drive his men into the most important, most controversial engagement of the war.

Given all this, we might be able to guess at Roberts's mindset as he received the call from General Casey requesting that Conrad be allowed to move out of Illingworth. Roberts's chances of affecting the outcome in War Zone C were dwindling; he only had a few weeks. He was a tough, brave combat paratrooper who had gone "balls to the wall" to beat the Germans in World War II. He career was writing its final chapters; the "young guns" (like Casey and Conrad) were taking over. Did he really care much about where his future was headed in the army? Or did he care more about charging up that one last hill? A more timid, more political general might have thought more about the media impact of a decision to pull out of FSB Illingworth. An old warrior sick and tired of the politics might have recognized that the enemy he had been chasing all over the region was, finally, right there in front of him. All he had to do was leave those men in place and tease the NVA out of hiding and smash them once and for all—one last hurrah before riding off into the sunset and the cushy job of heading a Reserve Army Corps in San Francisco, sporting a third star. The burdens of command are awesome, indeed, and always subject to second-guessing, no matter what the outcome might be.

There still exists much bitterness, even to this day, among the men who fought and survived the firestorms at FSB Illingworth. Too many good friends and comrades were lost. Their valor, however, cannot be denied, and although they may still feel as if they were pawns in a poorly understood war, aren't all soldiers ultimately pawns?

The game of chess, which contains more pawns than any other

type of piece, was most likely invented in Persia sometime around the sixth century. It was a game to mimic war—and to train its players in the art of war. Pawns are routinely sacrificed to try to take out the opponent's major pieces and ultimately corner or capture the opposing king. The sacrifice of one's pawns is always made better by victory. In the grand game of chess that the War in Vietnam ultimately became, we lost too many pawns, and there was no clear-cut sense of victory, only a feeling of defeat.

Illingworth was one battle of a hundred battles that occurred in a single day of a war that lasted more than seven thousand days. It was not the most significant engagement of the war, but neither was it the least significant. Illingworth had its place and its purpose, and it became a perfect microcosm of what the Vietnam War was becoming in the early days of Vietnamization. This book has been an attempt to see this portion of that war through this small window: what it was like under those conditions for those who fought the war during that time frame. What were those men thinking, feeing, doing? How were they reacting to and perceiving that war? It is also intended as a testimonial to all Vietnam veterans.

The War in Vietnam was not lost in engagements like FSB Illingworth. Ultimately, it was not lost at all. In a recent speech, retired U.S. Marine Corps Gen. Anthony Zinni spoke eloquently about this. In his talk he made note of the laudatory comments being heaped upon the "Greatest Generation," the men and women who fought in World War II. General Zinni certainly agreed wholeheartedly with those sentiments but also wondered why the "Vietnam Generation" is not now praised similarly. He pointed out that in all the long history of the Vietnam War, no American force ever lost a stand-up fight. He also wondered, if the Vietnam War is such a scar on our honor, why are there so many men today pretending to have fought in that war? He noted, with a touch of humor, that "I sure don't see too many out there pretending to have gone to Woodstock."

General Zinni is very adamant that the war was not "lost" on the battlefields of Southeast Asia. He contends it was ceded to the enemy in Washington and Paris by those who had more pressing political concerns than backbone. The contest at FSB Illingworth, albeit just one stark data point, would certainly bear out General Zinni's hypothesis.

Unfortunately, those who fought at FSB Illingworth have tended to subscribe to the concept that what they did there was unworthy of the same valorous accolades as those given to those who fought on other, more "honorable" battlegrounds. They should not feel that way in the least, but it is understandable given the overall general queasiness many Americans feel, to his day, relative to any topic that includes Vietnam. It is time to change that mindset. It is time to recognize how wrong we have been and to honor those who answered their country's call, like those brave men who endured, survived, and triumphed at FSB Illingworth. Welcome home, brave warriors.

14

EPILOGUE

Four-plus decades after the battle of April 1, 1970, it is still possible to make out a few faint outlines of the dirt-and-sand fort that was once FSB Illingworth. The former deadly battleground is now a small scar in a farmer's field. The mass grave of the NVA has settled peaceably into the earth. The world has moved beyond the events that took place there. So, too, have the men involved. A few went on to careers in the army. Several passed away in other fights before their time in Vietnam was over. A number have passed on since. Most of the men who fought there, thankfully, are still with us, and after they left Vietnam they folded themselves back into the fabric of America.

The names of those who gave their lives at FSB Illingworth are listed below in italics. An asterisk marks the names of those who have passed on since.

John Ahearn After two Bronze Stars, twelve Air Medals, the Army Commendation Medal, and two Purple Hearts, John was ready to leave Vietnam. He stayed in the army and completed the army's Career Course at Fort Sill, Oklahoma, and then went on to command an 8-inch nuclear battery in Germany. Like many other fine officers, he was caught up in the massive 1973 RIF (reduction in force) and left active duty. He joined Tenneco for three years, using the nuclear skills he attained in the service to work on a U.S. Navy submarine project. Scratching a different itch, he responded to a sales ad and went to work for Dan River in the carpet business. In 1980, he became a regional vice president in flooring for DuPont. In May 2009, he joined Commercial Surfaces, Inc., in San Antonio, Texas, where today he is in charge of project management and sales. John lives in San Antonio, raises horses, and participates, with his wife, in the annual San Antonio Rodeo.

Ray Armer Ray lives in Columbia, South Carolina, and laughingly refers to himself as a "retired world traveler." He and his wife do, indeed, enjoy gallivanting about and spend annual extended vacations in Italy and France, among other destinations. After his last Vietnam experience, in command of Company A 2/8, Ray was transferred back to Fort Benning, Georgia. He was caught up in another RIF after the Vietnam War ended in 1975, but he immediately volunteered for the Army Reserve. After twenty-eight years of combined enlisted, commissioned, active, and reserve service, Ray retired from the reserves with the rank of major.

Paul Baerman Paul was born in Lansing, Michigan, but was an army brat, whose father was a colonel of artillery. After a year at the Citadel he transferred to West Point, where he graduated with the Class of '68. He served with distinction in Vietnam, where he earned the Silver Star, Bronze Star, and Purple Heart. Baerman stayed with the army, but ten years after Vietnam he became afflicted with type 1 diabetes. Since Baerman was in top form otherwise, and there was no history of diabetes in his family, the best guess as to the cause was Agent Orange exposure. The army doctors treating him wondered whether Baerman should be allowed to remain on active duty or be medically retired. Baerman issued them a challenge: "Go get your PT clothes and we'll run the obstacle course. If you beat me, I'll retire." The doctors declined the challenge and approved Baerman for continuation on active duty. Just before Desert Storm, in 1991, Baerman had been given command of the 3rd Battalion, 2nd Armored Division, a plum assignment with tremendous possibilities for career enhancement and general's stars. As the Iraqi Army rolled over Kuwait, Baerman's battalion was told to deploy. The diabetes issue arose again. The army doctors were more insistent this time. There was no guarantee that the insulin he was required to take every day could survive the harsh desert environment—and what if he suddenly went into insulin shock in the middle of a battle? Reluctantly, Baerman handed over command. He also realized it was time to move on. He retired from the army as a full colonel in 1994. After the army he and his wife, Kerry, moved to Colorado, where Paul worked as an urban planner. He retired again in June 2012.

Corporal Bobby L. Barker, *Harvey, IL, April 9, 1949–April 1, 1970:* Randall Richards posted the following on the Vietnam Veterans Memorial online: "Bobby's death has brought pain to my life since April 1, 1970 when I crawled, through the dust, from Blue 3, to [the] FDC and found Bobby's lifeless body. Bobby was a hero in the greatest sense. He loved the people he served with, he loved life and I distinctly remember that Bobby loved his mother, above all. Bobby Barker was a great American hero. I'm proud, that I served with Bobby."

Charles Beauchamp Shortly after the battle at FSB Illingworth, SFC Beauchamp was recommended for a direct commission and awarded a Silver Star for his actions on April 1. He was approved for commissioning and made a second lieutenant in June 1970. He spent the next few years at Fort Ord, California, with the 4th Training Brigade and rose to Assistant S-3. In 1973, he got caught up in the massive, army-wide RIF. He reverted to his permanent non-commissioned rank of E-7. He went on to postings in Korea, the Sergeants Major Academy, and Fort Lewis, Washington. From 1983 to 1991 he taught ROTC at Oregon State University. He retired as a command sergeant major, an E-9, in 1991. After the army he worked for the State of Oregon, retiring again in 2005, and now divides his time between the Association of the U.S. Army in Oregon and acting as an area chairman for the National Guard and Reserve Affairs Program. He lives in Salem, Oregon, and can be contacted on Facebook.

Maynard "Bo" Boedecker Maynard Boedecker, Jack Illingworth's friend and last squad leader, was drafted into the army in 1968, right after he had gotten a good job at NCR. Work would have to wait. Boedecker was fast-tracked through the army's advanced NCO Academy, and by the time he landed in Vietnam in September 1969 he was an E-5 sergeant. In March of 1970, he was promoted to E-6 staff sergeant while he was soldiering in Ray Armer's Alpha Company of the 2/8. In August 1970, Boedecker received an "early out" from the army and, by October he was back home and at work, in Illinois. He spent the next thirty-three years working for Illinois Electric. He is now retired.

Private First Class Thomas R. Bowen, *Forestville, CA, November 19, 1949–April 1, 1970:* Private Bowen was killed in action by artillery or mortar fire while serving at his post among the 105 mm guns of the 1/77. Kimberly Kimmel-Ober posted this on the Vietnam Veterans Memorial online on Thomas Bowen's birthday in 2001: "For PFC/E-3 Thomas Bowen and all those who knew him and loved him, I just want to say thank you for your dedication and sacrifice! Please know that you have not been forgotten and always will hold a special place in my heart! It would have been nice to have known you as a person and I greatly appreciate your service! I just wish you did not have to pay so high a price! You forever will be a hero in my eyes!"

Patrick Boyle Father Boyle is still "kicking around," as he says. He is currently in residence as an associate professor in the Department of Christian Life, University of St. Mary of the Lake, Mundelein Seminary, which lies about 30 miles north of Chicago. He remains very active in the lives and reunion activities of his former "parishioners" at FSB Illingworth. His dog, No-Nuts, sad to say, has gone to puppy heaven, where, perhaps, he has a more active and satisfying life among the females of his species, since in heaven you (supposedly) get all your parts back, if you understand my meaning.

Morris J. Brady The Colonel Brady of our story attained his primary military ambition, general's stars—two, in fact—and retired after thirty-eight years of service as a major general. After his tour as division artillery commander in the 1st Cav he became, in succession, ADC of the 101st Airborne, commandant of the Command and General Staff College, commanding general of the 2nd Infantry Division in Korea, and director of operations for the U.S. Readiness Command. After retiring from the army, he managed and operated two aviation support companies in the Middle East and is chairman emeritus of the Army Aviation Heritage Foundation. In 2011, General Brady self-published a book entitled *A Night in the*

Dog's Head: A War We Didn't Want to Win. If anyone wants to get in touch with General Brady, you can contact him on Facebook.

First Lieutenant Cleaveland F. Bridgman, *South Dartmouth, MA, August 21, 1946–April 1, 1970:* Lieutenant Bridgman, as described in this book, died valiantly from wounds suffered in the artillery and mortar attack on the 1/77 FDC. Charles Brown, a friend and former army buddy, posted the following on the Virtual Wall: "Dear Cleave Today (3/10/10) a beautiful stone bench was dedicated to you in Dartmouth, Massachusetts. It's at the head of the harbor within sight of your former home. It's got your name and honors inscribed on it. Very beautiful bench and location. There were probably 80 people present including politicians and servicemen past and present. Quite a few flags from many of the service organizations. A very honorable presentation. I was honored to represent the men of Charlie Company, 1st Battalion, 5th Cavalry, 2nd Brigade, 1st Air Cavalry Division with whom you served as Forward Observer. You served with honor and the friendships you developed remain to this day. As soldiers we often refer to our 'Brothers' as a band of brothers. I want you to know that no soldier has a better brother than you have in your brother Tim. Tim loves and misses you very much to this day. His speech in your honor today showed his love, respect and enthusiasm for you. You must have been a special role model and big brother to Tim. Thank you for this. You may rest in peace knowing you are loved and missed and will never be forgotten by your friends and family and military brothers. Rest in Peace." At the small but nationally ranked independent Knox College in Galesburg, Illinois, an athletic scholarship is awarded annually in the name of Cleaveland Bridgman, Class of '68. We can only hope that those who win these stipends are told about the legacy of the brave soldier who once strolled that campus and excelled on its playing fields. Bridgman was awarded the Silver Star for his heroics on April 1, 1970, and posthumously promoted to captain. I note with some chilling irony that Cleve Bridgman was born August 21, 1946. Bill Clinton, former president and successful avoider of military service, was born two days before Cleave, and I was born three days after.

Tim Brooks Tim, a native of Milton, Massachusetts, graduated from Bowdoin College, Class of '67, and was immediately hired as the college's assistant dean of students. The draft, however, found Tim before he could really focus on his career. With a college degree, he was able to get into Army Officer Candidate School and when he graduated was commissioned as a second lieutenant and designated for the Armor Branch. After training and promotion to first lieutenant a year after commissioning, he was sent to Vietnam and ultimately to the 11th Armored Cavalry. He reported to 1st Squadron, D Company, in March 1970 and served with the company until January 1971, when he received an "early out" from both the army and Vietnam. Tim went back to school, earning a master's at Pacific Lutheran University and a doctorate in education at Oregon State. He worked in education for the rest of his career, spending many years at the University of Delaware, where he recently retired as dean of students. He still teaches and is very involved in the university's Center for Disability Studies.

George Burks George lives in Huntsville, Alabama, wife his wife, Elizabeth. They have six children and a growing group of grandkids. Burks grew up in Huntsville, where he was an avid fisherman and hunter. As a teenager, he decided to pursue a career in music. He played guitar, composed, and took off for "the big city lights." After a couple of years knocking around Nashville, he decided he needed to "do something different" and address his military obligation. He went to an army recruiting office and signed up. A year later, he was in Vietnam. April 1 turned out to be the worst day of the worst month of 1970 in terms of American casualties in Vietnam. George Burks describes the battle, for him, as an "out of body experience." He believes that at some point in the fighting he went into a psychotic state that he has never been able to shake. "My body was working on some higher level . . . I didn't even know who I was." Burks was taken to the medics at Tay Ninh but cleared to return to duty. Neither Burks nor the medics knew it at the time, but this was the beginning of a lifelong battle with PTSD. Burks reupped for another tour and was stationed in Germany for three years. After that hitch he decided he was not enamored with the new "Volunteer Army." He got out and returned to Huntsville, where he entered college for a degree in the emotional therapy field—perhaps so he could help others who had been afflicted, like himself. He got that degree and became a therapist but after six years found it too stressful. With a referral from the VA he obtained a job as a logistics manager at the army's Redstone Arsenal near Huntsville. His career at Redstone revolved around making sure that the army's far-flung commands were supplied with the operational missiles and spare parts that were developed and produced at Redstone. He worked there until his retirement in 2000. He still deals with the nightmares of Vietnam, his PTSD, and the medications, but enjoys his family-oriented band, Rewind, and his children and grandchildren.

Corporal Billy P. Carlisle, *Pelahatchie, MS, March 14, 1950–April 1, 1970:* As noted in the story, Billy Carlisle was a replacement headed to Alpha 2/8. He never got to his company. He was killed by fragments from a B-40 rocket blast while courageously defending his position along the berm. Fellow Mississippian Leslie Stapp posted the following on the Virtual Wall online: "My thoughts and prayers, to the family and friends. (W. Shakespeare) 'He which hath no stomach to this fight, let him depart. But we in it shall be remembered, we few, we happy few, we band of brothers, for he today that sheds his blood with me shall always be my brother.' Rest in peace brave soldier, you have not been forgotten. I served in Da Nang, 68/69, with the 1st, Marine Division." Billy Carlisle received a Silver Star for his actions on April 1 and was posthumously promoted to corporal.

George Casey Sr.* Shortly after the battle at FSB Illingworth George Casey Sr. was promoted to major general and assumed command of the 1st Cav from General Roberts. He would direct the division's plunge into Cambodia during the May–June 1970 invasion. He would also be standing on the tarmac to welcome the last troops back from Cambodia at the end of June. A week later, Casey climbed into his command helicopter to fly to Cam Ranh Bay to visit some of his wounded men. He never made it. The Huey flew into thick clouds along the way and disappeared. Casey and the crew were discovered two days later. The helicopter had flown into a mountainside, and all aboard were killed instantly. General Casey had asked Mike Conrad to go along on the flight. Conrad had just received his orders to rotate home and, anxious to see his wife, demurred. Lucky for Mike Conrad.

Major General Casey was one of the highest-ranking officers to perish in the Vietnam War. George Casey Jr. had been commissioned as a new second lieutenant shortly before his father's death. Many, at the time, believed that Major General Casey's star was on the rise and he would ultimately be propelled to the top as army chief of staff. He did not make it, of course, but his son did. Gen. George Casey Jr. would certainly have made his father proud. He led the troops into Iraq to topple Saddam Hussein and in 2007 was appointed chief of staff. He retired, after a long and incredibly distinguished career, in 2011.

Staff Sergeant Benjamin V. Childress, *Knoxville, TN, March 10, 1930–April 1, 1970*: Childress was killed during the initial NVA barrage of rockets, mortars, and artillery. "Chick," as he liked to be called, was an old hand, with sixteen years in the regular army. He had mentored many a young redleg. One of those was Jack Martin, who wrote this on the Vietnam Veterans Wall online: "As a young man in 1968 I met Chick at Fort Sill. He watched out for me and became a good friend. I got out of [the] army in 1969 [but] kept in touch with him until he shipped to [Vietnam] . . . To his wife and his two girls I will never forget him. God bless you."

Mike Conrad: Moving on from Vietnam, Mike Conrad, promoted to full colonel, served as executive assistant to the vice chief of staff, as chief of staff at the 9th Infantry Division, and as a brigade commander in the 9th Infantry; he also attended the Department of State's prestigious Executive Seminar in National and International Relations. Promoted to brigadier general, Mike Conrad went to Germany with the 1st Armored Division, served as principal adviser to the commanding general of V Corps, and then moved back to the Pentagon to the office of the chief of staff, Department of the Army. Promoted to major general, he commanded his old 1st Cavalry Division. His last posting was as assistant inspector general of the U.S. Army. After retirement from the army, Mike Conrad began a second career in the private sector. He joined EER Systems as a director of information technology, then moved up to vice president of the Federal Information Technology Group. After fifteen years at EER he moved over to L-3 Communications Services as vice president, Engineering and Scientific Services. Mike

Conrad retired a second time in 2005. In addition to the Silver and Bronze Stars, Air Medals, Distinguished Flying Cross, and Purple Heart he received in Vietnam, Mike was awarded two Legions of Merit and the Distinguished Service Medal. Mike lives in Alexandria, Virginia, and is president of his West Point Class (1956).

Sergeant David G. Dragosavac, *Meadville, PA, February 16, 1949–April 1, 1970:* David was regular army, having enlisted in 1969, designated as an infantryman, and was posthumously promoted to E-4. His sister Barbara placed this poignant message on the Vietnam Veterans Memorial online in 2002: "My Hero: David was one of 5 of my brothers. . . . I remember when he went into the service. I was very proud of him. I remember, too, when I learned of his death. . . . David was a fun loving brother—very artistic. He played guitar and attended the Art Institute of Pittsburgh prior to his enlistment. . . . He was a great brother. Thanks for giving your life so mine can be free in the United States of America. Love—Barb. P.S., I don't know that I ever told you that I loved you."

Corporal Leroy J. Fasching, *Wibaux, MT, July 28, 1945–April 1, 1970:* Posted as an infantryman to Charlie Company, Private Fasching was killed in the initial NVA barrage of artillery. He had been in Vietnam only eighteen days. Fraternity brother Larry Bruce posted the following on the Vietnam Veterans Wall online in 2009; it's fascinating to ponder Fasching's prescient comments on parting with his friend: "Still in my heart and lovingly remembered . . . I remember taking Leroy, along with two other friends to the plane in Missoula when he was leaving for 'Nam. He hugged us all and said he wished he was coming home but that he wasn't. He added not to worry about him though because he would be going to his permanent home. . . . Fasching was posthumously promoted to corporal.

Gordon Frank Major Frank took over command of FSB Jay after Lieutenant Colonel Hannas was gravely wounded. He helped tie off Hannas's arteries and was the first to give him CPR. Franks also pronounced him dead, a finding that, fortunately for Bob Hannas, proved premature. It was, nevertheless, a traumatic moment for both men. They were not only serving in the same battalion, they were very close personal friends. Earlier in their careers both had been stationed in Central America and had chased Che Guevara through the mountains and jungles of Bolivia. When Bob Hannas took command of the 2/7, he needed an S-3. He requested and got his friend Gordon Frank. Major Frank was widely credited with conducting a brilliant defense of FSB Jay after Hannas was knocked out of action. Several months after the battle, as Bob Hannas was recuperating at Letterman Army Medical Center in San Francisco, one of his former sergeants came for a visit and delivered the news that Major Frank was coming through San Francisco on his way to another assignment. Hannas insisted that he be allowed to greet his old friend at the airport, which he did, in a wheelchair still minus his legs (he had not yet been fitted with his prosthetics). It was a very emotional reunion for both men. "Sadly," Bob Hannas told me, "that was the last time I ever saw him. I don't know what happened to him and I have looked high and low for many years." Frank was a highly skilled soldier, a Ranger, Airborne qualified, and a bit of a clandestine operator. "I think maybe he became a mercenary," Hannas adds. "Some guys don't want to be found, you know. Gordon was like that."

Tim Hall Tim Hall, a Minnesota native, was drafted in February 1969, and by the following July he was in Vietnam, assigned to Alpha Company of the 2/8. He initially carried a rifle, but in November, Captain Armer made him a radio operator. In February 1970, he was transferred to battalion headquarters as an RTO for Colonel Conrad and Major Moore, men Hall says were "two of the best officers I ever saw." After his wounding at Illingworth, Hall was sent to Cam Ranh Bay to recover. After about two weeks, he regained his full sight and was ordered to return to the 2/8. On his way back to Tay Ninh, he passed through Phuoc Vinh, the 1st Cav's new rear headquarters. A friendly sergeant took pity on the still-bandaged Hall and escorted him to the mess hall. When the men there found out Hall was with the 2/8, an outfit the men had started calling "the Battalion of No Return," they treated him like a hero and piled his mess tray high with the best dishes they could offer up. As Hall sat down to eat more food than he could possibly consume, he noticed one lonely soldier sitting far apart from the other men. Hall recognized the man immediately: It was Pete Lemon, still recovering from his wounds. Hall went over to sit with Lemon and remembers that they chatted amiably enough before Lemon got up and wandered out. More men then came over to Hall and asked him if he knew who he had been sitting with, and he said, "Sure, that was Pete Lemon." It turned out everyone knew who Pete Lemon was, and they had heard of his deeds during the night along the berm at FSB Illingworth. The building of the legend had apparently already started. Hall made it back to Tay Ninh and soldiered on with his battalion, going into and out of Cambodia, after which, promoted to sergeant, he was shipped back stateside to complete his service obligation. After the army, Hall went to work for the U.S. Postal Service, enjoyed a long career, and retired in 2004. He lives in Minnesota with his wife, Sharon, and they have two children.

Robert Hannas Lieutenant Colonel Hannas survived the horrific wounds he incurred at FSB Jay, but it was a major miracle that he did so. He spent the next year in various hospitals but shortly thereafter was fitted for prosthetic limbs. It wasn't long before he was able to move around with the aid of crutches. The army sent him to the Monterey Institute of International Studies for a master's with a concentration in German (Hannas had spent a tour in Germany prior to going to Vietnam and was familiar with the language). He was then posted to the United States Military Academy to teach German. By the end of his four years at the Point, he was head of the German Department. By this time, Hannas was contemplating retirement from the army, and he and his wife wanted to move back to Monterey, California, where they had purchased a home. The army was not done with Bob Hannas, however. They offered him an appointment to the Defense Language Institute in Monterey, which he accepted. He eventually rose to commandant of the institute and attained the rank of full colonel before finally retiring.

When I asked Bob Hannas to comment on the tremendous risks that Generals Casey and Roberts had taken with FSBs Jay and Illingworth, he reminded me that the Americans wanted desperately to land a devastating blow on the NVA before having to retire from the field. Perhaps that was as much a matter of martial pride as it was an attempt to help our South Vietnamese allies, but in terms of disruption of the enemy it appeared to have worked, and it helped soften up the trails into Cambodia. Bob Hannas also told me not to omit the risks taken by the NVA; he feels very strongly that the NVA pushed so hard because they desperately wanted to capture a lot of Americans and use them as bargaining chips in the peace talks that were already under way in Paris.

Bob Hannas has few regrets. He says that even the loss of his legs gave him the opportunity to meet some really brave and wonderful people, challenged like himself, that he otherwise would never have had a chance to know.

***Sergeant Syriac Hebert**, Pine Bluff, AR, November 15, 1948–April 1, 1970:* Hebert died when the 8-inch ammunition blew apart a large portion of FSB Illingworth. He was less than two weeks from completing his yearlong Vietnam tour. He was posthumously promoted to sergeant.

Jerry Hensley The commander of 1st Squadron's D Company, 11th ACR, stayed in the army and retired in 1975 with the rank of major. Before commissioning, Jerry spent almost eight years in the ranks, where he was steadily promoted, attaining staff sergeant's stripes before deciding to become an officer. Jerry had been raised in the Texas oil fields, so after his retirement from the army it seemed natural to him to return to the oil business. It is the profession he pursues today, and very successfully so. He calls his command of D Company in Vietnam "the highlight of my military career."

***Sergeant Robert A. Hill**, Lowell, OH, October 17, 1948–April 1, 1970:* Hill had soldiered through some of the toughest fighting in War Zone C since he started his tour the previous August. This included the vicious struggle just five days earlier when Charlie Company had been surrounded within one of the NVA's local strongholds. He fought bravely at Illingworth but died during the savage pounding inflicted on the base by enemy rocket and mortar fire. Hill was posthumously promoted to sergeant.

George Hobson Charlie Company's commander stayed in the army. Over the course of the next twenty years, George held a number of command and staff assignments in Europe and the United States. His last active-duty posting was as inspector general at Fort Leonard Wood, Missouri, after which he retired, in 1990, as a lieutenant colonel. After the army George served on various community boards and started the first high school fly-fishing club in the United States. Through the assistance of the Federation of Fly Fishers, within four years there were additional clubs in seven states and Canada. He has been recognized for that and other conservation work by the Missouri Department of Conservation. Hobson now owns Eastwood Kennel and Farm; the kennel has an international clientele in France, Scotland, and Canada. He serves on the University of Missouri Bradford Research Farm Advisory Board and has recently participated in a new Vietnam veterans recognition project with the University of the Ozarks.

Sergeant Kenneth Ray Hodge*, Johnson City, TN, December 24, 1948–April 1, 1970:* Hodge died during the first moments of the battle at Illingworth as the NVA's initial barrage of rockets, mortar rounds, and artillery rained down. His friend Gary Collins posted this about him on the Vietnam Veterans Wall online: "I will never forget Ken. ROTC in high school, his humor, always happy. Some gave all, and all gave some. Have never got you out of my mind since my mom sent me Johnson City paper clipping and asked if I knew you. I knew you, and will always remember you."

Joe Hogg The former Blue Max pilot is retired and living in the mountains of North Carolina, "closer to Chattanooga than anywhere else," he told me. After Joe's first tour in Vietnam he was sent to Germany and assigned to a VIP airlift company. His main job was flying a general in a Huey wherever the general wanted to go and, as Joe further explained, acting as an escort to the general's wife. "Hell, I was single, six feet tall, blond, blue-eyed, and had some medals on my chest, so I got the job of taking the arm of the general's lady whenever he wasn't around." His final tour wasn't quite as pleasant: It was back to Vietnam in 1972 and flying along the DMZ. Joe left the army in 1973 with a Silver Star, Soldier's Medal, three Bronze Stars, forty-six Air Medals, the Purple Heart, Army Commendation Medal, Vietnamese Cross of Gallantry, and the usual collection of Vietnam campaign and service medals. He then started and sold several successful businesses in California, Florida, Washington State, and Georgia. In North Carolina he became the small business development director for the state's three westernmost counties and also an adjunct college teacher. In retirement, Joe does, as he says, "whatever the hell I want to" and enjoys attending reunions of his various army comrades and several commands from his Vietnam days.

Rick Hokenson Rick is retired and lives in Cotton Lake, Minnesota, with his wife, Gail, and their Weimaraner, Heather. Rick, originally from Detroit Lakes, Minnesota, was attending Fergus Falls Junior College when he got his draft notice. As he signed his induction papers, he remembers looking at the clock on a nearby desk. It read, "10:00, 26 November 1968." When he got out of the army, he signed his discharge papers at 10:10, so he likes to joke that he was in the army one year, nine months, nineteen days—and ten minutes. Rick grew up around guns and hunting, so he volunteered to be a sniper. He proved to be very good at it, earning a Bronze Star with "V," an Air Medal, a Purple Heart, his Combat Infantryman's Badge, and Expert Rifle status as a Sharpshooter and Machine Gun specialist. After the army, Rick got into steel construction, then heating and air-conditioning fabrication. He signed on with Northwest Bell, which changed to US West and finally Qwest. He worked at the phone company for twenty-six years before retiring out of the Qwest branch in Fargo, North Dakota. He and his wife now enjoy, as he says, "the laid-back life on the lake.

We are both retired. I also have some wooded property, and I go out to the woods and work on cutting wood, clearing trails, and enjoying nature. Our dog, Heather, is very spoiled, but she makes up for it by her great personality and hunting ability." Ricks says about his assignment to Charlie Company, "I was told at the Replacement Center that they called Charlie 'the Company of the Living Dead' and you did not want to be sent to that outfit. If I remember right, George Hobson is [another one] who told us that when he was sent out to our company. I would like to tell you that I feel very lucky to have survived all the battles we were in and I feel honored to have served with such a great bunch of soldiers and the great leadership skills of George Hobson."

J. C. (Joseph Colan) Hughes J. C. left the army shortly after his Vietnam tour and enrolled in a commercial aviation school. He obtained his commercial pilot's license and went to work for American Airlines. He flew with American for many years, becoming a senior captain and one of its premier instructor pilots. He retired from American in 2011. Since then, he has been a private pilot for a Saudi prince and a consulting pilot to Caribbean Airlines, flying in and out of Trinidad. J. C. lives in his original hometown of Delray Beach, Florida, with his wife, Carolyn Parker.

Ralph Jones After his army service ended, Ralph Jones went back to his native Cincinnati. His family owned a motel business, and Ralph joined the operation. After the family sold the motel, Ralph worked for the U.S. Postal Service for a number of years. He went back to Vietnam in 2008 on a pilgrimage to the site of the former FSB Illingworth. Ralph knelt and dug a small hole at the site, in which he buried a Celtic cross. He reverently took the soil he had dug up and placed it in a small bag and brought it home with him.

In 2010, Ralph was successful in spearheading a drive for a memorial for the men who died at FSBs Jay and Illingworth. The memorial was built and dedicated at Fort Sill, Oklahoma, the current home of Ralph's old unit, the 2nd Battalion, 32nd Field Artillery. The bag of dirt Ralph brought back with him from Vietnam was mixed into the ground at the Fort Sill memorial site. One more thing that Ralph related to me was this, and it really struck a chord: "When I was at the place, in 2008, where FSB Illingworth had once stood, I gazed out at the tree line, which looked very much the same as it did in 1970. As I stood there, the wind started gently moving those trees and I swore I heard the breeze whisper to me, 'Welcome back. It's been a long time.'"

Nguyen Tuong Lai Lai fought on with his NVA comrades until the end of the war. When the American forces left Vietnam completely, the weak and ineffectual South Vietnamese government collapsed swiftly. Colonel Lai was jubilant over the defeat of his enemies and looked forward to a period of peace and prosperity for his native country. He was to be sorely disappointed. As "Southerners" in a new country conquered by "Northerners" and their Soviet allies, Lai and many of his former comrades found themselves on the outside looking in. Even though he was lauded for his efforts during the long war, Lai was demoted in rank, in favor of a Northern "regular" more in tune with the ruling class in Hanoi. He was made head of security and counterintelligence in southwest Vietnam. He spent a great deal of his time evaluating who should go to one of the new government's many "reeducation camps." He reluctantly sent away many, some of whom were former colleagues in the Vietcong. Forced labor was a common fate, and over a half million would be executed by firing squad. Lai realized he had traded one class of oppressors for another, and a situation that was even worse than he could have ever imagined. This would lead him to a desperate gamble. In 1979, Lai gathered up eighteen members of his immediate family, including his wife and children, and crammed them into a small fishing boat. In the middle of a dark and moonless night, he cast the boat off from a dock and let it drift silently out to sea. This was a very risky business; pirates roamed the area. If the family was intercepted, they would be robbed, the women raped, the women and children sold off into slavery, the elders killed outright, and the men forced into working for the pirates or, if they refused, thrown overboard. There was also the Vietnamese Navy to worry about; they conducted constant patrols looking for just such "boat people." If Lai was caught, with his high profile, the authorities would make a horrible example of him. The group was lucky, however, and after a week of seaborne desperation, they landed in Malaysia, on Bidong Island, which at the time was a refugee camp for many escapees such as the Lai family. After he spent a period of time working for the Malaysians as an interpreter, Lai and his family were allowed to emigrate. They chose Switzerland. Today, the former high-profile Communist and tough old soldier lives a quiet, hermitlike existence in a small town near the Alps. He occasionally works as a journalist, and once in a great while he parts the curtain on his former life and lets writers, like me, take a peek inside, but only just a little.

Arnold W. Laidig* The censure that Arnold Laidig received from Col. Morris Brady immediately after the battle at FSB Illingworth did not, fortunately, prove fatal to Laidig's military ambitions. He stayed in the army and earned, among other decorations, a Silver Star and a Legion of Merit for his Vietnam service. After Vietnam, he was stationed at Fort Sill, Fort Lewis, and Fort Bliss, in Germany, and at the Pentagon and fought in Desert Storm before retiring, in 1995, as a lieutenant colonel. After the army he worked in private industry, primarily in human resources. He was an avid runner and competed in numerous marathons all over the United States and Germany. Unfortunately, he contracted leukemia and passed away, at the age of sixty-three, on January 1, 2008. He was buried with full military honors at Arlington National Cemetery.

Sergeant Robert H. Lane, *Concord, TN, September 17, 1950–April 1, 1970:* Robert Lane, just nineteen years old, sustained mortal shrapnel wounds while fighting among the guns of the 1/77. The following was posted on the Virtual Wall by "Sonja" on October 15, 2007: "The date is October 15, 2007 and today my family and I sponsored you as a fallen hero for the East Tennessee Veterans Memorial. We live in the same small town of Concord, Tennessee, probably just a walk away from where you grew up. Also my father's name is Robert Lane. With my donation to the memorial I will receive a dog tag with your name and info on it. It will hang from my mirror as a reminder of your service to your country. You will be thought of each day and my daughter will know your name and your story. I have worn a POW/MIA bracelet for 30 years, continue to pray for his family and will now add yours to our nightly prayers. YOU WILL NOT BE FORGOTTEN . . . we will never be able to repay you."

Specialist Fourth Class David H. Lassen, *Clarence, NY, March 17, 1948–April 1, 1970:* Lassen died when the 8-inch ammunition aboard Illingworth exploded. His widow, Bobbie, posted this on the Vietnam Veterans Wall online in 2008: "David and I were married on May 31, 1969, 8 days later he left to serve his country. I never saw him again. He was the love of my life and there is not a day that goes by that I don't think of all the happiness he brought to me through his fun loving ways or the letters he wrote while in Viet Nam. I hope there is a heaven and that one day I can hold my dear husband and tell him how much he has been, and always will be loved."

Peter Lemon Pete Lemon was absolutely typical of hundreds of thousands of eighteen- to twenty-year-olds who were fighting in the Vietnam War in the early 1970s. Born in Toronto, Canada, June 5, 1950, Pete became an American citizen at age twelve after his family moved to Michigan. Coming of age in the '60s, and attending an American high school, he was no doubt swept up in all the pros and cons of whether to support his adopted country and serve or to avoid the war and go back to his native Canada, as some natural-born Americans were doing. Pete chose to stay—and sign up. At 6'2" and well over 200 pounds, he was both a desirable catch for the U.S. Army and a potentially big target for its enemies. Nonetheless, he breezed through basic training and then signed on for Ranger School, after which he was sent off to Vietnam. He was originally posted to the 75th Infantry, but when that unit was sent home from Vietnam, Lemon still had months remaining on his obligated tour. He was sent back to the Replacement Center and ultimately reposted to Echo Recon of the 2/8. The heroics performed by Pete Lemon in the early morning hours of April 1, 1970, would nearly kill him, but they would also shape the rest of his life.

Shortly after he was finally medevaced from Illingworth, the stories of what he had done to defend the base and his comrades began to swirl around the division. His platoon leader, 1st Lieutenant Peters, first told his boss, Lieutenant Colonel Conrad, about Lemon's amazing feats of valor. The recitations were backed up by his surviving platoon mates. Conrad relayed the tale to Colonel Ochs and also to General Casey. Lemon would spend a month in the hospital recovering from his extensive wounds, but even as he did so, a petition for an award of the Medal of Honor would begin to circulate. With a Bronze Star, Air Medals, Purple Heart, Army Commendation Medals, and a slew of campaign medals and other awards, plus a meritorious promotion to sergeant, Lemon's potential for an army career was off to an excellent start. A Medal of Honor would ensure him acclaim and practically unfettered advancement. Lemon gave it some thought, but only briefly, and ultimately opted out of continued service. He left active duty soon after the completion of his recovery and moved to Colorado, where he enrolled at Colorado State University.

Lemon received his Medal of Honor from President Nixon at the White House in early 1972. The citation reads as follows:

> For conspicuous gallantry and intrepidity in action at the risk of his life above and beyond the call of duty. Sgt. Lemon (then SP4), Company E, distinguished himself while serving as an assistant machine gunner during the defense of Fire Support Base Illingworth. When the base came under heavy enemy attack, Sgt. Lemon engaged a numerically superior enemy with machine gun and rifle fire from his defensive position until both weapons malfunctioned. He then used hand grenades to fend off the intensified enemy attack launched in his direction. After eliminating all but 1 of the enemy soldiers in the immediate vicinity, he pursued and disposed of the remaining soldier in hand-to-hand combat. Despite fragment wounds from an exploding grenade, Sgt. Lemon regained his position, carried a more seriously wounded comrade to an aid station, and, as he returned, was wounded a second time by enemy fire. Disregarding his personal injuries, he moved to his position through a hail of small arms and grenade fire. Sgt. Lemon immediately realized that the defensive sector was in danger of being overrun by the enemy and unhesitatingly assaulted the enemy soldiers by throwing hand grenades and engaging in hand-to-hand combat. He was wounded yet a third

time, but his determined efforts successfully drove the enemy from the position. Securing an operable machine gun, Sgt. Lemon stood atop an embankment fully exposed to enemy fire, and placed effective fire upon the enemy until he collapsed from his multiple wounds and exhaustion. After regaining consciousness at the aid station, he refused medical evacuation until his more seriously wounded comrades had been evacuated. Sgt. Lemon's gallantry and extraordinary heroism, are in keeping with the highest traditions of the military service and reflect great credit on him, his unit, and the U.S. Army.

In the years since the war, Pete Lemon has been married twice, fathered children, and received his BA from Colorado State and an MBA from the University of Northern Colorado. He has been engaged in several businesses and for the last dozen years has been traveling the country as a professional motivational speaker. He still lives in Colorado.

Thomas H. Magness* Tom Magness received a Silver Star for his bravery at Illingworth and a Purple Heart for his wounds. The 1961 West Point graduate recovered and transferred to the Corps of Engineers in 1974. He spent the balance of his army career in environmental management positions within the Corps and even served on the White House Council of Environmental Quality. Before retiring as a full colonel in 1986, his last army posting was at the Pentagon as the chief of the army's Environmental Quality Office. In a second civilian career he worked for Tetra Tech in Fairfax, Virginia, primarily on environmental issues. He advised the National Guard on environmental assessments and taught courses on national environmental policy at West Point and Duke University. The Corps of Engineers honored him with its lifetime achievement de Fleury Medal in 2004. Two of his three sons went to West Point (Classes of

'85 and '86), and the third graduated from Norwich University. His daughter graduated from the University of Virginia. Colonel Magness passed away at the VA Hospital in Washington, D.C., on December 28, 2004, surrounded by many of his family and friends.

Corporal Nathan J. Mann, *Warsaw, MO, September 18, 1949–April 1, 1970:* Fellow Echo Recon buddy Allan Rappaport said this about Nathan: "I served with Nathan (Laredo) Mann in Echo Recon 2/8 1st Cav. I remember one time he got a care package of tequila and jalapeño peppers from home. The squad sat up one night drinking and crying, and laughing. He was my friend. He was a very brave and good man. He had great courage, and I mourn his loss." Nathan Mann, killed along the berm by artillery or mortar fire, received a posthumous promotion to corporal.

Private First Class Roger J. McInerny, *Richfield, MN, August 17, 1950–April 1, 1970*: Roger McInerny was in Vietnam eighteen days, had been in Charlie Company less than twenty-four hours, was only nineteen years old, and was blown away by a rocket on his first day of combat duty. Could there be a more sorrowful coda to this conflict?

Michael Moore Moore left the army shortly after Vietnam. At some point, he retired to a quiet life in the tiny eastern Arizona community of Alpine.

Specialist Fourth Class Thomas J. Murphy, *River Falls, WI, January 7, 1949–April 1, 1970*: Murphy died at the FDC after having sustained mortal fragmentation wounds from the NVA barrage. High school friend Leigh Livermore wrote this about Tom Murphy on the Vietnam Veterans Wall online: "Tom Murphy, a Man Who is Missed by All Who Know Him: Hi Tom! Man, I could not believe the news! . . . I was very dismayed when I learned from the Hudson paper about two weeks later that you had given your life to help your friends. That would be you though. You were loyal, courageous, honest, and principled. You were like that in real life and would stand tall to help others. Whether in friendship, on the athletic field, the field of combat, or in daily life, you stood head and shoulders above the crowd. I miss you my friend and will see you soon enough. Save me a place beside you. . . ."

Dave Nicholson Dave is a retired attorney who lives in South Burlington, Vermont. After returning from Vietnam, Nicholson went to law school, graduated, passed the bar exam and began a long and successful practice in family law, bankruptcy, and civil matters. In 1993 he became quite ill. After exhaustive tests it was determined that he had hepatitis C, contracted from the blood transfusions he had been given while hospitalized for wounds in Cam Ranh Bay in 1970. Nicholson struggled with the disease, a failing liver, and finally liver cancer, which was diagnosed in 2004. The VA classified him as 100 percent disabled due to combat-related illness. Miraculously, a donor liver came through for Nicholson in 2005. Today, Nicholson spends his time gardening, contacting old Army buddies, and writing. He completed a book about his Vietnam experiences in 2007—a manuscript he was kind enough to share with me. Dave has been invaluable to me in making contacts with some of the other men in Charlie Company as well as providing very useful background information.

William V. Ochs Jr.* William Ochs was a West Point graduate, Class of '45, too late to see service in World War II. He did serve in

Korea and, as depicted in this story, Vietnam. Ochs was appointed to brigade command in February 1970, taking over the 1st Cav's 1st Brigade. Already a bit behind the power curve in terms of advancement and assignment (his classmate George Casey Sr., for example, was about to get his second star and command of an entire division, whereas Ochs was still a colonel and a rookie brigade commander), Ochs got off to a rocky start. Fairly or unfairly, he received the largest dose of backroom criticism when events at FSBs Jay and Illingworth "went south," as the expression was. Then, shortly after Illingworth, a company from the 2/7, reeling from the loss of its CO at FSB Jay, but still part of Ochs's brigade, was involved in a very messy incident. It seemed that the company, under a new but experienced captain, had refused to obey orders concerning a particular mission it had been assigned. They were ordered to march down an NVA infiltration trail they had discovered, but the troops believed the trail was booby-trapped (as many were). They decided to take another route. The net result was that the company ended up at the wrong place at the wrong time and nearly got obliterated by a B-52 mission that was rerouted only at the last moment to avoid taking out the soldiers. Unfortunately for Ochs, the company was being shadowed by a film crew, and the whole affair ended up on the *CBS Evening News*. Ochs caught the brunt of this embarrassing fiasco. The net result was that by the middle of May, only three months after taking command of the brigade, Casey told General Roberts that if he didn't relive Ochs he would do it the moment he took over the division. Ochs was sent back to the States with a career-ending fitness report and the stain of being relieved of a combat command for cause. Ochs spent a year at the Pentagon and retired, as a colonel, in 1971. He then worked as a senior administrator for the Department of Energy for a number of years. After moving to

Annapolis, Maryland, he became a bailiff for the Circuit Court of Anne Arundel County—a job he thoroughly enjoyed and happily stayed in until two months before his death, at age eighty-seven, in 2011.

Corporal Michael R. Patterson, *Dearborn, MI, June 30, 1945–April 1, 1970:* Gary Duncan, who served with Alpha 2/8, posted this amazing message on the Vietnam Veterans Wall online on Veterans Day, November 11, 2009: "At our Veterans Day Service this weekend at our VFW a very sad, polite and beautiful woman came to me and asked me if I could help her find out about her father. She knew little except he was KIA when she was a baby. Knew name, where he was from and he is on the 'Wall.' I found you and your information and sent it to her. She is coming to see you. I know you have been her guardian angel all this time and you have done one hell of a job 'Trooper.' She's beautiful. God bless you brother." The very same day, the following message was posted by Corporal Patterson's daughter, Michelle: "Rest in peace my dear daddy: Michael Richard Patterson is my father. He died when I was one year old, so I didn't get to know him. I don't know anything about him but that he is a hero: my hero daddy. I wish you were here. I need you, dad. You have four grandchildren . . . and you have a great-granddaughter. We all love you." Patterson was twenty-four and married with a child when he landed in Vietnam. Eighteen days after arriving in country, he was dead—another of the Charlie Company replacements to die on their first day of combat duty. He was posthumously promoted to corporal.

Gregory J. Peters* The "Rooster," who so bravely defended the berm with E-Recon at FSB Illingworth, left the army shortly after his tour in Vietnam ended. He apparently struggled with his Vietnam "ghosts" after the war and fell into an unfortunate spiral of drugs and alcohol. He also suffered with a major case of PTSD. After many unhappy days, he passed away three years ago while under the care of the VA.

Sergeant Sidney E. Plattenburger, *Charlotte, NC, September 24, 1949–April 1, 1970:* Plattenburger was killed in the initial NVA mortar, artillery, and rocket attack and died from multiple fragmentation wounds. His sister, Bonnie, wrote the following on the Vietnam Veterans Memorial Wall online: "Eddie: There is not a day that goes by that I don't think of you. I remember when you were leaving and we sat on the bed and sang 'Leaving on a jet plane.' I try not to remember the day we received the news of your death. Instead, I remember the fishing trips we took and that smelly bait you used to make. I have told my son and granddaughter the stories about us growing up together and the good times we had. I still have some of your letters you sent to me. You always were and always will be "My Hero." It warms my heart to know there were people like you in my life. I miss you very much and often wonder where we would be today if you had not been taken from me at such a young age. Everyone tries to say God had a special plan for you. I still don't understand that plan, but want you to know how very PROUD I am of you and how much I miss you. I love you very much. Your little sis—Bonnie." From his brother, Howard, also from the Vietnam Memorial online: "Eddie, Not a year goes by that I am not thinking of you and remembering us growing up, fighting over Frances and other things brothers did. I will never forget the day the two Sergeants came to my door looking for Mom. Somehow before they even arrived, I knew. It broke my heart to have to go with them down to Mom's, but it had to be done. I go to your grave often to reflect and honor you as my best friend and my hero. Eddie, rest easy my brother. I will see you again one day."

John Poindexter Captain Poindexter quickly recovered from his wound, but his time in command of Alpha Troop and his obligation to the army were at an end. He left active duty and went to graduate school in June of 1970. He matriculated at New York University, earned a master's, and went to work on Wall Street. While engaged in the investment banking business he earned a PhD from NYU's Stern School of Business. After an extremely successful career in banking, John returned to his native Texas and purchased the first of several industrial companies he would acquire. He is currently CEO of John B. Poindexter & Company in Houston and owns a spectacular 35,000-acre ranch in the Big Bend area of West Texas. He is very active in the veterans causes that honor his former troopers and was instrumental in securing for his men a Presidential Unit Citation for their actions in the jungle on March 26, 1970.

Sergeant Gerald W. Purdon, *Cincinnati, OH, July 30, 1948–April 1, 1970:* From his cousin William via the Virtual Wall: "After my discharge in 1969 I joined the Ohio State Highway Patrol. . . . Jerry died April 1970 and I was at Kent State in May 1970. I thought to myself while standing there in riot gear shortly after the kids on campus were killed 'what a waste' for them and for Jerry. . . . He died so young. He had so much to offer." Sergeant Purdon received a posthumous promotion and a Silver Star for his bravery on April 1, 1970.

James Reed Jim Reed, a native Texan, was commissioned regular army right out of New Mexico Military Institute. He had, as he told me, "a wonderful career." His duties took him all over, including, of course, Vietnam, but also Germany and Hawaii. He was an ROTC instructor, operations officer, and War College graduate; he spent two tours at the Pentagon and commanded 1st Squadron, 11th ACR, at the time of the events covered in this book. Jim is a retired colonel and lives with his wife in San Antonio, Texas.

Cliff Rhodes The young soldier with the vivid vision made it back from Vietnam; just like in his dream, he got off the bus in his uniform, right in front of Pickering's General Store in Collins, Mississippi, rifle in hand. The only detail that differed from his dream was that he did not have his suitcase. The bus had been crowded when he boarded, and he had been given the choice of taking his suitcase or his rifle. He elected to keep the rifle at his side. The suitcase would be sent on the next available bus, and it was. He was sporting the Bronze Star he had won for himself for his bravery at FSB Illingworth, but he was hiding the terrors that would gnaw at him until the VA got him some help and designated him disabled with PTSD. Cliff eventually got into the sheet metal business, married and had two children, a boy and a girl (sadly, his son was killed in an accident at age 19) and today has four grandchildren. He is retired and spends a good deal of time in his shop where he tinkers, as he told me, "with a little bit of everything."

Randall Richards Richards is very active in veterans affairs, especially among those who shared with him the experiences of FSB Illingworth. Randall writes a very active blog about the battle, and it can be accessed at we-were-soldiers.com.

Elvy Roberts* A West Point graduate of the Class of '43, Roberts entered military service in World War II with the 101st Airborne Division and fought at both Normandy and the Battle of the Bulge.

After Vietnam, he was promoted to lieutenant general, and in 1973 he was named to succeed Gen. Richard Stilwell as commander of the 6th Army at the Presidio of San Francisco. General Roberts retired from the army in 1975 and spent two decades as an insurance and food industry executive and consultant. General Roberts spent the remainder of his years at home in Alameda, California, passing away peacefully shortly after his eighty-eighth birthday in 2005.

Mike Russell Mike left active duty after Vietnam but went home and joined the National Guard, from which he later retired with the rank of lieutenant colonel. Mike is working on his own notes relative to experiences in Vietnam, papers he's writing "just for myself." He lives in Bossier City, Louisiana, and is a member of VFW Post 5951.

Specialist Fourth Class Terry L. Schell, *Chicago, IL, August 1, 1948–April 1, 1970:* Terry Schell was a radioman assigned to the brave redlegs who manned the big 8-inch guns at Illingworth. When those guns could not be used effectively in the fight, he grabbed an M-16 and headed for the berm to defend his country and his friends. He was killed when the 8-inch ammunition exploded.

Corporal Klaus D. Schlieben, *Richmond, VA, September 14, 1949–April 1, 1970:* Schlieben was an infantryman assigned to Charlie Company and had soldiered with his mates from September 1969 all through the worst of the first three months of 1970, including the battle in the jungle on March 26. He was killed sometime during the NVA artillery barrage. Michael Janis served with Klaus in Charlie Company and posted this on the Vietnam Veterans Wall online: "I served with Klaus in 'Nam. He was just one of many heroes that gave their all that day April 1st 1970. I was on R&R and came back to 'Nam on April 2nd. The first thing I had to do that day was to try and identify as many of the casualties as I could. This was the worst day I spent in 'Nam and one I will never forget. It is impossible to say what [I] felt that day looking at faces of my fallen comrades. You could just see the hell they went through that day by the looks on their faces. When I came to Klaus's body it really shook me because he had been in my squad for about 8 months. He was quiet but a great guy and an even better soldier. God bless all who were at Illingworth that day." Schlieben received a posthumous promotion to corporal.

Corporal John Lee Smith, *Millbrook, AL, June 8, 1950–April 1, 1970:* Twenty-eight "John Smiths" died in Vietnam. There were even two John Lee Smiths who were KIA, although one was known as "Johnny." This John Lee was with Alpha Troop, 11th ACR, and had been in Vietnam less than two months. He was only nineteen, but he left behind two sons. One son, Steve, posted this simple note on the Virtual Wall in 2002: "I love my soldier." His other son, Tyrone Duncan, posted this in 2008: "Although I never gotta chance to meet you, I love you. Everybody say(s) I look just like you and that you were a wonderful person. You are my hero."

Francis "Bud" Smolich* Bud was one of the many heroes of the action on March 26, 1970, wherein Alpha Troop secured the release of Charlie 2/8 from the clutches of the NVA. Bud's singular contribution was to successfully light the way back for his troop, with illumination rounds, as they struggled to get out of the jungle after dark. "Sergeant Smo," as he liked to be called, helped me on many occasions with important details, excellent stories, and even some wonderful photos as I drafted *Blackhorse Riders*. He was very excited about the book and couldn't wait to see his friends and former buddies in print. He also wanted to share his legacy, in book form, with his family and friends. Sadly, shortly after I turned in the first draft of the manuscript, Bud and his wife of many years, Cheri, learned that Bud's life was going to be shortened dramatically and quickly by a combination of deadly cancers that proved resistant to treatment. He made a commitment to his family and to me that he was going to try to hang on until the book was published. Getting the hardcover into print and distribution was going to take almost a year, and the doctors had given Bud a prognosis of weeks, not months. Amazingly, this brave old warrior hung on and I was able to get to him a galley for the soon-to-be released book, so he could see the beautiful cover, the final product, and his story prominently featured. Happy and satisfied that the book was, indeed, a reality, Bud died the next day.

Greg Steege Greg is vice president of Hayden-Murphy Equipment Company in Minneapolis, Minnesota, a construction supply company that specializes in large cranes. Greg was in and out of college in 1969, which attracted the interest of his local draft board, and he was inducted in March of that year. He served two years, reaching the rank of E-5 sergeant before getting out and returning to his hometown of Denver, Iowa, where he still lives today with his wife, Susan. They have two sons. Greg has no immediate plans to retire.

Sergeant Brent A. Street, *Inglewood, CA, September 24, 1948–April 1, 1970:* In addition to the Medal of Honor awarded to Sgt. Peter Lemon, two Distinguished Service Crosses were bestowed for bravery at FSB Illingworth, both posthumously. Brent Street received one of the two. The survivors of Echo Recon remember Street tenaciously defending his position along the berm until he was cut down in a hail of shrapnel from either a grenade or a mortar. Fellow squad member Allan Rappaport posted this remembrance on the Virtual Wall in 2001: "Brent was my squad leader, and before that we served in the same squad of Echo Recon 2/8 1st Cav. He was a good and brave man. A good leader, and a friend. I mourn his loss." Street was posthumously promoted to sergeant.

Staff Sergeant Lawrence E. Sutton, *Portland, OR, August 13, 1938–April 1, 1970:* "Eddie" Sutton was regular army, almost fifteen years in service. He stood with the "big guns," the A-2/32 howitzers, on April 1 and died when the 8-inch ammunition cache exploded. His sister Marlene posted the following poem on the Virtual Wall in 2002:

I call out your name,
Not an answer do I hear
I call out your name
But I know you are near
I feel you in my heart
Your warmth and your love
For God has sent you to me
To give me comfort from above
Eddie, I love you and I miss you so very much
Your lil' sis,
Marlene

Staff Sergeant Sutton was awarded a posthumous Bronze Star with "V" for his service on April 1, 1970.

James Taylor* Staff Sergeant Taylor passed away several years ago. Sadly, not much could be learned about his post-Vietnam history. If anyone has more information, please contact the author.

Lou Vaca Miraculously, Lou Vaca survived the horrific wounds he suffered at FSB Illingworth. The medics on scene managed to stabilize him, but he didn't receive extensive treatment until he was dusted off later that morning. The doctors at Tay Ninh patched him up sufficiently to get him to the bigger, better-equipped hospitals in Japan. Vaca lost part of his stomach and a good portion of his intestines. From Japan, he was medevaced to Brooke Army Medical Center in San Antonio, where he spent the better part of another year rehabilitating. Vaca decided to reenlist, which he did, but after another year both he and the army realized that continued active duty was going to be too stressful on his weakened system; he was allowed to medically retire as an E-5 sergeant. Vaca kicked around for a while, got married, divorced, and remarried (thirty-two years and counting), and has five children. For the last twenty-four years he has worked in software quality for Sysco Food Services. He has no immediate plans to retire but is "maybe thinking about it." Even with all that happened to him during his army service, Lou Vaca has no regrets. He says, "I did what I was called upon to do, and I was proud to do it."

Ken Vall de Juli Ken joined the Washington, D.C., Police Department in 1973 and became a member of the department's SWAT team.

Sergeant Casey O. Waller, *Cumberland, VA, August 19, 1949–April 1, 1970:* The second DSC for heroism at FSB Illingworth was awarded, posthumously, to Casey Waller. He died fighting next to Peter Lemon. Michael Kilgore, a former platoon sergeant of Casey's, wrote this about him on the Vietnam Veterans Memorial Wall online: "Casey came to my platoon at the bridge on the Song Bay River. He was small in stature but big in heart. He loved music, especially the Glenn Campbell songs. He was with my platoon until I left in February, 1970 while we were on LZ Mary. I only learned of his death when I attended a reunion in 1998 with the guys from mortars, recon, and heavy weapons. They were on the LZ with Casey when he died. He stayed with me for the last three months of my tour, he became my little brother, I tried to watch out for him until I left. War brings men together where a brotherhood and alliance is bonded for life. May God bless you Casey. We talk about you at every reunion, your memory will always live with us." Waller was posthumously promoted to sergeant.

Lee Weltha (known today as Lee Velta) Twenty-seven years after FSB Illingworth, Lee Velta wrote the following about his experiences: "I returned to a safe area near our military area by the village of Phuoc Vinh. As a multi-decorated veteran I wasn't expected to really do anything, just recuperate, which I did daily in the village and nightly at the famous motor pool parties. Three weeks later I was back in the US—out of the army and 20 years old—too young to drink or vote. Every veteran has a story to tell. I only talk about Viet Nam to another vet or to select special others if the moment seems clear. People don't believe what they can't understand, and their assumptions create unique problems which label survivors unfairly. Sometimes it's best to just accept where someone is, rather than knowing where they've been. Viet Nam is remembered more for shorter moments of intense horror than much longer moments of peace and beauty. Somehow over time the human spirit denies enough of one to survive with the other." In one of the more unique and interesting career changes made by the veterans of FSB Illingworth, Lee Velta became a well-known and established opera singer in New York, where he continues to perform today.

Staff Sergeant Steven J. Williams*, Portland, OR, August 31, 1948–April 1, 1970:* Steve Williams served the 105 mm howitzers of the 1/77 at

FSB Illingworth. He was cut down by shrapnel during the bombardment of the base. The following was posted on Staff Sergeant Williams's memorial page on the Vietnam Veterans Memorial Wall online, and it is a fitting tribute not only to Williams but to all of the fallen at Illingworth: "Remembering this First Team Hero, SSgt. Steven James Williams, with a Multitude of Thanks for his Service and Dedication to our Country and for Freedom. Rest well and know that you will NEVER BE FORGOTTEN. I am the sister of another young 1st Cav. Hero, who made the Supreme Sacrifice in Vietnam 1967 . . . They shall grow not old, as we that are left grow old; age shall not weary them, nor the years condemn. At the going down of the sun and in the morning, We will remember them."

Ken "Mississippi" Woodward Ken is now retired and living in Pachuta, Mississippi. For his services in Vietnam, Woodward was awarded the Air Medal, Purple Heart, Army Commendation Medal with Combat "V," Combat Infantryman's Badge, and Expert Medals for both the M-14 and M-16. After his army service he returned home and successfully completed radiology training. For thirty-two years, until his retirement in 2005, Woodward was a radiology administrator, including twenty-two years with the Saudi Aramco Medical Services Organization in Riyadh, Saudi Arabia. Ken was an invaluable resource, providing me with background information on life as an infantryman in Vietnam and with Charlie Company in particular.

ACKNOWLEDGMENTS

I owe a profound debt of gratitude to all the veterans of FSB Illingworth who helped me with this story. I have tried, as best I could, to accurately reflect the events that surrounded them before and after that terrible April Fool's Day in 1970. I hope I have done them justice.

A special thanks goes out to retired Maj. Gen. Mike Conrad. We, all of us, owe Mike Conrad for the heroic and successful stand he directed on that fateful day. He did his very best to defend his men, his country, and his honor, and I absolutely believe he succeeded in superb fashion. I recognize that he was awarded a very prestigious Silver Star for his actions at FSB Illingworth, but after having thoroughly researched this story, living it for almost two years, and then writing it down, I believe today that he deserved at least a Distinguished Service Cross, if not more. He was the glue that held all the pieces together. He also gets a big "gold star" from me for all that he did to help me with this book. He patiently answered all my requests, never failed to try to track down those details that completely baffled me, and guided me through a thicket of terms and reminiscences that were of great value. Thank you, Mike, for everything.

The Illingworth family was a wonderful resource. Acting primarily through sister Laura (Illingworth) Phillips, I was provided with insight into the dynamics of the family as they grew up together in New Haven. Laura was so kind as to gather a complete dossier of family photos and the family's records of Jack's military service, including the sad but powerful death notices and letters of condolence. With Laura's permission, I have included some of these letters in appendix 2 so that readers can get a sense of what it was like for the tens of thousands of families who received similar missives during the Vietnam era.

There's a retired colonel out there to whom I owe a big "thanks," but he specifically requested that I not name him or give him any credit. He knows who he is, and if he sees this he will know that the guidance he gave and the reams of documentation he provided were extraordinarily helpful to my research. Thank you, sir.

Then there's my "literary wingman" J. C. Hughes. J. C. didn't fly in Vietnam, he drove a tank. I did fly in Vietnam to avoid doing risky things like driving a tank. J. C. got out of the army after Vietnam and became one of the top-rated airline pilots in all of commercial aviation. He's also a great storyteller and, for me, a provider of extremely useful information about the cavalry and the 11th Armored, especially in regard to how his detachment experienced the horrors of FSB Illingworth. Thanks, J. C., and I sure wish I could have flown with you. I bet you'd have been a hell of a nonliterary wingman, too.

Another Blackhorse buddy deserves a nod: George Burks. George has been with me through two books, *Blackhorse Riders,* where he was fighting with Alpha Troop to rescue Charlie Company, and now *Illingworth,* where he was once again at the heart of the storm. George is a constant, faithful source of support, tracking things down, contacting people, and providing a "boots on the ground" level of detail that has been immensely helpful.

I also want to express gratitude to former captain John Ahearn. Through the research and writing I've done in the past few years I have enjoyed excellent and highly valuable contacts within the Armor and Infantry branches, but I had no "go-to" guy in the Artillery until being introduced to John Ahearn. John has been a wonderful resource for all things artillery, especially as it functioned and performed in Vietnam. Through several long, into-the-night conversations with John I learned what it was like to be in a TOC under bombardment. I found out how challenging it was to try to direct fire effectively across a broad spectrum of artillery resources that are being bombarded themselves. John described what it was like trying to coordinate with airborne and remote resources simultaneously while standing out in the open, exposed to hails of lead, because your primary radios have been rendered ineffective. Nice work if you can get it, eh, John?

My thanks to Russ Horner, Joann Illingworth-Bates, Charles Brown, Sonja Page, Allan Rappaport, and Marlene Reid for permission to quote their tributes posted on the virtualwall.org; and to Randall Richards, Kimberly Kimmel-Ober, Jack Martin, Gary Collins, Bobbie (Lassen) VanderMeer, Gary Duncan, Michelle Patterson, Bonnie Bridger, Howard Plattenburger, Michael Janis, Michael Kilgore, and Garnet Jenkins for permission to quote their tributes posted on the Vietnam Veterans Memorial online at thewall-usa.com.

My remarkable agent, Nat Sobel, continues to find me gainful employment in this increasingly competitive business, and I am grateful for his steady counsel and excellent guiding hand. I know that Nat loves these kind of stories, and I am so proud that he allows me to associate with his experiences and the marvelous authors he has shepherded over the years.

This is my second book with St. Martin's executive editor Marc Resnick. I am a very fortunate guy to have Marc on my side. He is never too busy to answer a question or point me toward a resource. His suggestions, amazingly, are always "right on," and I would like to do as many books with Marc as Father Time and Marc's patience will allow.

My most steadfast, enduring, and utterly faithful partner, Laura Lyons, was once again at my side. Her love and support sustain me and get me through the difficult times as well as the fun times. How many "author's nights" can one person sit through, especially when you're not the author? How many book signings can she endure? Yet she is always there. It's a wonderful thing.

Then there's the "daughter of my heart," my dearest Lauri. She has seen me through the most difficult times of my life and has watched me move through many incarnations until now, at last, there is some peace. I don't know how to express the love I have for this girl.

In this tricky writing business it's always good to have a circle of steadfast friends with whom you can hoist a glass in celebration or drown your sorrows at the latest rejection. I am most grateful to my literary commiseration circle that we playfully call "Nights at the Round Table." Thanks, guys, for your wonderful support: Tom Clavin, Bob Martin, Ken Moran, Dave Winter—and ex-officio, Bob Drury.

I save the last paragraph for you, "Dude!" My buddy, my pal, my wonderful, talented, oh-so-smart son, Pierce. You are the best gift I ever could have had, the best "production" I have ever been involved with, the best that I can ever give the world. These books are intended to honor the brave men whom you will find herein, but they are your legacy, son, and every word I write is penned with you in mind.

APPENDIX 1

Letter of April 5, 1970, from
Major General Elvy Roberts to
General Creighton Abrams.
5/April 1970

General Creighton W. Abrams, Commander
US Military Assistance Command, Vietnam
APO 96222

Dear General Abrams:

You asked me to take a good, hard look at the contacts we have had in the Dog's Head area of Western War Zone *C* to see what can be derived as "lessons learned" for the benefit of others. We have conducted a study of the action in the form of detailed critiques with participation by all units involved. From these critiques I have gleaned some points which I think may be worthwhile to pass on.

As so often is the case we have not come up with very many new lessons, but there are several old ones that deserve reemphasis. I have taken the liberty to briefly recap the character of the action as a backdrop for the experiences gained.

During the first week in March the 9th Division, along with some COSVN elements, began to slip down toward Base Area 354 northwest of Tay Ninh City. The 1st Cavalry Division moved units to cut off the main routes between the 9th Division's former area and Base Area 354. The (first) major contact occurred at mid point of the route system, in the center of the Dog's Head, on 26 March. The results of this fight were 88 enemy KIA from the 3d Battalion, 95C Regiment. Also identified very close to that contact was the 66th COSVN Security Guard Regiment and the proselyting section of COSVN Headquarters. US losses were three killed.

The fight at Fire Support Base Jay on the morning of 29 March was the second major contact of the operation, resulting in 74 enemy killed, three FIT's, and 12 AK-47's captured. The enemy units were the 1st and 3d Battalion of the 271st Regiment. Thirteen US soldiers were killed.

The attack on Fire Support Base Illingworth early on 1 April was the third major contact, with 71 enemy KIA, 28 AK-47's and three crew-served weapons captured. Documents on the enemy dead indicated that the unit making the attack was the 1st Battalion, 272d Regiment. Twenty-four US soldiers were killed in this contact. Other fighting in the same area included the engagements of A and B Troops, 1st Squadron, 11th ACR, in which 42 enemy from the same 272d Regiment were killed and 17 captured. The enemy loss total now stands at 662 KIA and 21 PW's. 1ACD losses have been 50 killed and 203 wounded. ARVN Airborne losses have been two killed and 25 wounded. The enemy obviously decided to move sizeable forces into or through the Dog's Head and back into

Base Area 354. It is now apparent that he is determined to carry this out, regardless of the cost. Our actions I think have set back his time schedules and probably disrupted his plans to some degree.

In the attack on Jay, the performance of the US infantry and artillery troops was magnificent. Major Gordon Frank, the S-3, took over when the battalion commander (LTC Robert Hannas) was hit, losing both legs. Although wounded himself, Major Frank led the defense in a manner that can only be described as brilliant. One of the first enemy rounds struck the command bunker and swept away all antennas, cutting off communications except between Jay and Illingworth, but artillery defensive targets were fired from Illingworth and Camp Hazard immediately, since it was known from these locations that Jay was under attack. Communications came up within three minutes and the fires were adjusted.

Jay was a small fire base, and with six 105's and six 155's the personnel and materiel density was greater than usual. Incoming fires were 107mm rockets, 122mm rockets, B-20's, B-40's, 120mm mortars, 82mm mortars, and 75mm recoilless rifles. A ground probe of company size on the south side was driven back, leaving four enemy killed just inside the berm. The balance of the enemy force committed to the attack never got out of the wood line. The 105 ammo dump was hit and exploded. In addition to the artillery ammo, 3000 pounds of composition "C" which was to be used for clearing trees the next day also went up. The dump was well dug in and little damage resulted from this explosion. Shadow, Nighthawk, ARA, and flare ships supported the defense in addition to the artillery, which fired 3518 rounds. . The firing became sporadic by 0600, and ceased altogether by 0650. Artillery and air support by this time was shifted to withdrawal routes.

The attack against Illingworth on 1 April was expected, and the defenders all were ready and waiting. In fact, as the first enemy rounds were landing in the area, the battalion S-3's alarm clock signaled the time for the practice alert. The battalion commander, LTC Michael Conrad, and his S-3, Major Michael Moore, did an absolutely outstanding job during this attack, and not enough can be said in praise of the conduct of the troops on this fire base. The first enemy volley, again as at Jay, cut down the antenna array and reduced commo capability. The Air Force FAC immediately began to operate as a relay and did such a fine job bridging over the communications gap plus directing all fires in the difficult environment he was in that I have put him in for the DFC. The incoming rounds caused a heavy curtain of dust, making observation and the employment of night observation devices very difficult. This had also happened at Jay.

The ground attack at Illingworth, consisting of about two enemy companies, began at 0235 and reached the edge of the berm but not a single enemy soldier got inside the position. Most of the enemy bodies were strung out from 50 to 100 meters from the berm and extending back into the wood line. Here the attack foundered. At 0318, as the attack began to slacken, the 8-inch ammo dump, which had been on fire, exploded with tremendous force, blowing a large crater and covering everything with dirt. The immediate effect of this was to stun the defenders in the bunkers on the southwestern quadrant of the fire base and the crews on the 8-inch and 105 Howitzers in that sector. Although it could not be positively determined, certainly a major portion of our casualties came from this explosion and the rounds which intermittently "cooked off" for the next hour. The 155's which were located in another sector of the fire base continued operational. It was fortunate that Illingworth was a relatively large base with less density of personnel and materiel than there was at Jay.

Contact ceased and pursuit fires began at 0515. Forces were committed along possible withdrawal routes at first light. An armored Cav troop had been moved in earlier to sweep around the fire base. Support such as artillery, air, scouts, flares, and Shadow was "across the "board" as it had been at Jay. Preemptive fires early in the evening probably weakened the enemy ground probe, but the indirect fire against Illingworth was significantly more intense and of longer duration.

The most significant points that come out of this which I believe may be useful in the experience bank are as follows:

OBSERVATION: The enemy in the Dog's Head area, because of his location close to large cache areas in Cambodia, has an increased capability to mass fire in support of his attacks.

LESSON LEARNED: The enemy has great capability to mass artillery fires in this particular area. Being close to the border, he has more ammunition and of heavier caliber than is generally expected. Therefore fire bases either have to be exceptionally hard (and I doubt if any fire base can be hardened sufficiently to withstand without unacceptable casualties a standoff attack of the magnitude as occurred at Illingworth) or else they must be relocated more often than we did here. The problem with either course becomes, as always, a matter of blade time and continuity of operations. In the case of Illingworth we tried to compromise between a medium heavy base and a longer term occupancy. This base stayed too long for this area. I think we will have to go for an even lighter base with occupancy no longer than five days. Even five days, however, does not carry with it any guaranteed immunity from heavy standoff attacks by fire in this area. To remain in position longer must be recognized as an obvious tactical risk, and any advantages to be gained by remaining on site longer than five days must be carefully weighed against the increased possibility of attack. If the enemy can be forced to attack without the necessary time for a proper reconnaissance, his chances for a strong and well coordinated operation are lessened. This can be achieved by continuous movement of fire bases. Mutual support between these rapidly-moving bases remains an essential requirement.

OBSERVATION: Ammunition storage and level of ammunition in the fire base require special attention.

LESSON LEARNED: Ammunition and explosives must be dug in and overhead provided. This of course will be a real problem in the wet season in this area. Our ammunition at both fire bases, while largely below ground, was not well protected. In particular the 8-inch Howitzer ammunition was not dug in deep enough at Illingworth, and there was too much of it in one place. I believe several smaller dumps dug in at different quadrants in the fire base should be the pattern.

OBSERVATION: At any given time, the enemy can knock out generators and destroy antenna systems, thus hindering rapid and effective response to an attack.

LESSON LEARNED: The retention of at least four spare AN/P-RC 25 or 77 radios in the TOC is a necessity. These radios, equipped with fresh batteries, backpacks, and both long and short whip antennas, can provide adequate communications with support agencies and base defense. Battalion must communicate with brigade, the base defense company, and units in the field. There should be standby radio relay aircraft at brigade which can be put up immediately to bridge the communication gap in the initial onslaught and to make it possible to communicate over long ranges with the standby PRC 77's. Backup generators and 292 antennas should also be retained in the fire base to reconstitute normal communications once the attack has abated. When planning fire base defense, the assumption must be that in the initial stages of an attack the antennas will be swept away and generators will be put out of commission. Plans should be made accordingly.

OBSERVATION: The dust thrown up by incoming rounds on a fire support base in dry weather obscures vision to a significant degree and makes the defense of the fire base more difficult.

LESSON LEARNED: Night vision devices may prove unusable during the attack. Employment of defensive fires based on sectors and primary direction as an alternate means should be prepared, using the old stake and marker method. Units should be ordered to cover assigned sectors with fire if their area becomes obscured.

A final comment on the lessons we learned:

The situation in the Dog's Head is a special one in which the enemy is strong and has very short lines of communication plus the ability to slide back into sanctuaries in Cambodia: the observations and lessons learned apply to such a situation but may not apply elsewhere.

We shall continue to review our techniques and procedures in the light of the experiences from these two attacks, and I am certain we shall profit from our experience.

Sincerely,

E. B. Roberts

E. B. ROBERTS
Major General USA
Commanding

APPENDIX 2

LETTERS THAT NO FAMILY EVER WANTS TO RECEIVE

The following are copies of some of the communications that the Illingworth family received after the death of Cpl. Jack Illingworth.

The telegram that every family with a soldier in Vietnam dreaded receiving:

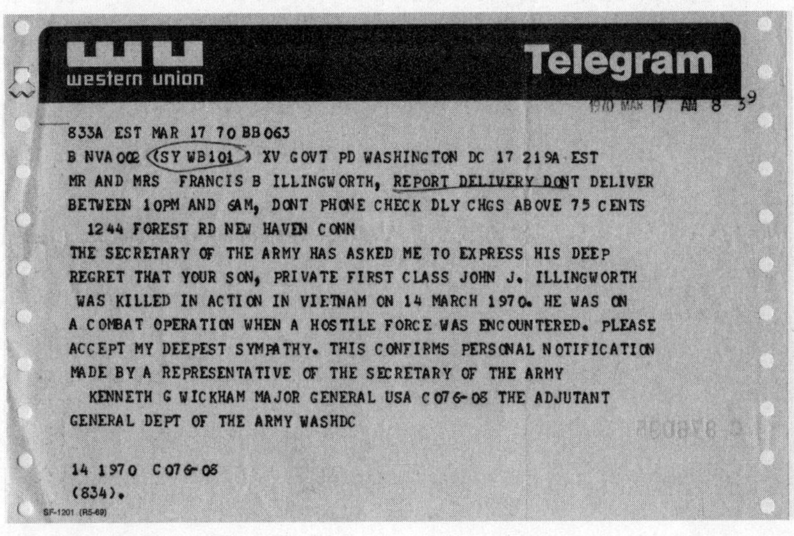

western union Telegram

1970 MAR 17 AM 8 39

833A EST MAR 17 70 BB063
B NVA002 (SY WB101) XV GOVT PD WASHINGTON DC 17 219A EST
MR AND MRS FRANCIS B ILLINGWORTH, REPORT DELIVERY DONT DELIVER
BETWEEN 10PM AND 6AM, DONT PHONE CHECK DLY CHGS ABOVE 75 CENTS
1244 FOREST RD NEW HAVEN CONN
THE SECRETARY OF THE ARMY HAS ASKED ME TO EXPRESS HIS DEEP
REGRET THAT YOUR SON, PRIVATE FIRST CLASS JOHN J. ILLINGWORTH
WAS KILLED IN ACTION IN VIETNAM ON 14 MARCH 1970. HE WAS ON
A COMBAT OPERATION WHEN A HOSTILE FORCE WAS ENCOUNTERED. PLEASE
ACCEPT MY DEEPEST SYMPATHY. THIS CONFIRMS PERSONAL NOTIFICATION
MADE BY A REPRESENTATIVE OF THE SECRETARY OF THE ARMY
KENNETH G WICKHAM MAJOR GENERAL USA C076-08 THE ADJUTANT
GENERAL DEPT OF THE ARMY WASHDC

14 1970 C076-08
(834).

SF-1201 (R5-69)

Appendix 2

The letter of condolence sent by President Nixon:

THE WHITE HOUSE

WASHINGTON

March 21, 1970

Dear Mr. and Mrs. Illingworth:

It is with great sorrow that I have learned of the death of your son, Private First Class John J. Illingworth.

Of all the hardships of war, the cruelest are the losses of men such as your son. The only consolation I can offer is the profound respect of the nation he died to serve, and the humble recognition of a sacrifice no man can measure and no words can describe. Those who give their own lives to make the freedom of others possible live forever in honor.

Mrs. Nixon joins me in extending our own sympathy, and in expressing the sympathy of a saddened nation. You will be in our prayers, and in our hearts.

Sincerely,

Richard Nixon

Mr. and Mrs. Francis B. Illingworth
1244 Forest Road
New Haven, Connecticut

Appendix 2

The letter sent by Secretary of the Army Stanley Resor:

SECRETARY OF THE ARMY
WASHINGTON

March 27, 1970

Dear Mr. and Mrs. Illingworth:

Please accept my deepest sympathy for the death of your son, Private First Class John J. Illingworth, in Vietnam on March 14, 1970.

We are proud of his military accomplishments and grateful to him for his contribution to our Nation's strength. All members of the United States Army join me in expressing the hope that the memory of his dedicated service will help to ease your sorrow.

Sincerely yours,

Stanley R. Resor

Stanley R. Resor

Mr. and Mrs. Francis B. Illingworth
1244 Forest Road
New Haven, Connecticut 06525

Appendix 2

The letter sent by General Abrams:

HEADQUARTERS
UNITED STATES MILITARY ASSISTANCE COMMAND, VIETNAM
OFFICE OF THE COMMANDER
APO SAN FRANCISCO 96222

13 APR 1970

Mr. and Mrs. Francis B. Illingworth
1244 Forest Road
New Haven, Connecticut 06525

Dear Mr. and Mrs. Illingworth:

On behalf of the U. S. Military Assistance Command, Vietnam, I wish to extend my sympathy to you over the loss of your son, Private First Class John J. Illingworth, United States Army, and express my condolences during your time of sorrow and bereavement.

It is my hope that you will find a measure of solace in knowing your son gave his life for a noble cause, the defense of liberty in the free world. Rest assured that we who remain here in Vietnam will continue our efforts to bring peace to this troubled land so that your son's sacrifice will not have been in vain.

Sincerely,

Creighton W. Abrams

CREIGHTON W. ABRAMS
General, United States Army
Commanding

Appendix 2

The letter sent by General Roberts:

DEPARTMENT OF THE ARMY
HEADQUARTERS 1ST CAVALRY DIVISION (AIRMOBILE)
OFFICE OF THE COMMANDING GENERAL
APO SAN FRANCISCO 96490

15 APR 1970

Mr. and Mrs. Francis Illingworth
1244 Forest Road
New Haven, Connecticut 06515

Dear Mr. and Mrs. Illingworth:

Please accept my heartfelt sympathy on the recent loss of your son, Private First Class John J. Illingworth, who died in the service of his country on 14 March 1970.

As a member of Company A, 2nd Battalion, 8th Cavalry, John was well liked by his fellow servicemen. He was an excellent soldier who performed his duties in a cheerful and effective manner. His untimely passing deeply touched those who knew him. I hope that you may find some consolation in this and in the fact that your grief is shared by John's friends.

Our sympathy and prayers are sincerely extended to you in your bereavement.

Sincerely,

E. B. Roberts

E. B. ROBERTS
Major General, USA
Commanding

Appendix 2

The letter sent by Captain Ray Armer, Corporal Illingworth's company commander:

DEPARTMENT OF THE ARMY
COMPANY A, 2D BATTALION (AIRMOBILE) 8TH CAVALRY
1ST CAVALRY DIVISION (AIRMOBILE)
APO San Francisco 96490

15 APR 1970

Mr. and Mrs. Francis Illingworth
1244 Forest Road
New Haven, Connecticut 06515

Dear Mr. and Mrs. Illingworth,

I extend my most profound sympathy to you on the recent loss of your son, Private First Class John J. Illingworth, who died in the service of his country on 14 March 1970. At about 6:45 A.M. on 14 March, John was with his company on a protective reaction mission when they became involved in a firefight and he was fatally wounded. It may afford you some comfort to know that death came quickly and he was not subject to any unnecessary suffering.

The news of your son's death came as a shock to all who knew him, and his loss will be keenly felt throughout this organization. I sincerely hope that the knowledge that he was a exemplary soldier and died while serving his country will comfort you in this hour of great sorrow.

John's enthusiasm and devotion to duty, no matter how difficult the mission, identified him as a outstanding soldier. As a rifleman, he commanded the respect of his superiors as well as that of his fellow soldiers. I am extremely proud to have served with him.

Your son received the ministrations of his church by the Battalion Chaplain. A memorial service will be held when the company returns to base camp.

Once again, personally and for the officers and men of this company, our sincere sympathy is extended to you in your bereavement.

Sincerely yours,

Raymond B Armer

RAYMOND B. ARMER II
CPT, Infantry
Commanding

GLOSSARY

.50 CAL (MACHINE GUN) The .50 caliber machine gun used at FSB Illingworth (and throughout the Vietnam era) was a heavy machine gun based on the model originally crafted by John Browning toward the end of World War I. The basic M-2 model, which dates to the 1920s, has been in use and in inventory longer than any other small arm other than the basic .45 caliber pistol (designed in 1904, also by John Browning). It used a belt-fed .50 caliber cartridge and, depending on the model, could fire hundreds of rounds a minute with an effective range out to approximately 2,200 yards.

8-INCH HOWITZER (SELF-PROPELLED) The big 8-inch guns at Illingworth, the M-110 models, were, at the time they were introduced (1963), the biggest self-propelled guns in the army's inventory. They fired a 207-pound shell out to an effective range of 25,000 meters. The M-110s were immensely powerful guns and remained in the army's inventory until the 1990s. After the M-110s were phased out, many of the barrels were cut apart and used as casings for the twenty-first-century "bunker buster" bombs used to great effect in Iraq and Afghanistan.

81 MM MORTAR (see also: mortar) The 81 mm mortar, in Vietnam, was an effective infantry support piece that weighed roughly 90 pounds, making it a reasonably portable field piece for its normal crew (four or five men). It fired a variety of charges out to a range of about 5,000 yards.

105 MM HOWITZER The army developed the M-102 105 mm howitzer during the early 1960s, and it quickly became the primary artillery field piece used in Vietnam. It could be towed by truck, slung underneath a helicopter, or even dropped by parachute. It fired a relatively small 4.1-inch projectile, but its rapid rate of fire—ten rounds per minute, initial; three rounds per minute, sustained—more than made up for the size of the shells. The 105 could also fire a wide array of munitions including high explosive, canister, and illumination rounds. The gun could be used in indirect fire as well as direct fire operations, and the crew could service the weapon while lying down, if under fire.

155 MM HOWITZER The army used the M-114 model 155 mm howitzer extensively in Vietnam, including at fire bases like Illingworth. Bigger than the 105, the 155 fired a 6.1-inch shell that could range up to 16,000 yards. It could fire 4 rounds per minute in a burst and up to forty rounds per hour in a sustained mode. It required a larger crew, at least six men, preferably eight. It could be towed, but at 6 tons plus, only by the biggest trucks. It could also be airlifted, but only by the heaviest helicopters or large fixed-wing aircraft. The 155 was used primarily in the indirect fire mode but could be used for direct fire. Since the crew needed to stand and was very exposed while working the weapon, direct fire was not very practical, however. The 155 fired a wide variety of shells including high explosive, smoke, illumination, and chemical rounds.

ACAV Armored cavalry assault vehicle. The ACAVs described herein were M-113 tracked vehicles armed with one .50 caliber heavy machine gun and two M-60 light machine guns (see M-113, below).

ADC Assistant division commander. At the divisional level in the U.S. Army, the division commander was usually a two-star major general assisted by one ADC for operations, an ADC-O; and one ADC for support, ADC-S. Both ADCs were usually brigadier generals.

AK-47 The AK-47 was a selective-fire, gas-operated 7.62 mm assault rifle, first developed in the Soviet Union by Mikhail Kalashnikov. The designation AK-47 stood for "Kalashnikov automatic rifle, model of 1947." Even after six decades, due to its durability, low production cost, and ease of use, the basic model and its variants have remained the most widely used and popular assault rifle in the world. The AK-47 was the standard operating rifle for the NVA, supplied in quantity by the former Soviet Union.

AN/PPS-5 The "Pipsy-Five" was a small, two-man, portable surveillance radar system able to detect groups of people moving across the ground or the movement of vehicles, even transports as small as jeeps. It could pick out a squad or platoon of enemy soldiers either by sound or by radar image. The effective range was out to approximately 6 kilometers for personnel and out to 10 for vehicles.

AO Area of operations. The area in which a military unit has operational responsibility.

ARA Aerial rocket artillery (see also: Blue Max). Airborne artillery, primarily rockets and miniguns placed aboard helicopters.

ARVN The Army of the Republic of Vietnam or an individual South Vietnamese regular army soldier.

B-40 The B-40 was a variant of the dreaded RPG. Both fired an 82 mm grenade. Although primarily an antiarmor weapon, the NVA often used them against troops. They were very effective at terrorizing massed infantry. If a B-40 round hit a solid object it could send a deadly shower of shrapnel across an area of several yards. If it hit a group of soldiers, it could wipe out an entire squad in an instant.

B-52 The B-52 was the workhorse, long-range U.S. Air Force bomber of Vietnam. Originally designed and built in the early 1950s, some are still in service today, sixty years later.

BANGALORE (TORPEDO) An explosive charge that could be placed inside a long, thin tube, connected to other tubes, and used to clear a path through obstacles, such as minefields or barbed wire.

BEEHIVE (PROJECTILE) The "beehive round" was an artillery or tank cannon projectile used primarily as an antipersonnel weapon. The shell contained 8,000 to 10,000 tiny darts called "flechettes." When the round was fired, a mechanical time fuse would cause the round to burst and release the flechettes, which spread out in an expanding pattern until they reached terminal velocity and maximum range. Soldiers who experienced the power of this weapon in Vietnam called it the beehive round because, after it was fired, the sound of the flechettes flying through the air mimicked the noise made by a hive of angry bees.

BLIVET A portable fuel storage container. In Vietnam, these were large, cylindrical, heavy-duty rubber fuel bladders that contained approximately 550 gallons of diesel fuel or petroleum. They were often delivered by helicopter to tanks and trucks in the field so they could be refueled on station.

BLUE MAX "Blue Max" was a generic term for the 2nd Battalion, 20th Artillery, also known as the Aerial Rocket Artillery (ARA). The 2/20 ARA had been flying in Vietnam in support of the 1st Cav since 1965 and had initiated their campaign with specialized UH-1 Huey helicopters equipped with rocket pods and machine guns. The idea was that these units would be used for "danger close" or very close-in infantry support. By the time of Illingworth, the 2/20 ARA had transitioned to the faster, better-equipped Cobra attack helicopter. The Blue Max Cobras were equipped with four under-the-wing pods of 2.75-inch rockets and the nose-mounted XM-28 gun system. The rockets (76 in total) sported a variety of warheads, depending on the mission, and the XM-28 could fire either 40 mm grenades or 7.62 mm machine-gun ammo. The grenades could be fired at up to 400 rounds per minute (although max capacity was only 300 rounds), and the machine gun could fire at 2,000 to 4,000 rounds per minute (4,000 round capacity). "Blue Max" was a call sign that the 2/20 adopted for itself in 1968. Although the unit was known by many call signs during their Vietnam service (for example, at the time of the Illingworth battles they were call sign "Silver Dagger"), it was "Blue Max" that they preferred; or, just "Max" for short. The moniker stuck, and most 1st Cav units called them by their preferred name.

BUST JUNGLE A slang term to define the act of transiting thick vegetation by using brute force to smash through the greenery. Sometimes, busting jungle was done by infantry as they pushed through; in this book, the term is most often used in context with mechanized tracks smashing down the jungle.

C-130 The C-130 Hercules, a large four-engine turbo-prop aircraft, was originally designed and built in the early 1950s. Its airframe and basic design, which have spread over forty different configurations, are still in production today. In Vietnam, the C-130 was often used on short or unprepared runways. Among its many versions were cargo hauler, troop transport, gunship, flare ship, medical transport, search and rescue platform, refueling ship, and more.

C-RATS (OR C-RATION) Commonly called "C-rats," C-rations were the standard-issue field meals. They came in three basic types and were packaged inside a thin cardboard container. They could be eaten cold, since all the food was precooked, or they could be heated by any local means, most often by placing a can on a warm engine or by taking a Chiclet-sized piece of C-4 explosive and using it as a heat source. Ham and lima beans was the most despised ration, spaghetti and meatballs the favorite. Each C-ration also came with a plastic spoon, salt and pepper packets, instant coffee, sugar, nondairy creamer, two real Chiclets, and a pack of four cigarettes.

CHICOM GRENADE A hand grenade similar to the old German "potato masher" of World War II; that is, a small explosive charge attached to the end of a short wooden or bamboo handle. It would be activated when the cork or wooden top cap was pulled off, at which point the soldier would toss the grenade.

CHINOOK Production designation for the CH-47 medium-lift helicopter manufactured by Boeing and first deployed in 1962. It became a workhorse helicopter in the Vietnam era, lifting and resupplying everything from troops to tanks, beans to bullets. The grunts of Vietnam sarcastically referred to it as the "Shit-hook."

CLAYMORE An antipersonnel mine containing seven hundred small ball bearings that became shrapnel when the mine exploded. The mine was shaped to throw its large volume of metal bits across a 60-degree arc.

Effective range was about 100 meters. The mine could be control detonated, set with a timer, or set off by trip-wire, step-plate, or (in later designs) laser.

CO Commanding officer (of a unit).

COBRA The AH-1 Cobra helicopter gunship was deployed to Vietnam beginning in 1967 and quickly became the army's principal helicopter gunship. In various versions, the Cobra could mount machine guns, aerial cannons, or rockets.

COMMAND AND CONTROL Sometimes called "C2," command and control, in a military organization, specified who was in command of specific resources and forces as they were applied to a specific mission. For example, Lt. Col. Mike Conrad, in the Illingworth story, was C2 of the infantry and its supporting components but not, interestingly, the artillery or the cavalry aboard his base.

CONEX Abbreviation for "container, external," or a large, usually corrugated, metal shipping container. It was designed to be used in overseas shipping aboard large container vessels. In Vietnam the military used the containers, which kept piling up at the docks after they disgorged their military cargoes, for a myriad of purposes. Their size and heavy construction made them readily adaptable to "bunkers," protected medical spaces, operations centers, temporary living quarters, and more.

COOK OFF When ammunition spontaneously explodes, usually as a result of its proximity to a high heat source, it is "cooking off."

COSVN Central Office for South Vietnam. At various times during the Vietnam War, American commanders referred to COSVN as being the hub and nerve center for all PAVN (see below), Vietcong, and NVA activities in South Vietnam. Some referred to it as "the NVA Pentagon in the Jungle." The Americans fought against it, tried to eradicate it, and made many attempts to locate it; in reality, it probably never even existed. It may, in fact, have been more of a concept than a physical reality. Many experts now believe it was a loosely connected network of Communist officers and party functionaries widely scattered across the South who coordinated with one another only when necessary.

DEUCE-AND-A-HALF Slang for the standard U.S. Army 2.5-ton truck. The deuce-and-a-half came in dozens of versions and served the army as troop transport, cargo vehicle, tow truck, mechanics' shop, medical supply vehicle, ambulance, and more. The design, from 1951, was rugged and versatile. The standard load for cargo was 5,000 pounds off road and 10,000 pounds on road. The truck was originally produced by REO Motors, then by Kaiser, and finally AM General. Kia Motors produces a version today (for Korea).

DI DI MAU Vietnamese slang for leaving quickly or running away.

DIRECT FIRE Direct fire—and direct-fire weapons—require line-of-sight aiming and an unobstructed view from the gun to the target. Artillery in a direct-fire mode was aimed at targets that were directly in view and in range. Direct-fire weapons also included handguns, rifles, grenades, machine guns, etc.

DSR Daily Status Report. In the army, in Vietnam, all units of company size and larger were required to keep DSRs. Most were handwritten on preprinted forms.

DUST-OFF A helicopter-borne medical evacuation.

F-4 The F-4 Phantom II was a tandem, two-seat, twin-engine, all-weather, long-range supersonic jet interceptor fighter/bomber originally developed for the U.S. Navy by McDonnell Douglas Aircraft. It was introduced into the U.S. Navy inventory in 1960. Proving highly adaptable, it became a major part of the air combat strategy of not only the navy but also the Marine Corps and the U.S. Air Force. It was used extensively by all three services during the Vietnam War, primarily as an air-superiority fighter but also for ground-attack and reconnaissance operations.

FAC Forward Air Controller. FACs were the "eyes" of the artillery and also TACAIR (see below). They acted primarily as visual spotters so artillery assets and air strikes could be targeted accurately. Sometimes FACs were on the ground, and usually well out in front of the ground forces; or they could be airborne.

FB Fire base (see FSB, below).

FDC Fire Direction Center. In a field artillery team there was usually one FDC for each battery of six guns (at the division level). The FDC plotted the targets for the guns, decided what ammunition to fire, and directed the firing of the batteries (all under the guidance of an artillery LNO, or liaison officer.) At FSB Illingworth, each battery of artillery had its own FDC, and Captain Ahearn was the LNO at the tactical operations center.

FLAK JACKET A sleeveless jacket with a collar designed to provide protection from shrapnel and other indirect, low-velocity projectiles. It was made of a nylon material into which small steel plates were sewn.

FLARE SHIP In Vietnam, several C-47 and C-130 aircraft were modified by the U.S. Air Force to act as flare ships. The sole purpose for these ships was to drop illumination on targets as directed. Most of the flare ships operated out of Da Nang, South Vietnam, or Naha, Okinawa. In the beginning, the flare dropping was mainly an ad hoc exercise with jury-rigged devices. Later in the war, the C-130s, in particular, began to be equipped with internal flare tubes.

FLECHETTE The dart inside a beehive round (see above).

FNG "Fucking new guy," a newbie.

FRAG Fragmentation grenade or hand grenade: a small, metal, handheld munition primarily used as an antipersonnel weapon. "Frag" could also mean "to frag," as in using a grenade or other explosive device to "blow away" an officer or NCO who was not liked by the troops (230 documented cases in Vietnam).

FRIENDLY FIRE Being fired upon by one's own troops—an occurrence all too frequent in Vietnam (over 8,800 cases).

FSB Fire support base: a military encampment designed to provide artillery support to infantry operating beyond the normal range of direct-fire support from their own base camps. FSBs were originally propagated by South Korean troops during the Vietnam War. The United States adopted the technique after South Korean troops proved its usefulness. Most FSBs were temporary encampments, but some became famous—or infamous, as the case may be (FSB Illingworth, in this story).

G-2 Designation for the division intelligence office(r).

GOOK Derogatory term for a North or South Vietnamese soldier or civilian; etymology suggests the word was originally Korean and refers to a "country" or "rural" person.

GRUNT Slang term used in Vietnam for an American infantryman; a regular GI.

H&I "Harassment and interdiction," an artillery firing tactic: annoying the enemy with random fire to disrupt their movements and activities.

HUEY The UH-1 basic utility helicopter transported eight to ten soldiers, flew small cargos, was employed in command and control, and was also used as a gunship. In the medevac version it was called a "slick" because its outside configuration, without guns, was "clean."

IN COUNTRY Army slang for being in Vietnam. The standard tour for a U.S. soldier during this period was twelve months in country (thirteen months for the marines).

INDIRECT FIRE As used in this book, artillery fire that was directed at targets that were not in line of sight; that is, targets that were over the horizon or out of view. With indirect fire, firing solutions had to be plotted based on intelligence provided by others (see also "direct fire").

KA-BAR The standard issue, 7-inch combat utility knife. It originated in World War II and was manufactured by the KA-BAR Knife Company. A Vietnam version had a double edge versus the original single-edged weapon. Ka-Bars also had a standard non-slip hard plastic handle and hard plastic sheath.

KC Kit Carson Scout. Named after the famous American frontiersman, the KCs were almost exclusively former NVA or Vietcong who had, for one reason or another, defected and agreed to work for the ARVN or American forces as scouts or sometimes as interpreters.

KIA Killed in action (akin to MIA, missing in action, and WIA, wounded in action).

KILLER JUNIOR, KILLER SENIOR Both "killer junior" and "killer senior" were terms of art for the artillery and refer to types of guns and their uses. "Killer junior" normally referred to the 105 and 155 mm guns and "killer senior" to the large 8-inch howitzers. The terms referred to direct-fire defensive programs of the field artillery. Both techniques were designed to defend fire bases against enemy ground attack and used mechanical, time-fused projectiles set to burst approximately 30 feet off the ground at ranges of 100 to 1,000 meters. This technique proved more effective in many instances than direct fire with "beehive" ammunition, because the enemy could avoid the beehive ammunition by lying prone or crawling.

KIT CARSON See KC above.

KLICK Slang for "kilometer," or .625 miles.

LOACH Nickname for the OH-6 Light Observation Helicopter.

LZ Helicopter landing zone.

M-14 The M-14 rifle was a standard-issue rifle of the U.S. Army from the late 1950s to 1970. It was heavier and longer than the M-16, and had a wooden stock, which tended to swell in the steamy jungles of Vietnam; but, many troops still preferred the M-14 over the lighter, shorter M-16, especially during the M-16's first years, when it had significant challenges with jamming and fouling of the barrels. Once the M-16's deficiencies were overcome (with better ammunition and chrome-plated barrels) the M-14 was withdrawn from service, except for those used as sniper's weapons.

M-16 The M-16 entered service as the M-16 A-1 and was put into action for jungle warfare in Vietnam in 1963, becoming the standard U.S. rifle of the war by 1969. Initially, it was poorly suited to the conditions of jungle warfare and often jammed or malfunctioned in the heat, high humidity, and dirt-filled environment of Southeast Asia. The main problems centered on the powder used in the cartridges and dirt accumulating in the rifle barrels. The ammunition problem was solved quickly and rifle barrels were lined with chrome to make them smoother and less susceptible to collecting dirt. Once these changes were made, the M-16 performed better, and soldiers started preferring the M-16 to any other standard-issue rifle. The M-16 became, in fact, the second most widely adopted infantry firearm in the world after the rugged AK-47 (the M-16 being more accurate, however).

M-48 Patton Tank Officially classified as a "medium" tank, the M-48 Patton was the main battle tank for the U.S. Army during the Vietnam War. It replaced the older M-47 Pattons and the M-4 Shermans. It served admirably throughout the war, mainly in an infantry support role. The M-48 carried a 90 mm gun and both .50 cal and .30 caliber machine guns (one each). It could travel at speeds up to 48 mph and had a crew of four.

M-60 The M-60 was a general-purpose machine gun firing 7.62 × 51 mm NATO cartridges from a disintegrating belt of links. There were several types of live ammunition approved for use in the M-60, including ball, tracer, and armor-piercing rounds. Introduced in 1957, it has served with every branch of the U.S. military and still serves with other armed forces. It was the largest and heaviest machine gun employed by the infantry. It was a weapon usually serviced by two soldiers: One man would carry the 23-pound weapon; the other would "hump" the ammo. When firing, the two soldiers would work as a team: one gunner, one loader. It was one of these weapons that PFC Illingworth was using when he was fatally wounded.

M-113 The U.S. Army, who commissioned them and had them built starting in the early 1960s, initially called them Armored Personnel Carriers, or APCs; as the M-113 morphed into more of a fighting vehicle than a simple troop carrier, the term "armored cavalry assault vehicle," or ACAV, became more common. The ACAV was the ubiquitous U.S. Army fighting vehicle in Vietnam.

The first batches of M-113s arrived in Vietnam in early 1962. They were immediately turned over to the ARVN, who promptly reconfigured them as light tanks or assault vehicles capable of carrying a few troops *and* blasting away at the enemy.

By 1965, the U.S. Army was deploying the M-113 with belly armor, a shielded turret for a .50 cal., and two M-60 machine guns mounted internally, with shields. The M-113 had become a fighting vehicle, and so it would remain for the rest of the war.

M-551 SHERIDAN TANK The Sheridan was not a true tank at all; it was designated an ARAAV, or Armored Reconnaissance Airborne Assault Vehicle. Although its main gun turret was steel, its hull was made of aluminum. This allowed the Sheridan to be light and fast, but it could not absorb anything like the punishment the M-48 Patton tank could take. Mines and RPGs often proved deadly to the Sheridan in Vietnam, and heavy-caliber machine gun bullets could penetrate the thin aluminum skin. It was, without question, maneuverable and reliable. The 300 hp Allison diesel engine could drive the machine all day at speeds in excess of its top-rated 43 mph. The developers of the Sheridan had decided to equip it with an outsized main gun—a whopping 152 mm cannon. This was much bigger than the 90 mm main guns on the M-48 Patton. The Sheridan was equipped with two smaller supporting guns: a faithful and powerful Browning automatic .50 caliber machine gun was mounted in the turret, and a secondary 7.62 mm machine gun was placed in the belly of the tank.

M-577 Army designation for the Mobile Command Post tracked vehicle, a variant of the M-113 ACAV. The M-577 typically acted as a mobile office and radio center for a troop of cavalry.

MACV Military Assistance Command, Vietnam. Created in 1962, MACV was the overall command and control structure for all U.S. forces in Vietnam. It was headquartered at Tan Son Nhut Air Base. The first and only commanders of MACV were Gen. William Westmoreland (1964–68), Gen. Creighton W. Abrams (1968–72), and Gen. Frederick C. Weyand (1972–73.) MACV was disestablished when the role of U.S. forces in Vietnam ended (1973).

MAD MINUTE Prearranged, simultaneous discharge of all the weapons in the unit at unspecified but suspected targets nearby. It was meant to be a deterrent to opposing forces and to disrupt any enemy attempting a covert attack.

MEDEVAC Medical evacuation, which in Vietnam was often carried out by helicopter. Only used for nonambulatory cases, as a general rule.

MIA Missing in action (see also KIA and WIA).

MORTAR An indirect-fire weapon that launched several types of munitions at low velocities, short ranges, and high-arcing ballistic trajectories. It was typically muzzle-loading and had a barrel length less than 15 times its caliber.

NAPALM A jellied gasoline that was thick and syrupy, used in flamethrowers and incendiary bombs. It burned at a temperature of about 800 degrees. In Vietnam, napalm was often used as an antipersonnel weapon and was greatly feared by the NVA.

NCO Noncommissioned officer, typically an enlisted sergeant ranked E-5 or above (to E-9).

NDP Night defensive position (the cavalry also called it a laager). Overnight defensive formation wherein all forces were arranged in a circle, weapons pointing outward. Support and noncombat tracks were placed in the circle's interior.

NEWBIE Slang term for a new replacement soldier, officer or enlisted.

NVA North Vietnamese Army or an NVA regular soldier.

PATTON (TANK) See M-48, above.

PAVN People's Army of Vietnam. The PAVN was the overall armed forces structure of the former North Vietnam. The Americans distinguished between the NVA (forces from the North) and the Vietcong (Communist forces from the South). The PAVN, in reality, coordinated all Communist forces throughout the Vietnam War.

PRC-25 The PRC-25 was a backpack, portable, VHF FM combat-net radio transceiver used to provide short-range, two-way radio-telephone voice communication.

PSP Pierced steel planking: flats of perforated steel planks, often used for making temporary runways, parking areas, and steel mats.

PUC Presidential Unit Citation, the highest U.S. military award for valor given to a unit (as opposed to an individual soldier).

POW Prisoner of war.

QUAD .50 A gun mount consisting of four .50 caliber machine guns rigged to fire in unison and mounted in the rear flatbed of a deuce-and-a-half truck. The quad .50 was a powerful, mobile machine-gun platform and was most often used to provide defense for artillery batteries.

R&R Rest and relaxation. During a typical tour in Vietnam each soldier was guaranteed between five and ten days off the line, on R&R, and usually in Thailand, Hawaii, Australia, or some other close-by but exotic location designed to get their minds off the intensity of combat.

REDLEG Slang for an artilleryman. The provenance goes back to the American Civil War; to distinguish themselves from the regular infantry, those assigned to the artillery had a distinctive narrow red stripe, made of piping, down the outside of each trouser leg.

REMF Acronym for Rear Echelon Mother Fucker: a popular derogatory phrase to describe someone who spent their time in Vietnam behind the lines; or, "in the rear" areas, as opposed to being on the front lines and in combat.

RIF Reduction in force. The U.S. Army had ramped up to force levels not seen since WW II in response to the manpower needs of Vietnam. After the peace talks started and U.S. forces started to relocate stateside, the army began to revert to peacetime levels at all ranks. This would require the involuntary cutting of hundreds of thousands of officers and enlisted men. Career NCOs and regular army commissioned officers were spared, by and large, from the RIFs.

ROE Rules of Engagement. The rules of war by which combat was conducted, or not conducted, as the case might be. The "rules" often changed as combat conditions changed.

RPG Rocket-propelled grenade: a shoulder-launched, shaped-charge grenade. It was a staple of the NVA. Most were manufactured in the former Soviet Union, but by 1969–70 many were being made in China.

RTO Radio telephone operator. Typically a unit's radioman.

SATCHEL CHARGE Satchel charges have been around since WW II. The NVA and Vietcong used them frequently. Most satchel charges consisted of various quantities of dynamite or C-4 explosive carried in a canvas sack with a shoulder strap. They could be remotely detonated, but most were activated with a simple pull-cord, then flung at or into a target area.

SHAKE 'N BAKE The savageness of the Vietnam War created thousands of vacancies in the ranks of NCOs, primarily at the E-5 (sergeant) and E-6 (staff sergeant) levels. The army could not keep up with the need for these critical positions in the ranks. In an effort to catch up, the army created an Advanced NCO Academy at Fort Knox, Kentucky. Enlisted soldiers of above-average aptitude were accelerated through a program to create "instant sergeants," and the program became known colloquially as "shake 'n bake," after a then popular instant fried chicken cooking product: Raw chicken ("recruits") was tossed into a bag of ready-made coatings and flavorings (the NCO Academy), quickly baked (the advanced training), and made into instant fried chicken (sergeants). Like several men in this book, some soldiers went from E-1 (newly drafted privates) to E-6 staff sergeants in under a year, something that normally took regular army soldiers seven years or more to achieve.

SHERIDAN TANK See M-551 Sheridan, above.

SHIT-HOOK The CH-47 helicopter was commonly referred to as a "Shit-hook," a bastardization of the helicopter's formal name of Chinook (see page 264).

SHIT SANDWICH A very tough spot. It was a bad place to be in.

SHRAPNEL Metal fragments produced by the explosion of a round.

SLICK Army jargon for the UH-1 Huey version that was used for transport, dust-off, and logging (resupply). The helicopter was "slick" because it was "smooth," i.e., it was unarmed, and not bristling with weapons.

SPOOKY The "Spooky" gunship. The Spooky in Vietnam came in two versions: First, the U.S. Air Force converted a number of aging C-47 cargo aircraft into gunships. "Spooky" was the radio call sign, but the men also called them "Puff the Magic Dragon." The C-47 was modified to place a powerful minigun in the open cargo door. The gun could fire thousands of rounds a minute and place a devastating fire on selected ground targets, usually concentrations of enemy troops. As the C-47s aged out of usefulness, they were replaced by a C-130 version of the "Spooky" (starting in 1968).

STARLIGHT (SCOPE) A type of sniper's scope that could be fitted to a variety of rifles and would allow the shooter to see targets in very low-level light conditions, even total darkness. It functioned by picking up faint heat signatures.

TACAIR Tactical air (support): airborne assets, typically fixed-wing fighters, bombers, fighter-bombers and helicopters.

TANGLEFOOT A configuration of concertina or barbed wire that was usually placed at midcalf or knee level and in wide bands. It was meant to slow down and "tangle" enemy troops. Some FSBs used tanglefoot, but since it was labor-intensive to erect and take down, only those sites that were to be of more than a few days' duration might erect it.

TC Track commander: the individual in charge of a tracked vehicle, usually a sergeant (E-5) or above.

TET (HOLIDAY) In Vietnam, Tet is the celebration of the New Year according to the lunar calendar. It usually occurs in January or February. In the Vietnam War, the Tet Holiday in 1968 became infamous. All parties had agreed to a two-day cease fire in observance of Tet. The Vietcong decided to break the agreement and launched a surprise offensive. The NVA threw 80,000 troops against 100 targets. Most attacks were quickly beaten back with terrible losses for the Communists. The one exception was the monthlong battle for the city of Hue.

TOC Tactical Operations Center: the point of command and control for the unit engaged.

TRACK Slang term for a tracked vehicle such as the M-113 or M-551 Sheridan, that is, one that moves on a continuous band of treads rather than on wheels.

TROTTER A trail in the jungle wide enough for two men to march along side by side.

VIETCONG The Vietcong were members of the PAVN (see page 274) who operated primarily out of locations in South Vietnam and were generally indigenous South Vietnamese fighting for the Communist forces. Some were characterized as irregular forces, or guerrillas in "black pajamas," but many were regular NVA soldiers as well.

VIETMINH Originally formed in 1941 to oppose French colonial rule of Vietnam, the Vietminh took over the North after the accords of 1954 divided Vietnam into two countries, North and South. They became active again in opposition to the South but eventually merged into the Vietcong (see previous page).

WAR ZONE C The operational area in and around Tay Ninh City, northwest of Saigon and up to and including the Cambodian border. It was the primary AO for the 1st Cav and the 25th Infantry Division at the time of the events at FSB Illingworth.

WIA Wounded in action (see also KIA and MIA).

XENON SEARCHLIGHT (JEEP) A modified jeep equipped with a 30-inch high-power xenon searchlight. It was used primarily for artillery spotting during nighttime operations.

XO Executive officer.

SELECTED BIBLIOGRAPHY

Coleman, J.D. *Incursion*. New York: St. Martin's Press, 1991.

Hay, Lt. Gen. John H., Jr. *Tactical and Materiel Innovations*, Vietnam Studies. Washington: Dept. of the Army, 1974.

Keith, Philip. *Blackhorse Riders*. New York: St. Martin's Press, 2012.

Laurence, John. *The Cat from Hué*. New York: Public Affairs, 2002.

Nicholson, David A. *Tales from the 'Nam*. Manchester, NH: Oak Manor Publishing, 2008.

Nolan, Keith. *Into Cambodia*. Novato, CA: Presidio Press, 1990.

Stanton, Shelby. *The 1st Cav in Vietnam*. Novato, CA: Presidio Press, 1999.

INDEX

Index

Index

Index